MACROBIOTIC COOKING FOR EVERYONE

Macrobiotic Cooking for Everyone

Edward & Wendy Esko

Japan Publications, Inc.

Published by JAPAN PUBLICATIONS, INC., Tokyo

Distributors:
UNITED STATES: *Kodansha International/USA, Ltd., through Harper & Row, Pub-
lishers, Inc., 10 East 53rd Street, New York, New York 10022.* SOUTH AMERICA:
Harper & Row, Publishers, Inc., International Department. CANADA: *Fitzhenry &
Whiteside Ltd., 150 Lesmill Road, Don Mills, Ontario M3B 2T6.* MEXICO AND
CENTRAL AMERICA: *HARLA S. A. de C. V., Apartado 30–546, Mexico 4, D. F.*
BRITISH ISLES: *International Book Distributors Ltd., 66 Wood Lane End, Hemel
Hempstead, Herts HPZ 4RG.* EUROPEAN CONTINENT: *Boxerbooks, Inc., Limmat-
strasse 111, 8031 Zurich.* AUSTRALIA AND NEW ZEALAND: *Book Wise (Australia)
Pty. Ltd., 104–8 Sussex Street, Sydney 2000.* THE FAR EAST AND JAPAN:
Japan Publications Trading Co., Ltd., 1–2–1, Sarugaku-cho, Chiyoda-ku, Tokyo 101.

First edition: November 1980

LCCC No. 79–89344
ISBN 0–87040–469–5

Printed in U.S.A.

Foreword

Cooking is the highest form of human art. It not only pleases the senses, but has the power to cause sickness or health; to enhance or destroy our appreciation of life; and to increase or decrease our ability to participate fully in our own destiny. The importance of cooking has long been neglected, and it is now more and more obvious that the preparation and selection of our food should be a main priority of life.

Over the past ten years, it has become evident that the way we eat is one of the prime factors in the rapid increase of degenerative disease. This knowledge has led to a wide-spread reassessment of food consumption. Hundreds of books on diet and nutrition have been published, most of which stress the analytical approach to nutrition, which is difficult to apply in the kitchen. The beauty of the macrobiotic approach to nutrition and cooking is that the principles are easy to understand and apply, and also to relate to events in our lives. The seasons of plant growth, the local environment, and individual health needs, are all taken into account, thus creating a dynamic and comprehensive system to be used in any situation. Macrobiotic cooking serves as a bridge between sensory satisfaction and personal needs. It is a tool for creating health and happiness for ourselves and our families.

Edward and Wendy Esko are well aware of the fact that the importance of cooking extends far beyond the dinner table. For many years they have been active in sharing their experience and knowledge with hundreds of students, who have been grateful for their ability to translate the simple but profound wisdom of traditional cooking and nutrition into an approach which can be used creatively within our present society.

A book like this can help us to better understand the relationship between ourselves and our environment, and how to live harmoniously within it. After discovering the power food has to heighten our experience of life, it is difficult not to be profoundly grateful to nature for providing us with such wonderful gifts. The simple information contained within these pages can help in the process of creating a healthy society and give us the vitality needed to enjoy life to the utmost.

My thanks to Edward and Wendy for all the work they have put into preparing this invaluable guide for us all; and my encouragement to you, the reader, in applying the information presented here to enrich your own life, tonight—in the kitchen.

WILLIAM TARA, *Director,*
Community Health Foundation
London, England

Preface

One of the most profound experiences I have had took place not too long ago on a clear October day in Japan, in the mountains and rice fields which surround the city of Kyoto. During an afternoon walk through the suburbs of the city, I decided to stray from the main road onto one of the paths that led into a large clearing at the foot of the mountains. The plain was overflowing with fields of ripening rice, and as I continued walking, I soon found myself surrounded on all sides by acre after acre of golden grain. The sun was shining in a warm, late afternoon yellow and the sky was a crystal blue. The pine-studded mountains off in the distance were a brilliant green.

In this beautifully natural setting, everything seemed in perfect harmony—living, breathing, vibrant with the energy of heaven and earth. Underlying this harmony, which seemed to extend throughout the universe, was the deep sense of attraction and oneness that I felt for the ripening rice, not unlike the attraction between a man and a woman. After eating brown rice and other whole-grains for nearly ten years, this was my first opportunity to actually see and experience them growing in the fields.

The magnetism that I experienced very vividly that afternoon is based on the natural attraction that exists between human beings and the vegetable kingdom, especially with the cereal grains, which are our biological counterparts in the vegetable world. Without this relationship we literally would not exist, since without food there is no life. However, as fundamental as it is, this is only one of a countless number of complementary and antagonistic, or yin and yang relationships existing throughout nature.

One of America's greatest thinkers, Ralph Waldo Emerson, expressed this in his essay titled *Compensation* when he wrote:

> "Polarity, or action and reaction, we meet in every part of nature; in darkness and light; in heat and cold; in the ebb and flow of waters; in male and female; in the inspiration and expiration of plants and animals; in the equation of quantity and quality in the fluids of the animal body; in the systole and diastole of the heart; in the centrifugal and centripetal gravity; in electricity, galvanism, and chemical affinity."

At the same time, the duality which bisects nature originates within the wholeness or oneness of the infinite universe, and comes into being when the oneness of the universe polarizes itself into two complementary and antagonistic forces. This process is without beginning or end, and occurs in the form of a vast spiral, which is the most basic form of everything in the universe.

This unified spiral of life, which flows unbroken and continuously through time and space, is readily apparent in the hills and rice paddies in Japan. The rice, the sacred blood of the Far Eastern peoples, gives itself, changes itself into human flesh and spirit. The rice, along with all other products of the vegetable kingdom, is in turn produced by the sky, wind, earth, water, and the other elements which give birth to the vegetable world. These elemental forms owe their existence to the pre-atomic particles, or plasma, in which form more than 99 percent of the matter in the universe exists. This world is symbolized in Japanese mythology in the form of the sun-goddess, Amaterasu-Ōmikami. All of these manifestations are alive with spirit, or vibration, out of which the entire visible universe comes into being. This process was expressed by Jesus in the *Gospel According to Thomas* when he said, "If they say to you: 'From where have you originated?', say to them: 'We have come from the Light, where the Light has originated through itself. It stood and revealed itself in their image.'" This world of vibration is in turn the product of the everlasting and imperishable forces of centrifugality and centripetality, or yin and yang, which emanate continuously from the oneness of the infinite universe or God, and which create all phenomena.

Macrobiotic cooking is simply the art of balancing these universal forces as they appear on earth and in the biological world so as to achieve harmony with our immediate environment in nature and with the universe as a whole. Biologically, this condition of balance or equilibrium is referred to as *health*, while psychologically, we refer to it as *happiness*.

As you will discover in these pages, macrobiotic cooking is not at all difficult to learn, nor is it too expensive or complicated to apply. After nearly ten years of studying, practicing, and teaching macrobiotics in America, Europe, and Japan, I am convinced that it offers not only a practical and common sense approach to the problems of individual health and development, but also a fundamental method for achieving the imperishable dream of social harmony and world peace.

Since returning from Japan in May of last year, we have settled in the Boston area and have established a macrobiotic student house here. I have also begun to lecture in the Boston-Cambridge area on various aspects of macrobiotics, and am presently advising a growing number of people about diet and way of life.

New England is one of the leading regions in the United States for the spread and development of macrobiotics and the natural food movement, due largely to the patient efforts of Michio and Aveline Kushi. There are now a number of fine restaurants in the Boston area, notably the Seventh Inn, Sanae, the Last Chance cafe, and Open Sesame, along with Paul and Elizabeth's in the Amherst area, where one can order a wide variety of deliciously prepared natural food dishes. At the same time, Erewhon, which is the world's largest distributor of natural and macrobiotic foods, is located here, with a large warehouse facility and several retail stores which employ more than 100 people. Educational activities are also being conducted on a regular basis through the Kushi Institute and the East West Foundation.

Last summer, more than 100 delegates from various regional centers throughout the United States and Canada met in Boston for the first North American Congress of Macrobiotics. Just as the movement for American Independence began in this area more than 200 years ago, I am confident that the macrobiotic activities now centered here will produce an equally significant revolution in our eating habits, agricultural practices, concept of health, and in many other aspects of daily living. Interestingly, this new revolution in diet and consciousness is a totally peaceful one, and unlike many previous social movements, is largely in the hands of women and is centered in the kitchen of every home. It is to further this peaceful, worldwide movement for better health, social harmony, and world peace that we humbly offer this book.

In the Part One, we have presented basic explanations of the fundamental principles of macrobiotics, including methods for balancing meals according to yin and yang; the importance of using primarily whole grains and local vegetables as principal foods; the standard macrobiotic way of eating; how to modify the standard diet; nutritional considerations; food for spiritual development; and others. The second part contains a wide selection of recipes arranged by food type, along with additional practical information about food and cooking. We hope that you will enjoy preparing these dishes as much as we, and our many friends around the world, have also enjoyed them.

There are now a number of excellent texts available on the subject of macrobiotics, and we hope that you will use this book in combination with them. These include the *Book of Macrobiotics* which is the leading classic on this subject to date, in which many of the fundamental principles of macrobiotics included in this book were first introduced, *How to See Your Health: The Book of Oriental Diagnosis* by Michio Kushi, *How to Cook with Miso* by Aveline Kushi, Wendy's first book, *Introducing Macrobiotic Cooking*, and many others.

EDWARD ESKO
Boston, Massachusetts
February, 1980

Contents

Foreword by William Tara
Preface

Introduction   11

Part One: Macrobiotics: a way of life for everyone

1.   The Harmony of Opposites   19
2.   Macrobiotics: East and West   42
3.   Food for the Past, Present, and Future   57

Part Two: Cooking for Health, Happiness, and Freedom

1.   Cooking with Whole Grains   83
2.   Special Grain Dishes: Seitan, Fu, and Noodles   110
3.   Soups and Soup Stocks   123
4.   Cooking with Vegetables, including Salad-Making   147
5.   Bean Dishes, including Tofu and Natto   179
6.   Cooking with Sea Vegetables   192
7.   Natural Baking including Whole-Grain Bread, Waffles, Pancakes and Doughnuts   200
8.   Natural Desserts   207
9.   Seafood   217
10.   Condiments   223
11.   Pickle-Making   228 ′
12.   Dressings, Spreads, Sauces and Dips   236
13.   Beverages   244
14.   Holiday Cooking   249
15.   Menu Suggestions   256

Appendix A: Principles of the Order of Universe   261
Appendix B: Yin and Yang Guidelines: The Vegetable and Animal Kingdoms   263
Appendix C: North American Macrobiotic Congress, Case History Project   265
Glossary   267/Bibliography   271

Introduction

When I began to study macrobiotic cooking more than eight years ago, I had
no idea of the important change that I was making in my life. We all seem to
take food very much for granted, as it is always there, but seldom consider the
profound effect that it has on our mental, spiritual, and physical condition. How
wonderful it was then, and still is now, to begin feeling stronger and more alert,
and to watch various sicknesses change into health. Some changes in our condition take place very quickly, while others are more gradual and subtle.

During childhood, life is so new, fresh, exciting, and wonderful. When I was
younger I often wondered why life could not remain in some way like that.
After eating whole foods for only a few days, however, life suddenly began to
look different to me. Again it seemed exciting, challenging, and interesting. My
view of life was changing along with my physical health.

After practicing macrobiotics for several years in upstate New York, I moved
to Philadelphia and became involved with macrobiotic activities there. I met
my husband in Philadelphia, and moved to Boston in 1973 in order to study with
Michio and Aveline Kushi, while helping to establish the East West Foundation,
an educational institution which had been founded by the Kushis. I was very
busy with various Foundation activities until I became pregnant with my second
baby in 1976. At that time, I felt that I was ready to begin teaching others some
of the wonderful things that I had learned. For me, teaching was, and still is, a
very enjoyable experience, as it places me in direct contact with other people.
My students are also my teachers, as I continuously learn from their questions,
points of view, and experiences. They have also helped me develop the ability
to express myself in a clear, orderly, and simple manner.

I continued teaching in Boston until September 1978, at which time my husband, two children, and I went to Japan for further study and experience. During
our 10 month stay there, we had the opportunity to teach macrobiotic cooking
and philosophy both at the Kyoto YMCA and in our home. This proved to be
quite an interesting and challenging experience, as most of our classes were presented through a translator. It also required a period of time before I adjusted
my cooking to the new environment in Japan, where I found a number of unfamiliar vegetables and other foods.

Interestingly, most Japanese women study cooking in school or college, or at
home. In many cases, their actual cooking techniques are very refined. During
class, we would often spend a great deal of time discussing the principles of
macrobiotics, rather than studying many of the cooking techniques that they
already were familiar with. Many of the women in our neighborhood attended
these classes, and after a while, began sending their daughters to study with me.

Cooking for my family on a daily basis has also been essential in helping me to learn, change, become flexible, and experience the practical aspects of macro-biotics. This is especially true if you have children, since you must be continually aware of their changing needs and adapt your cooking accordingly. There is nothing like practical experience to teach you.

From the beginning of my macrobiotic practice I have often thought that someday, after I had gained experience, I would like to write a cookbook. So, in 1978, I began to write a short booklet about macrobiotic cooking, largely at the urging of friends, even though I felt that I needed further development and refinement of my cooking and teaching abilities. That original idea gradually expanded into a full-fledged book, simply because there were so many important things to talk about and to share. I had wanted to write a cookbook that was basic, uncomplicated, and easy to use, yet comprehensive enough to serve as a complete introductory guide. This book is available through Japan Publications, Inc. under the title *Introducing Macrobiotic Cooking*, and has generally been well received throughout the United States, Canada, and Western Europe.

This new book, *Macrobiotic Cooking for Everyone*, is basically an extension of my first book. It includes an additional collection of both basic and advanced recipes, along with an introductory section about the principles of macrobiotics.

Both books were written in New England during the autumn and winter months. Depending on where you live, you may need to modify some of the recipes which they contain so as to adapt your cooking to your own climate, environment, and season. In the near future, as macrobiotics continues to spread, I hope to see many cookbooks available which reflect the unique environmental conditions and customs of the regions in which they are written. It would be so wonderful to have regional cookbooks such as these available in a number of languages, as this would make it much easier for many people to begin the practice of macro-biotics.

There are many benefits which result from eating well, and I would like to briefly mention several of these. First, proper eating is the most fundamental way to establish our health. In order to enjoy life and function as productive members of society, we must have good health. Once our health has been established, our thinking becomes clear and our judgment and intuition become keen. If enough people begin to restore their health and happiness in this way, the world will automatically change into a happy and peaceful place in which to live, work, play, and raise our families.

Secondly, as we begin to establish good health, our sense of beauty begins to change. Not only does our appearance begin to change into one of more natural beauty, but we also begin to appreciate and desire a more simple elegance and natural beauty in our home and surroundings. Through macrobiotics, our skin becomes softer and more beautiful, and we begin to look and feel more youthful. Our expression also begins to change, making our voice more beautiful and pleasant to listen to.

Thirdly, macrobiotics makes it possible to enjoy the experience of natural preg-nancy, childbirth, and childcare, including the natural practice of breastfeeding.

I know from experience that children who are raised in this manner are very healthy and strong, and are rarely troubled by many of the sicknesses that effect children today.

Aside from being better for your health, a diet based on whole, natural foods is much more economical than the usual supermarket fare. As everyone knows, food prices have increased tremendously over the last several years. Interestingly, about 87% of the increases in food prices since 1973 are the result of rising transportation and processing costs. The solutions to these problems are simple. Whole foods require a minimum, if any, processing. What little processing they may require usually takes place in very small factory or home-based situations where costs are very low. For example, the *miso*, *tamari*, and other processed items that we use are still made according to traditional methods which do not require huge machines, complicated production techniques, or large staffs of people. Transportation costs could be substantially reduced by shifting in the direction of a more regionally based agriculture. As they were in the past, grain, bean, and vegetable cultivation should become the most important part of every community's agricultural program. Needless to say, these essential food items should be grown primarily for human consumption rather than as feed for livestock.

From my experience in Japan, I can see that huge tracts of land are not really necessary to provide people with a steady and reliable supply of food. In Japan, there is no wasted space. If for example, a family owns some land, it is almost always used for growing rice or vegetables. The entire country is literally dotted with family and community gardens of this type, while the average size of commercial farms is only about two and a half acres. Some of these gardens produce enough grain and vegetables for an entire family to live off of, while others produce enough surplus to sell at local markets. If we could create a situation like this in America, our country would become much more healthy and self-sufficient. This is the type of independent spirit that America was founded on. For example, New England used to produce such a large output of grain that it was referred to as the "breadbasket" of America. As food and energy costs continue to spiral upward, the time is rapidly approaching when a more traditional type of home and community-based agriculture will become increasingly necessary.

When we cook for ourselves, our families, or our friends, we should always maintain a healthy, positive, and peaceful state of mind. I find cooking to be the most wonderful and rewarding part of my day. It makes me very happy to prepare and serve nourishing food to my family and friends, and to see them grow healthier and happier. I feel that I am really benefiting mankind by making others healthy and happy through my cooking, since by cooking for others, you are creating life. Much depends on the proper nourishment of mankind, and this joyful task is largely in the hands of women.

At this time, we would like to acknowledge our deepest gratitude to Michio and Aveline Kushi for their continual dedication to the teaching and development of macrobiotics both in this country and throughout the world; to George and Lima Ohsawa, who dedicated their lives to bringing this wonderful way of life from the East to the West; to our parents, who have given unselfishly of them-selves to provide and care for us and who have given us the opportunity to be born on this earth; to our ancestors, who are also responsible for our lives and who have instilled us with the dream of macrobiotics; and to our children, who bring us continual joy and who teach us daily by providing us with many oppor-tunities for self-reflection and growth. We would also like to thank our friends, seniors, and students in America, Japan, and Europe who have provided us with the opportunity to learn and develop along with them, and would also like to express our gratitude to those who grow the grains, vegetables, and other foods which we eat daily, along with all of our friends in the natural food industry who work very hard to make these foods available to us.

This book has truly been an international project involving the friendship and cooperation of a number of people throughout the world. In Japan, we would like to thank Mr. Iwao Yoshizaki, President of Japan Publications, Inc. for pro-viding us with the opportunity to write this book and for his kind assistance from the very beginning of this project. We would also like to thank all of the members of the Kushi family in Japan for their friendship and kindness during our stay there, and for making it possible for Michio Kushi to come to this country many years ago. We would also like to extend a very special thank you to Mrs. Lima Ohsawa, who at the age of 80, continues to teach the art of cooking in Japan and throughout the world, and who serves as a continuing inspiration and example of the benefits of health and beauty that this way of life bestows upon us. We would also like to thank the macrobiotic centers in Tokyo, Kyoto, and Osaka for their continuing dedication to spreading macrobiotics in Japan, and extend special thanks to Mrs. Sachiko Shimooka for her kindness in contributing to the pickle section of this book.

On the other side of the world, in England, we would like to extend our deepest gratitude to William Tara, founder and President of the Community Health Foundation and the Kushi Institute in London. Through his continuing social and educational activities, he has inspired and helped thousands of people in Europe and America. We would like to thank him for taking time from his active schedule of teaching, writing, and consulting to contribute a foreword for this book.

In the United States, we wish to thank our friends Tom and Toby Monte in Washington, D.C. for their kindness, hospitality, and assistance in preparing part of this book, and would also like to thank our many friends in the Philadelphia and Baltimore macrobiotic communities for their warm hospitality during our stay in that area last summer. We also thank Joe and Diane Avoli in Worcester, Mass., for their kindness and hospitality during our stay with them last fall, and for their comments and advice while we were writing this book. We would espe-cially like to thank Peter and Bonnie Harris for their efforts in producing dia-grams and illustrations both for this book and for *Introducing Macrobiotic Cook-ing*, and also thank Patricia Davis for her effort in typing the manuscript. We also wish to thank Steve Gagne for taking time to review part of the manuscript, along with Karin Jones, Sarah Loring, Lynn Fradkin, and our many other friends at the Kushi Institute, the East West Foundation, the *East West Journal*, and Erewhon for their friendship, guidance, and assistance.

WENDY ESKO
Boston, Massachusetts
January, 1980

Part One

Macrobiotics: a way of life for everyone

1. The Harmony of Opposites

"There are no fixtures in nature. The universe is fluid and volatile. Permanence is but a word of degrees. Our globe seen by God is a transparent law, not a mass of facts."
—Ralph Waldo Emerson in his essay, *Circles*

The macrobiotic way of life is based on achieving and maintaining a dynamic balance with our environment in nature and the universe, beginning most fundamentally with the proper selection and preparation of our daily foods. This is actually the secret of life and the key to our health, happiness, and freedom.

Throughout history, people have understood that life, nature, and the universe are based on the continual interplay of complementary, yet antagonistic, forces which are produced out of one, indivisible and infinite universe. This process is explained in the opening lines of *Genesis* in the words, "In the beginning, God created Heaven and Earth." A similar explanation can be found in all of the great religious and spiritual teachings in both East and West, while an awareness of these two primary forces is also universal and common to everyone, and lies at the base of our native intuition and common sense.

Before we are born, each of us becomes aware of these forces in the alternating expansion and contraction of our mother's heartbeat. After we are born, we begin to detect the difference between coldness and warmth, hunger and fullness, darkness and light, and other similar pairs of opposites. Usually, we come to prefer some of these conditions, such as fullness and warmth, while disliking others. Through experience, however, we soon come to realize that nothing is static, and that conditions eventually change into their opposites.

In the beginning, common occurrences such as these are not taken for granted; they are new discoveries. After repeated experience of and continual adaptation to our environment, we begin to realize that, on the most fundamental level, life is a process of change. We also begin to sense that this process occurs in an orderly and predictable manner, as we gain the confidence, or faith, that day will eventually change into night, and vice-versa; that hunger will change to fullness, and that movement will change into rest. This intuitive realization is possibly the most important one in our lives, since it precedes the understanding of language and is the underlying basis for the accumulation of all other forms of knowledge. However, just as these realizations begin to crystallize, our formal education usually begins, and most of us tuck them somewhere below our everyday, surface consciousness.

As obvious as they seem, basic realizations such as these are actually the starting point for a comprehensive understanding of life. This type of fundamental understanding is referred to in the *Bible* as the *Tree of Life*, while the accumulation of knowledge or facts, without a unified perspective, is referred to as the *Tree of Knowledge*. The *Bible* also symbolically depicts mankind's fall from paradise as being the result of abandoning the *Tree of Life* and eating fruit from the *Tree of Knowledge*.

However, even our modern pursuit of knowledge has its origin nowhere else

Fig. 1 Sayings of Heraclitus and Lao-Tzu

From the *Fragments* of Heraclitus:

From the *Tao Te King:*

From the *Fragments* of Heraclitus:	From the *Tao Te King:*
We should let ourselves be guided by what is common to all. Yet, although the *Logos* is common to all, most men live as if each had a private intelligence of his own. Listening not to me but to the *Logos*, it is wise to acknowledge that all things are one.	The *Tao* is like an empty bowl which, in being used, can never be filled up. Fathomless, it seems to be the origin of all things. It blunts all sharp edges, It unites all tangles, It harmonizes all lights, It unites the world into one whole.
Cool things become warm, the warm grows cool; the moist dries, the parched becomes moist. Immortals become mortals mortals become immortals; they live in each other's death and die in each other's life. It (the universe) throws apart and then brings together again; it advances and retires.	In fact, for all things there is a time for going ahead and a time for following behind; A time for slow-breahing and a time for fast-breathing; A time to grow in strength and a time for decay; A time to be up and a time to be down.
Everything flows and nothing abides; everything gives way and nothing stays fixed. You cannot step twice into the same river, for other waters and yet others go ever flowing on.	Look at it but you cannot see it! Listen to it but you cannot hear it! Grasp it but cannot get it! Continually the Unnameable moves on, Until it returns beyond the realm of things.
It is by disease that health is pleasant; by evil that good is pleasant; by hunger, satiety; by weariness, rest.	Difficult and easy complement each other. Long and short exhibit each other. High and low set measure to each other. Voice and sound harmonize each other.
To God, all things are beautiful, good and right; men, on the other hand, deem some things right and others wrong.	Back and front follow each other. The Sage has not interests of his own. He is kind to the kind; he is also kind to the unkind. He is faithful to the faithful; he is also faithful to the unfaithful

but in the awareness of the eternal order of change. For example, in ancient Greece, where the processes of logic and reasoning were first studied, an early philosopher named Heraclitus devoted his life to perfecting this awareness. Heraclitus lived around 500 B.C., and influenced many later thinkers such as Plato and Aristotle. One of his main tenets was that "everything flows and nothing abides; everything gives way and nothing stays fixed." He referred to the process of change as the *Logos*, and stated that it was universal, or common to all things. The *Logos*, or a systematic understanding of the order of change was later developed as the concept of *logic*, or the attempt to identify an order or pattern within our constantly changing environment.

Interestingly enough, at about the same time, a Chinese philosopher named Lao Tzu developed a similar view of life. Lao Tzu referred to the order of change as *Tao*, and also understood that it was eternal and universal. Lao Tzu arrived at this conclusion after a lifetime of studying more ancient Chinese classics, especially the *I Ching*, or *Book of Changes*, which had been compiled more than five hundred years earlier. The *I Ching* is one of the most well-known and respected of all Far Eastern texts, and has had an effect on Oriental thought and culture not unlike that of the *Bible* in the West.

Lao Tzu's philosophy was recorded in a small book entitled the *Tao Te King*, and his teaching led to the development of *Taoism*, a school of thought which has since influenced millions of people throughout Asia, and, more recently, in the West.[1] As we have seen, Heraclitus' study of the *Logos* was developed by later Greek philosophers into the concept of logic. However, several of these later thinkers, especially Aristotle, lost the more comprehensive outlook of their predecessor, and, instead of pursuing an understanding of the order which creates everything, concentrated on the classification and collection of data on individual phenomena, leading to the general misconception that the world is made up of a countless number of separate and independent entities. Out of this developed the separation of religion, or the study of the invisible world, and science, or the study of the visible, material world, as well as the tendency to think of our sciences, arts, religions, philosophies and other areas of knowledge as separate fields of study with no common principles. This tendency has been accelerated in the modern age by the rapid development of technology, so that at present the over-

---

[1] Confucius also studied the *I Ching*, and he based his philosophy and ethical teachings around it. He referred to the order of change as *Ten-Mei*, or *heavenly order*, and taught that the highest virtue was to live in harmony with it. He also taught that the ideal society would come when governmental affairs were conducted in accord with the order of the universe, and when people cultivated it in their daily lives. Another well known Chinese classic, *Monkey*, is also based on the understanding of the order of change. Written almost as a fairy tale, this book describes the mythical adventures of a magic stone monkey who develops the ability to change himself freely into a variety of forms. This folk novel continues to delight people of all ages throughout the Orient. For example, one of the most popular songs that we heard last year during our stay in Japan was entitled *Monkey Magic*, and was about Monkey, the hero of the novel.

whelming tendency is to specialize or compartmentalize our understanding within increasingly narrow limits.[2]

However, even scientific research, which has become one of the most highly specialized fields of modern knowledge, is, according to Albert Einstein, ultimately an attempt to perfect our understanding of the order of the universe as a whole. As he states in one of his essays, "The scientist is possessed by the sense of universal causation. His religious feeling takes the form of a rapturous amazement at the harmony of natural law, which reveals an intelligence of such superiority that, compared with it, all the systematic thinking and acting of human beings is an utterly insignificant reflection. This feeling is the guiding principle of his life and work, in so far as he succeeds in keeping himself from the shackles of selfish desire. It is beyond question closely akin to that which has possessed the religious geniuses of all ages."[3]

When combined with the chaotic dietary practices which prevail throughout the world, the lack of a unifying principle has resulted in our modern crisis, which is biological, psychological and spiritual in nature. We are now in a situation in which the major degenerative illnesses continue to affect larger and larger numbers of people; in which religion, the family, education and other traditional institutions have lost much of their former stabilizing influence; in which the end of human civilization through nuclear destruction is an ever-present possibility; and in which the very fabric of society is being threatened by a seemingly endless number of conflicts. Our modern predicament is largely the result of abandoning the *Tree of Life*, or the understanding of the order of nature, and pursuing almost exclusively the *Tree of Knowledge*. In order to overcome the many challenges that we as individuals and as a society will confront both now and in the future, we must first re-establish a unified understanding of life, and apply that understanding on a practical, day to day basis for the creation of our health and happiness.

---

[2] *On Independent Thinking in the Age of Science*:

"With modern instruments we can analyze starlight, and find out what substances are there; we can send men to the moon and dispatch rocket probes to our neighboring planets. But when we ask first how the earth and the rest of the universe came into being, we have to admit that we are totally ignorant. The atoms which make up you, me, this book, the kitchen sink, Aunt Emily, the sun and the galaxies must have come from somewhere; but where? If we begin with a universe filled with homogenous gas, we can work out an evolutionary sequence; but we cannot decide how the gas got there in the first place. Neither can we understand the nature of time, and we are very uncertain about the origin of life itself. In fact, modern science is strong on details, weak on the essential fundamentals. What the independent thinker usually does is go to the grass roots and question *everything*. This is why he cannot be refuted by conventional argument."

From *Can You Speak Venusian? A Guide to the Independent Thinkers* by Patrick Moore.

[3] Many of our present sciences have their origins in attempts to understand and apply the order of change. For example, the science of chemistry, and, to some extent, physics, originated largely with the ancient practice of alchemy, or the attempt to transmute one element into another. Practiced thousands of years ago in China, India and other parts of the Orient, alchemy was also attempted by the Alexandrian Greeks and, until the 18th Century, in many parts of Europe.

The Orderliness of Nature

In macrobiotics, we use the Chinese terms *Yin* (▽) and *Yang* (△) to describe the two most basic forces in nature. A similar concept can be found in practically every culture. Arnold Toynbee, the British historian, also utilized these terms to describe the alternating rhythm of the universe and its manifestation in human affairs. In Japan, these terms are used frequently in daily conversation and are pronounced *In-Sei* (陰性), or "yin nature," and *Yo-Sei* (陽性), or "yang nature." For example, the sun is referred to in Japanese as *Tai-Yo* (太陽) or "great yang," while the moon is called *Tai-In* (太陰) or "great yin." The solar system is referred to in Japan as *Tai-Yo-Kei* (太陽系), or "great yang system."

Yin and Yang refer to the two most basic, relative forces in the universe; that of centrifugality and that of centripetality. The more yang force of centripetality arises within the infinite depth of the universe and produces such relative tendencies as contraction, fusion, more rapid motion, a more inward position, heat, brightness, the male sex, a positively charged pole, and others. The complementary force of centrifugality (yin) manifests out of the primary expansion of the universe, and creates the tendency toward expansion, slower motion, a more outward position, coldness, darkness, the female sex, a negatively charged pole, and numerous others. Everything in the universe comes into being, is maintained, develops, and ultimately disappears as a result of these two primary forces. The basic polarity which they represent can be found at every level of existence— from the intergalactic to the sub-atomic and beyond, into the invisible worlds of vibration and consciousness. A more complete classification of phenomena according to yin and yang is presented at the back of this book in the Appendix, "Principles of the Order of the Universe."

An understanding of how these universal forces operate fulfills the ultimate concept of science as defined by Einstein, and is also the underlying principle on which Christianity, Judaism, Buddhism, Shintoism, Taoism, Vedantic thought, Greek philosophy and most of the world's great religious, cosmological, spiritual, and philosophical systems are based.[4] Since they involve a fundamental understanding of the principles of cause and effect which govern the whole universe, any problem, no matter how seemingly complex, becomes readily understandable when viewed in terms of these universal laws. These unifying principles are especially relevant in our modern world, since in order to deal with the many complex

---

[4] In one of his essays, Albert Einstein defined science as an attempt to "bring together by means of systematic thought the perceptible phenomena of this world into as through-going an association as possible." Through the synthesis of traditional Far Eastern and other spiritual and philsophical modes of thought with modern philosophical and scientific understanding, George Ohsawa, Michio Kushi and other macrobiotic associates have developed a comprehensive outline of the universal order of nature, presented at the back of this book in the Appendix, "Principles of the Order of the Universe." The macrobiotic way of life is simply the application of this universal order to the art of longevity and rejuvenation through proper food. Similar applications were practiced in many traditional cultures throughout the world.

problems that we are now facing, we must seek the most basic causes and most fundamental solutions.

We can easily see that everything in nature alternates between antagonistic yet complementary states. Day changes into night; and night changes into day. Winter becomes spring; spring becomes summer; summer changes into fall, and fall again becomes winter. In the morning we awaken to begin the day's activity and at night we return home to rest. Common sense, daily cycles such as these are actually examples of a universally occurring pattern. In the *Gospel According to Thomas*, Jesus referred to this process when he said: "If they ask you, 'What is the sign of your Father in you?', say to them, 'It is a movement and a rest.' "[5]

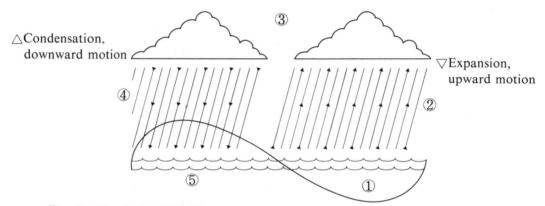

Fig. 2 The Cycle of Water
Within the biosphere, water alternates between a more yang, or condensed state, and a more yin or diffused state. Yin changes into yang, and yang changes into yin. This process occurs universally throughout nature.

A familiar example of this universal process is found in the cycle of water, in which it passes through a continual process of transformation from a more yang, or condensed stage to a more yin, or diffused stage. Most of the estimated 53 billion cubic feet of water on the earth exists at any given time in the ocean. Fresh water accounts for a small portion of the total, only about three percent, and roughly three-fourths of this is locked into glaciers and polar icecaps. These forms, including other stable bodies such as lakes and ponds, correspond to the most yang, or condensed state in the cycle, shown in the diagram as (1). With the process of evaporation, (2), yang changes into yin, as water is transformed into a gas (water vapor), and rises upward into the atmosphere. Only about 0.0001 % of the total volume of water is present in the atmosphere at any given time. While in the atmosphere, high above the surface of the earth, lower temperatures cause this more yin gas to condense back into liquid form, forming tiny

---

[5] "Motion or change, and identity or rest, are the first and second secrets of nature: Motion and Rest."—Ralph Waldo Emerson in his essay, *Nature*.

droplets which are still light enough to be suspended in the air. This more yang process of condensation results in the formation of clouds (3) high above the earth's surface and, when it occurs at lower altitudes, in mists, fog, dew and frost. Within these cloud formations, increasingly lower temperatures cause the tiny cloud droplets to condense into ice-crystals, resulting in the formation of snow, rain, hail or other types of precipitation (4) which falls to earth in a more yang, or downward, direction. Some of the water which falls as precipitation collects into streams, rivers, brooks, and other moving bodies (5), and eventually gathers in the larger, more stable bodies mentioned above. Here the cycle begins again.

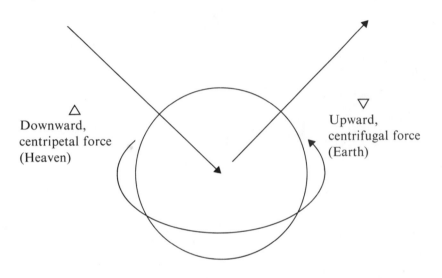

△
Downward,
centripetal force
(Heaven)

▽
Upward,
centrifugal force
(Earth)

Fig. 3   Heaven's and Earth's Forces
The more yang, centripetal force of heaven is strongest at the Poles, while the earth's centrifugal, expanding force is strongest at the equator. That is why the earth is somewhat flattened at the Poles and bulges slightly at the equator. Heaven's force spirals in from space in a counterclockwise direction, while the force of earth spirals outward in a clockwise direction. (Directions are opposite in the Southern Hemisphere.)

There are numerous other cycles within the biosphere, such as the carbon and nitrogen cycles, which generally follow a similar pattern. As the example of water illustrates, these cycles are governed by two huge forces: that of centrifugality, or expansive force or motion, which causes movement in an upward direction away from the earth; and that of centripetality, or movement in a downward direction toward the earth's surface. The more yang, centripetal force is generated inward toward the center of the earth by the sun, stars, planets, constellations and other heavenly bodies, and by space itself. This comprehensive force creates the tendency of objects to stay on the earth's surface, while at the same time causing the planet to rotate and revolve around the sun. Isaac Newton named this force *gravity*, but did not understand that it originates in the universe rather than with physical bodies. In other words, Newton thought that the earth "pulled" the apple to the ground when actually space was "pushing" it. At the equator, the earth rotates at a speed of about eleven hundred miles per hour, and this motion generates an opposite, expanding, centrifugal force which is strongest at the equator, becoming progressively weaker toward the poles. In the *I Ching*, as in the *Book of Genesis*, these relative tendencies are referred to as *heaven* and *earth*. In macrobiotics we also use a similar terminology, referring to the more yang, downward or centripetal force as *heaven's force* and to the more yin, expansive or upward force as *earth's force*.[6]

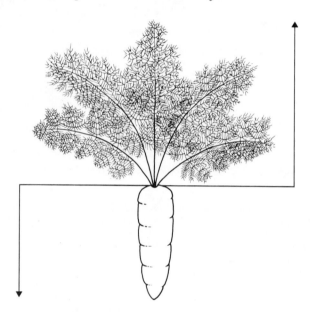

▽More yin
(Created by Earth's Force)

△More yang
(Created by Heaven's Force)

Fig. 4   The Influence of Heaven's and Earth's Forces in the Vegetable Kingdom

All things on the planet are created and held in balance by these two complementary forces. For example, most vegetables contain two major sections: a more compacted root portion and a more expanded stem or leafy portion. In a carrot, for instance, the root portion grows in a downward direction toward the center of the earth, and is governed more by heaven's force. The leafy carrot top grows in an opposite direction, upward toward the sky. It is governed more by the expanding force of earth. Therefore, within the complete vegetable we have two large sections—the more yang root portion and the more yin, leafy green portion. When eaten, the root portion will produce a more yang, or contractive, effect, while the leafy portion produces a more yin, expansive effect.

---

[6] In the *Book of Macrobiotics: The Universal Way of Health and Happiness*, Michio Kushi introduces and further explains the dynamics of the forces of heaven and earth, elaborating on their roles in the formation of the human body and in determining the development of male and female sex characteristics.

At the same time, each of these contains further yin and yang divisions. In the root portion, for example, the narrow tip is more yang than the expanded upper part, while in the leafy top, the compact branches and stems are more yang than the expanded leaves. Therefore, to create balance in cooking, vegetables such as carrots, *daikon*, burdock and others are cut diagonally rather than horizontally so that each piece will have a more even balance of yin and yang factors.

A similar complementary and antagonistic structure can be found in the human body. The body can be divided into a number of complementary yet antagonistic sections, all of which reflect the structure of the universe. These include the upper and lower sections, the left and right sides, the front and back sides, the parts which move actively and those which are more stationary, and others. Of these, the relationship between the upper and lower parts of the body, especially between the head and the rest of the body below the neck, offers a clear illustration of the interaction of heaven's and earth's forces.

Structurally, the head is smaller and more compact than the rest of the body. In terms of structure, therefore, we would classify the head as more yang, while the larger and more expanded body would be classified as being more yin. In terms of their growth and development, however, the opposite is true. The head develops in a more yin, or upward, direction (taking the mouth as the central point of balance), while the rest of the body develops in a more yang, or downward, direction. Although more yang in structure, the head develops more as a a result of the earth's more yin, upward force, while the structurally more yin body develops primarily under the influence of heaven's more yang, downward force.

All of the major organs and systems within the body can also be classified according to yin and yang. With the major organs, for example, two primary types can be identified—the more yin, hollow or expanded organs such as the stomach and intestines, and the more yang, solid or compact organs such as the liver, heart, and kidneys. In traditional Oriental medicine, which includes the theory and practice of acupuncture, *shiatsu* (finger-pressure) massage, herbal medicine, and other techniques, each of the bodily organs is viewed as part of a pair which contains a more yin organ in combination with a more yang organ. This classification was first recorded several thousand years ago in China in the *Yellow Emperor's Classic of Internal Medicine*, or *Nei-Ching*, one of the oldest medical texts in existence throughout the world. In this volume, the major organs are classified as follows:

△Yang (Solid or Compact Organs	▽ Yin (Hollow or Expanded) Organs
Lungs	Large Intestine
Heart	Small Intestine
Kidneys	Bladder
Spleen/Pancreas	Stomach
Liver	Gall Bladder

We can better understand this classification when we consider several of the complementary functions shared by these organ pairs, such as (1) the complementary digestive enzymes secreted by the stomach and its partner, the pancreas (those of the stomach have a more acid reaction, while pancreatic enzymes are generally more alkaline); (2) the kidney function of blood filtration and the complementary function of storing and discharging the filtered waste products by the bladder; and (3) the liver's secretion of bile and other digestive juices, and their subsequent storage in the gall bladder.

This structural classification is still utilized in many types of Oriental diagnosis and treatment. For example, if a person visits an Oriental doctor with a lung sickness such as asthma or lung mucus, the practitioner will invariably check the large intestine, its complementary partner, for some type of related difficulty. Often, when treating an organ with acupuncture, *shiatsu*, palm healing or some other traditional technique, the Oriental doctor will place just as much emphasis on treating its complementary partner.

The basic illustrations presented above and in the Appendix represent only a few of the countless examples of the complementary, yet antagonistic, structure of the universe. We hope to offer additional examples throughout this book, and hope that it will serve as a guide to the application of this universal order in the kitchen for the establishment of health and happiness. For, as we shall see, it is on the proper balancing of yin and yang that our life depends.

Yin and Yang: Universal Guides for Food Selection

> "Food represents the very essence of the power of creation. It stands at the crossroads between the infinite forces of nature and the biological wonder of man." From an Erewhon product label.

Like everything else in the universe, we can classify foods into those which are more yin and those which are more yang. However, our definition of food should not be limited to what we eat at our tables every day, but should include our total environment from the more immediate, physicalized component to the invisible, vibrational component and beyond, into the infinite universe itself.

As Michio Kushi and other associates have pointed out, our total environment manifests into two complementary forms: (1) as the invisible fields of energy and vibration which permeate the universe, which we interpret as sound, light, heat, charged particles, cosmic rays, electromagnetic waves and in other ways; and (2) in the form of physically detectable matter, existing in the form of solids, liquids, and gases. Both the more yin, vibrational components and the more yang, physicalized components of the environment are constantly coming into us in the form of food. Our life is fundamentally a process whereby we attract and transform our multiple environments into ourselves.

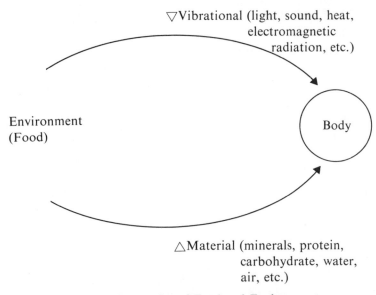

Environment
(Food)

∇Vibrational (light, sound, heat,
electromagnetic
radiation, etc.)

Body

△Material (minerals, protein,
carbohydrate, water,
air, etc.)

Fig. 5 Two Categories of Food and Environment

The brain and central nervous system acts as a receiver for the countless variety of vibrations which originate both within our immediate environment on the earth and in our distant environment in space. Our physicalized environment is eaten in the form of minerals, protein, carbohydrates, water, air, etc., and is being continually processed by the digestive and respiratory systems. Structurally, the digestive system is a soft, hollow tube which branches into the lungs and respiratory organs. These organs are more yin relative to the more compact brain and central nervous system. As a result, the nervous system attracts and processes the more yin, vibrational form of the environment, while the digestive system processes our more yang, physicalized environment. The circulatory and excretory systems are classified as being in between these two primary divisions. The relationship between these two broad categories of food and the human body can be seen in the following chart:

Two Broad Categories of Food

Type of food:	Processed by:
∇ Vibrational (solar and stellar radiation, electromagnetic waves, light, sound, etc.)	△ Nervous System
△ Physicalized (minerals, protein, carbohydrate, water, air)	∨ Digestive and Respiratory Systems

The relationships listed above are complementary and antagonistic. If, for example, we eat too much, we activate the digestive and respiratory systems, while supressing the activity of the nervous system. As a result, we begin to lose our

sensitivity to the more subtle forms of vibrational food, and our powers of thinking and imagination decline. On the other hand, when we eat less, our nervous
system becomes more active and we become progressively more senstitive to finer
and subtler vibrations emanating from the depths of the universe. These vibrations
are in turn translated into images, thoughts, ideas, imagination and insight, similar
to the way in which a television set catches the waves being broadcast from the
station, and produces an image and sound. This is one of the primary reasons
why fasting or moderate eating are often recommended as means of achieving
spiritual development, which we can interpret as an increased sensitivity to a
wider range of vibrations.

As George Ohsawa pointed out many years ago, the most primary complementary and antagonistic relationship existing within the realm of biological life as a
whole is that between the animal and vegetable kingdoms. Generally speaking, the
animal kingdom is more yang, and is governed more by heaven's downward force,
although both forces are involved in all life forms existing on the planet. This
active, centripetal force has the effect of causing animal cells to generally be more
condensed or compact in structure, and also enables most animal species to generate self-movement. In the more advanced animals, this more yang influence
produces the generation of body heat.

The vegetable kingdom is governed more by the opposite, upward or expanding
force generated by the earth. As a result, vegetable cells usually have a more
hollow or expanded structure, while vegetable species lack the ability of self-
movement and do not generate their own heat. Animals take a more active role
within their environment and are able to gain some degree of independence from it,
while vegetables are passive and totally dependent on their immediate environment.

The vegetable kingdom is the matrix out of which the animal world is produced.
The essence of the primarily green vegetable kingdom is the compound chlorophyll,
which is yin relative to the hemoglobin which lies at the base of red-blooded
animals. At the same time, all animals depend on the vegetable world for their
existence. Since the vegetable kingdom is generally yin, foods from this category
tend to produce more yin effects, for example slowing the rate of metabolism and
producing an overall relaxation of bodily functions. Animal foods, for the most
part, produce an opposite effect, causing a general "tightness" in the body and
often accelerating the speed of metabolism. Since they are complementary in
structure and function, the animal and vegetable kingdoms are naturally attracted
to one another, in the same way that men are attracted to women, a positive
charge attracts a negative charge, and more yin oxygen atoms attract more yang
hydrogen atoms to create water molecules. This process is universal, reflecting the
natural tendency toward equilibrium through the unification of all complementary
phenomena. In a similar way, overall harmony is maintained in the universe
through the tendency of similar factors, such as two positive charges, to repel
one another.

An overall classification of food from the most yang items to the most yin

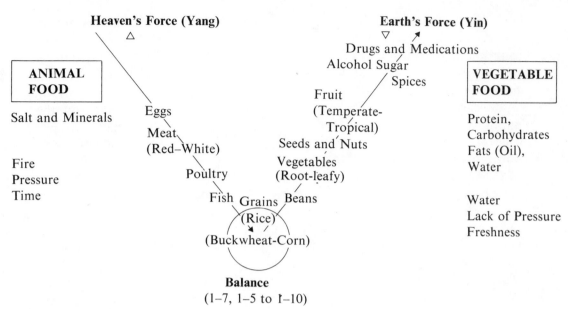

Fig. 6 Yin (▽) and Yang (△) Classification of Foods
Among nutritional factors, salt and other minerals would be classified as more yang; while proteins, carbohydrates, fats, oil, and water are more yin. Among the environmental factors utilized in cooking, fire, pressure, and time are more yang; while water, lack of pressure, and freshness are more yin. Cooking is the art of adjusting these various factors to adapt the qualities of our foods to the environment, season, and to each person's needs.

is represented in Figure 6. In general, the more yang items such as eggs, meat, poultry, and fish, are animal foods, and are representatives of heaven's more downward force. The foods listed on the opposite side of the scale—vegetables, nuts, fruits, spices, sugar, and drugs and medications—represent the more yin, expansive force of the earth. Generally speaking, the foods presented near the center of the scale, especially cereal grains, have a relatively more equal balance of heaven's and earth's forces.

There are also more yin and more yang varieties within each category of food. For example, as pointed out in the *Book of Macrobiotics*, there are at least fifteen factors which should be taken into consideration when judging whether a particular vegetable is more yin or more yang. Among fruits, for example, those which grow in a more tropical or warmer climate, such as bananas or pineapples, are more yin than northern varieties like apples and strawberries. Vegetables with a softer or more watery texture or consistency such as zucchini or summer squashes are more yin than those with hard or more fibrous textures such as carrots or fall squashes. More yin vegetables generally have a high ratio of potassium and other more yin elements to sodium and other more yang elements.

In general, root vegetables such as carrots and burdock are more yang than leafy green vegetables such as kale and Chinese cabbage. As we saw earlier, the root protion of a vegetable grows primarily under the influence of heaven's more yang force, which produces growth in a vertical direction below the ground. Therefore, although vegetables on the whole are relatively more yin, within the overall category of vegetables, root varieties are more yang. Vegetables which grow in an opposite manner—vertically above the ground—are generally more expansive or yin. However, vegetables which grow underground in a horizontal direction, such as potatoes, are more yin, while those which grow above the ground in a horizontal manner, such as fall squashes and dandelions, are more yang.

The color of a vegetable is also an important consideration when judging its yin or yang quality. In general, vegetables which have a purple, blue, green or white color are more yin, while those with a yellow, brown, orange or red color are usually more yang. Therefore, red strawberries are more yang than yellow bananas, while burdock, a relatively dry, dark brown root, is more yang than daikon, which is a juicy, white root vegetable. However, color alone is not enough to determine whether a particular vegetable or variety of fruit is more yin or more yang. For example, tomatoes, which are red when ripe, are actually one of the most yin vegetables, due largely to their chemical composition (high in potassium), place of origin (in a semi-tropical region), and high water content. For similar reasons, fruits such as oranges, grapefruits, and papayas (which have an orange color when ripe) are also very yin, although they appear to have more yang colors.

Overall guidelines for judging the yin and yang qualities of vegetable foods are presented at the back of the book in Appendix B, "*Yin and Yang Guidelines— The Vegetable Kingdom*," adapted from the *Book of Macrobiotics*, while the following chart may be helpful in applying these classifications in your kitchen:

Yang △	Food	More Yin	More Yang
	Grains	Corn Rice	Millet, Buckwheat
	Rice	Long grain, Medium grain,	Short grain
	Wheat	Summer wheat	Winter wheat
	Beans	More fat or oil, i.e. soybeans	Less fat or oil, i.e. chickpea, lentil, azuki
	Vegetables	Leafy Ground	Root
	Seaweed	Harvested in warmer water or closer to shore	Harvested in colder, deeper water
	Nuts	More oily, i.e. peanuts	Less oily, i.e. almonds, chestnuts
	Fruits	Tropical origin, i.e. citrus, pineapple, mango, papaya	Temperate origin, i.e. apple, cherry, strawberry, etc.
Yin ▽	Sweeteners	Refined sugar, honey, maple syrup	Barley malt, rice honey

A similar situation applies to various animal products. For example, more primitive forms of animal life such as shellfish, fish, and birds are generally more yin than more biologically advanced species such as mammals. At the same time, animals which inhabit a more yang, fluid environment are generally more yin than those which live on the surface of the earth in a more yin, air environment. Therefore, whales and other mammals which live in the ocean are generally yin—large and expanded—in comparison to the mammals which live on land. Red meat varieties of animal food are more yang than white meat varieties, while animal products which contain more sodium are more yang than those with a lower sodium content. The major criteria for determining the yin and yang qualities of animal foods are also listed in Appendix B.

The Principle of Balance

> "For 15,000 years, the epoch of grain has been one with the epoch of man."
>
> —H.E. Jacob, *6,000 Years of Bread*
>
> "The destiny of nations depends on how they eat."
>
> —Brillat-Savarin, *The Physiology of Taste*

Our environment on earth is a highly complex, delicately balanced system within which the essential factors exist which make life possible. As human beings, we obviously require certain environmental conditions in order to live and develop. Fortunately, each of the almost infinite variety of chemical, physical, electromagnetic and other factors which make life possible are presently maintained on earth in the proper life-supporting balance.

For example, the earth is surrounded by a number of protective layers, all of which are of the proper density and composition to filter potentially harmful radiation from the sun, especially X-rays and ultraviolet light. This protective envelope includes the earth's magnetic field, which deflects or captures many of the highly energized particles which flow continuously from the sun; the ionosphere, which absorbs high-frequency radiations; the ozone layer, which absorbs most of the ultraviolet light which comes from the sun; and the atmosphere itself, which filters the remainder of these harmful radiations and permits the passage only of beneficial light and heat. If, for example, any of these protective layers were to become more yin—weaker or less dense—a greater number of these solar radiations would penetrate to the earth's surface, eventually making life impossible. On the other hand, if they were to become more yang by increasing in strength or density, not enough solar radiation would penetrate, and life would also diminish.

The molecules of air which comprise the atmosphere are not all electromagnetically neutral. Certain molecules carry a positive charge, due to the loss of a negatively charged electron, while others carry a negative charge as a result of picking up an extra electron. These charged molecules are known as *ions*, and it is estimated that, on the average, a cubic centimeter of air contains between one and two thousand of them. Human life evolved within this electrically charged atmosphere, which generally maintains a delicate balance of more yang, positive, and more yin, negative ions. If this balance is disturbed, human life becomes more difficult, and a variety of physical and mental illnesses can result.[7]

In regard to temperature, there are certain parameters within which we must remain in order to survive. At the same time, within the maximum range of temperatures on earth, certain climatic conditions exist, especially those with an alternating balance of four seasons, within which more advanced human culture and civilization have flourished. This temperate climatic belt extends around the globe, and encompasses most of present day Europe, North America, the Near East, China and Japan.

In respect to our environment, two broad sets of conditions can be identified:

1. *The entire range of conditions within which human life is possible.*

2. *A more balanced, or moderate, range of conditions which offer the optimum environment for human development.*

For example, the maximum range of temperatures on earth would correspond to the first set of conditions listed above, while the temperate climatic zone, which exists within this maximum temperature range, would correspond to the second. It is here that the most ideal balance of yin and yang factors exist within the environment. As we go outside of this more balanced region, for example toward the poles, it becomes necessary to expend increasing amounts of energy just in meeting the demands imposed by climate. Therefore culture and civilization do not develop as actively in these regions. If we proceed toward the equator, the lack of colder temperatures produces a less active pattern of development. However, once we pass out of the range of life-supporting conditions, for example by going to a desert or polar region, it is impossible to survive unless artificial measures are employed. Examples of this are apparent in the tremendous technological efforts required to sustain human life under the ocean, at the North and South Poles, and in outer space.

The following similar categories can also be identified within the realm of foods:

1. *The entire spectrum of possible food items, from the most yin to the most yang.*

2. *Foods which are near the center of the yin/yang scale.*

Among daily food items, cereal grains are generally classified as being nearest to the center of the yin/yang scale. However, the average ratio of the more yin to more yang factors among the cereal grains is not one to one. This comprehensive ratio actually approaches seven to one (between 10:1 and 5:1), and this is the

---

[7] A number of scientific studies have been conducted on seasonal winds which contain an overabundance of positively charged ions and which have been found to produce harmful effects. These include the Foehn winds in Switzerland and southern Germany, the Santa Ana wind in California, the Chinook winds in Canada, the Sharav winds in Israel and the Middle East, and others. During the times when these winds are active, there have been documented increases in problems such as respiratory ailments, headaches, anxiety, tension, etc. In one region of southern Germany, the traffic accident rate was found to increase by more than 50 % during the Foehn season.

most ideal for our present environment on earth. An approximate ratio of seven yin to one yang is the inverse of the average ratio of centripetal (yang) to centrifugal (yin) force existing on the earth at present. In other words, heaven's force is generally seven times stronger than earth's force. By basing our diet around foods which naturally maintain this ratio, we enter a state of relative equilibrium with our surrounding environment. If properly maintained, this condition of balance means that we can remain free of sickness, which is the condition resulting from an excess of yin or yang factors in our diet or environment.

As Michio Kushi pointed out in the *Book of Macrobiotics*, the proportions of the human body also generally reflect an overall seven to one ratio. This "golden proportion" can be seen in such factors as the average length of the body versus the average length of the head; the average height and width of the waist; the approximate ratio of the body's more yin chemical components to its more yang chemical components, and others.

Perhaps it was as many as thirty million years ago when the average ratio of heaven's centripetal force to earth's centrifugal force began to approach the ratio of seven to one. At that time a new species—the ancestors of present-day cereals —began to appear within the vegetable kingdom. It was by eating these relatively compact, seed-bearing grains that our ancient ancestors began to develop toward homosapiens. As they began eating these new foods, their physiological structure began to develop toward the "golden proportion" which the cereal grains represented, and upon which our human form is presently based. This is the primary reason why the cereal grains have constituted mankind's most important staple food from the origin of the species up to the present.[8]

In all but the most extreme polar climates, whole grains comprise the optimum primary food for man, while the most ideal secondary foods are locally grown, seasonal vegetables, beans and sea vegetables. The most preferable supplementary items include some animal food, preferably the more yin forms such as fish and shellfish, local fruits in season, and various types of seeds and nuts. By selecting our daily foods from these groups, it is relatively easy to maintain a more moderate balance of yin and yang factors. Foods such as these are relatively near the center of the yin and yang scale, and correspond to the second, or most ideal, set of environmental conditions listed above. A diet that encompasses this range

---

[8] "No civilization worthy of the name has ever been founded on any agricultural basis other than the cereals. The ancient cultures of Babylonia and Egypt, of Rome and Greece, and later those of northern and western Europe, were all based on the growing of wheat, barley, rye and oats. Those of India, China and Japan had rice for their basic crop. The pre-Columbian peoples of America—Inca, Maya, and Aztec—looked to corn for their daily bread." Paul C. Mangelsdorf in "Wheat," *Scientific American*, July, 1953.
"Because of their low cost, cereal grains are the major source of food energy for 97 % of the people of the world; they make up more than 82 % of world food output and 73 % of actual food consumption. Worldwide, 53.7 % of the population eat mainly rice, and 35.5 % rely largely on wheat products." Ed Edwin, *Feast or Famine: Farming and Farm Politics in America.*

of foods not only enables us to comfortably maintain our health but will also secure our evolutionary status, as well as our potential as human beings.

However, man has the capacity to eat almost anything—from the most yin items through to the most yang. However, as with our environment, the further we proceed from the most ideally balanced region, the more difficulties we begin to encounter. In the case of food, these difficulties appear as various physical, mental and spiritual illnesses. As we eat further out along the yin and yang scale, our body must deal with these extreme or excessive factors by either: (1) discharging them through some abnormal method such as fever, coughing, sneezing, allergies, skin diseases and others, or (2) storing them internally in the form of mucus, fat, cholesterol deposits, kidney or gall stones, cysts, tumors, and so on. In some cases, these extreme factors are so excessive that they become explosively out of control. This condition is otherwise known as cancer. The entire range of foods—including the extremes of yin and yang—correspond to the first set of environmental conditions listed above. Although it may be possible to live by eating such a wide range of foods, the excessive factors contained in such a diet will eventually result in the development of sickness, while our life becomes a process of continual decline and degeneration as we lose our adaptability to our environment.

An examination of the changing eating patterns over the last century in the United States offers a clear illustration of the large scale dynamics of yin and yang. Statistics compiled by the United States Department of Agriculture reveal that the American way of eating has undergone tremendous changes during this century. Several of the more outstanding examples of these changes are presented below:[9]

1. More Centrally Balanced Items
In 1976, the average person ate roughly half as many grain products as average person did in 1910. Seventy years ago, grain products provided an estimated 38 % of the average caloric intake, while in 1976 they provided only about 19 %. Most of the grain presently being eaten in Western Europe and the United States is consumed in the highly unbalanced form of refined and processed wheat flour, such as that used in white bread, while in the past a variety of whole or partially refined grain products were eaten much more frequently. At the same time, the consumption of other grain products like rye, barley, buckwheat and corn flour have all declined substantially.

---

[9] These statistics, along with the accompanying graphs, are reprinted from *The Changing American Diet*, which is available from the Center for Science in the Public Interest, P. O. Box 7226, Washington, D. C. 20044, for $2.50.

2. More Yang Items

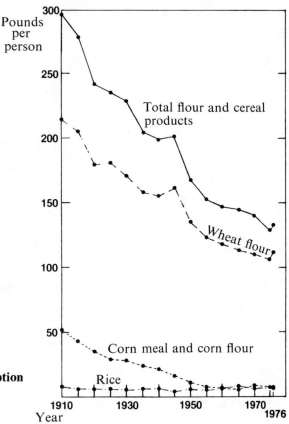

Pounds
per
person

Total flour and cereal
products

Wheat flour

Corn meal and corn flour

Rice

1910   1930   1950   1970
1976
Year

**Fig. 7   Flour and Cereal Product Consumption
in the United States (1910–1976)**

A. Meat. The consumption of meat has increased substantially in the last
fifty years. In 1976, the average person ate nearly 165 pounds, compared to an
average consumption of 120 pounds in 1930. (In the early 1970s the average person
ate slightly over 190 pounds of red meat per year; the decrease toward the end of
the decade is due largely to price increases.) The rising popularity of beef is largely
responsible for the overall increases in meat consumption. For example, in 1910,
the average person ate about 55 pounds of beef. In 1970, this figure had risen
to over 113 pounds per person, while 1976 consumption levels were estimated
at 95 pounds per person.

B. Poultry. Poultry consumption has increased about three times in the last
seventy years. In 1976, people in the United States ate an average of 53 pounds
per person compared with 18 pounds in 1910. During this period, chicken consumption (which represents about 80% of the total poultry consumed) increased
about 179%, while the consumption of turkey increased by about 820%.

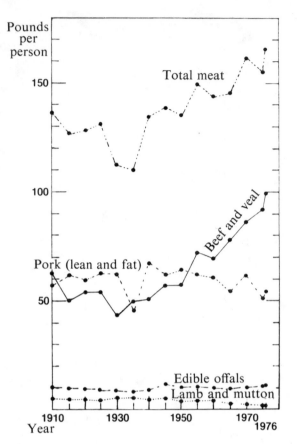

Fig. 8   Meat Consumption in the United States (1910–1976)

3.   More Yin Items

A.   Orange Juice and Other Processed Fruits.   The consumption of items such as dried, canned and frozen fruit and fruit juices has increased an estimated 300% since 1930. The average person drank 110 four-ounce servings of frozen orange juice in 1976, compared to one four-ounce serving in 1948 and 42 four-ounce servings in 1952. Many of these highly processed items contain sugar as well as a variety of chemical additives.

B.   Sweeteners.   The consumption of sweeteners has increased dramatically in the last hundred years. In 1976, the average American ate 94 pounds of sugar, an increase of over 100% over the 1876 consumption level, and about 29% higher than the 1909 estimate of 73 pounds. Corn syrup use rose from ten pounds per person in 1960 to about 32 pounds in 1976, while the use of saccharin, which is several hundred times more yin than sugar, increased about 400% from 1960 to 1976.

C.   Soft Drinks.   In 1976, the average person drank about 493 eight-ounce servings of soda, a 12.3% increase over the year before. This represents nearly a 500% increase in the consumption of soft drinks since the turn of the century.

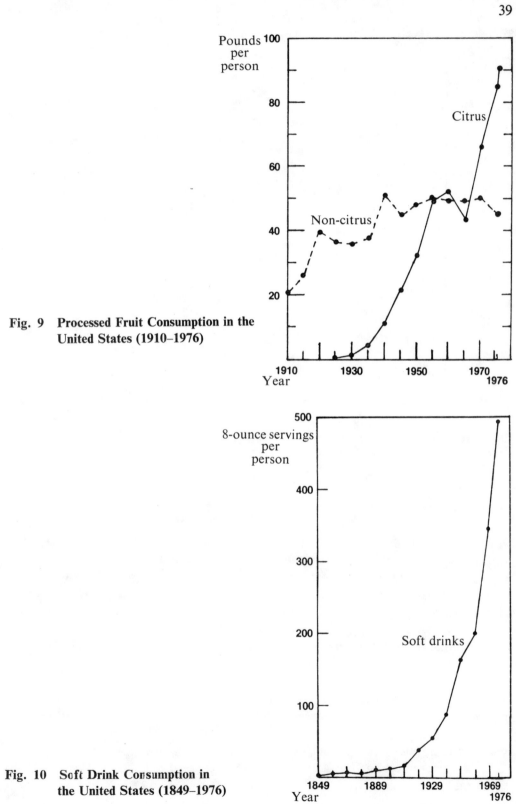

Fig. 9 **Processed Fruit Consumption in the United States (1910–1976)**

Fig. 10 **Soft Drink Consumption in the United States (1849–1976)**

40

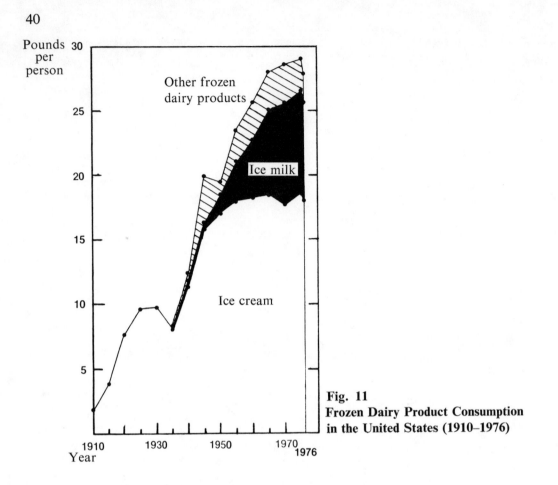

Pounds per person

Other frozen dairy products

Ice milk

Ice cream

Year

1910   1930   1950   1970   1976

Fig. 11
Frozen Dairy Product Consumption in the United States (1910–1976)

Many people in the United States receive more than 25% of their total sugar intake in this form.

D. Ice Cream and Frozen Dairy Products. The consumption of ice-milk, which is used mainly in products such as ice cream cones and milk shakes, rose from a 1950 average of 1.2 pounds per person to an average of 7.8 pounds in 1976. In 1976, the average person ate 18 pounds of ice cream, a substantial increase over the 1.9 pounds consumed in 1910. The total per capita consumption of various frozen dairy products was almost 30 pounds in 1976.

Now, what does this general pattern mean in terms of yin and yang? Several basic conclusions can be drawn. (1) Many people in the United States, and other modern nations as well, eat far fewer centrally balanced foods than in the past, reflected most apparently in the overall decline in the direct consumption of grain products. (2) There have been substantial increases in the consumption of more yang items such as beef and poultry. (3) These increases have triggered an explosive rise in the consumption of extremely yin items such as sugar, soft drinks, ice cream, frozen orange juice, and others. At the same time, even more extremely yin items such as marijuana, cocaine, birth control pills and other drugs and medications, some of which the hundreds and even thousands of times more yin than sugar, are all being consumed widely, while we are presently adding as many as 2,500 substances to our foods in the form of synthetic coloring and flavoring agents, preservatives, texture agents, etcetera. A large number of these artificially produced chemical products are extremely yin, and many were either relatively unknown or nonexistent before World War II.[10]

What are the consequences of continuing to eat in such an extreme manner? Senator George McGovern, chairman of the Senate Nutrition Committee, stated in the foreword to *Dietary Goals for the United States* that he felt that "the eating patterns of this century represent as critical a public health concern as any now before us." Using the statistical evidence documenting the links between our modern diet and the increasing incidence of degenerative illnesses, *Dietary Goals* went on to recommend that people in the United States and other modern nations reduce consumption of extremely yin foods such as sugar, as well as extremely yang items such as eggs, meat and salt, and begin moving toward a more centrally balanced diet based on such traditional staples as whole grains and fresh vegetables and fruits. In place of meat, *Dietary Goals* advised us to use more yin forms of animal foods such as poutry and fish. These conclusions generally corroborate those of macrobiotics, and were echoed in the Surgeon General's report on Health Promotion and Disease Prevention released in 1979 entitled *Healthy People*.

Whether we approach the problem of proper diet through the modern scientific methods which underlie *Dietary Goals*, the Surgeon General's report, and other similar investigations, or through the traditional, intuitive concept of yin and yang, our conclusions are surprisingly similar. From both the traditional and modern point of view, it is becoming increasingly clear that, in order to secure our health and happiness as human beings, as well as a sound future for our families and the world, we must begin to eat a more natural, centrally balanced diet more in accord with the laws of nature and with our universal dietary heritage.

---

[10] On an individual level, there are countless examples of the balancing of yin and yang in daily eating. For example, steak or other types of meat are usually eaten along with more yin items such as potatoes, onions, wine or other alcohol, or salad. A breakfast which contains meat or eggs is usually balanced with coffee, potatoes, or some type of sugary pastry or bread with jam. At lunch, hamburgers are usually accompanied by French fries, soda, milk shakes or ice cream, all of which are extremely yin.

2. Macrobiotics: East and West

In the East: Food for Spiritual Development

Our first anecdotal account takes us to the Far East, to the ancient Japanese city of Kyoto. Designed originally according to a Buddhist mandala, or chart of the universe, this old capital city is considered by many to be the cultural center of Japan, with more shrines and temples than any other location in the country. The city is also surrounded by mountains, and contains many rice fields and small vegetable farms within its boundaries. Fortunately, it was spared by the bombing of World War II, and so many of its ancient structures remain. Several of the leading schools of Zen Buddhism have their main centers in Kyoto, and, as Zen has continued to grow in popularity in the West, an increasing number of people from America, Europe, Australia and other places have gone there to study.[1]

Wendy and I became friends with a number of these young students during our stay there, and often discussed some of the similarities between macrobiotics and Zen during the open house dinners which we presented in our home. One of these students, a young English woman named Lisa, was especially interested in this relationship. Lisa had gone to Japan several years before following a year of Yoga studies in India, and at the time we met, she was studying and practicing Rinzai Zen at the Dai-Toku-Ji temple in Kyoto. Although she found her way of life to be fulfilling, she had nonetheless developed a number of health problems which, among other things, were interfering with her practice. Her major problem had been periodic attacks of sharp pain in her middle back, for which the original medical diagnosis had been pancreatitis and later kidney stones. Her Japanese physician had advised surgical removal of the stones, but, at the urging of her

---

[1] The high concentration of shrines and temples in Kyoto may be due to its unique environmental conditions, especially the surrounding mountains, which have the effect of intensifying the local charge of atmospheric and electromagnetic radiation, known in Japanese as *Ki*. For example, during a three-day trip outside of the city, Wendy left her steel cutting knife on the metal sink of our house. The blade had become dull, but upon our return, we were surprised to find that it had again become sharp enough for use. This effect is similar to that observed to occur in pyramids, and results from an intense generation of environmental *Ki*. In many European countries, ancient cathedrals were often constructed on even more ancient worship sites which were later discovered to have particularly vibrant charges of energy. When we visit places such as these, we experience an overall sense of well-being as a result of revitalization of our physical, mental and spiritual energies.

husband, a businessman from Atlanta, she decided to postpone such a drastic procedure and to try macrobiotics.

Kidney stones, as well as many other types of stone or cyst formations, develop through a very simple mechanism which is dependent on how we eat and drink. The repeated intake, over an extended period, of foods such as milk, cheese, butter, yogurt and other dairy products, as well as eggs, sugar, refined flour, saturated fats and oily or greasy foods, produces a "sticky" and fat-filled bloodstream. This condition, which affects to some degree practically everyone who consumes the so-called "modern diet," is the general, underlying cause of most major illnesses, including, along with kidney stones, heart and cardiovascular disease, blood disorders, cancer, diabetes, arthritis and many others. The development of an unhealthy blood condition opens a veritable Pandora's Box of potential illnesses.

All of the above-mentioned foods had formed the basis of Lisa's diet during her childhood and young adult life in London. However, due to her interest in Yoga, she had stopped eating meat a number of years before going to Japan, and had begun a semi-vegetarian regime which included white rice, chemicalized vegetables and fruits, eggs, dairy foods and sugar. As a child, she had suffered from frequent illness, and her semi-vegetarian way of eating had not reversed this trend. Her continuing consumption of dairy products, sugar and eggs, as well as poor quality grains and vegetables, had produced an unbalanced condition in her body, resulting in the development of a sticky blood condition. This had in turn led to the gradual formation of deposits of fat and mucus throughout her body, especially in and around organs like the heart, lungs, liver, kidneys and others. This condition provided the underlying base for the development of kidney stones.

Kyoto is well known for having one of the hottest summers in Japan, due mostly to the tendency of the surrounding mountains to hold in heat and moisture. During the summer months, following the rainy season in June, ice-soda, milk, fruit juices, beer and ice cream are consumed in great quantities. In this environment, where vending machines proliferate, there were many opportunities for Lisa to find the additional factor required to crystallize these deposits into hard stones. This additional factor is the tendency of these fluid-like colloidal deposits to freeze or solidify when cold or iced foods or beverages are consumed.

The macrobiotic approach to this condition is quite simple, and, in most cases, higly successful. It involves two principal elements: (1) approaching the problem from the inside by causing the blood to clean and regenerate itself through the intake of proper food, and (2) accelerating the breakdown and discharge of existing stones through the use of simple external applications, in combination with the natural cleansing effect of clean and healthy blood.

When Lisa first contacted us, she was in tremendous pain. It seemed that a stone had dislodged itself and gotten caught in the urinary tube. To provide quick, although temporary, relief, I advised her to apply a hot ginger compress over the painful area.[2] The heat generated by this compress has the effect of activating the circulation of blood and producing a general expansion or relaxation of the blood vessels and tissues in the area where it is placed. This simple home remedy is especially effective in the case of kidney or gall stones, particularly to bring relief from pain that results when a stone becomes blocked in a duct or tube, since it causes the tube to expand and allows the stone to pass. In situations like this, it is also advisable to further dilate the blocked tube by drinking several cups of hot *bancha* tea. In some cases, a special beverage can be made by grating fresh daikon (about a tablespoonful) into a teacup, adding several drops of *tamari* soy sauce and then filling the cup with hot bancha tea.

These simple remedies brought Lisa immediate relief, and within several days she called for advice about her way of eating. In order to eliminate her existing stones and prevent new ones from developing, it was necessary for her to eliminate the intake of sugar, dairy food, white rice, saturated fats, chemicalized foods and iced or cold foods and beverages, and begin the standard macrobiotic way of eating. I also advised her to continue the ginger compresses for ten days and to take the daikon-bancha drink once a day for several days. (It is usually not advisable to continue with this very effective tea for more than three days at a time.)[3]

Lisa improved steadily over the next several months, so much so that the painful attacks in her back began to disappear. Impressed by her improvement, she then began to introduce macrobiotics to her friends at Dai-Toku-Ji, many of whom were experiencing health problems of various sorts.[4] Lisa's situation was not unlike many others which I have seen over the last several years in Boston and other parts of the United States. In many of these cases, young women who had been practicing meditation or who were involved with one or another of the popular spiritual movements came for advice for problems ranging from kidney stones to breast and ovarian cysts, due largely to their lacto-vegetarian diet high in sugar, honey, dairy products, fruit and fruit juices, spices and other items. However,

---

[2] *Ginger Compress:* To prepare this natural remedy, place grated, fresh ginger in a cheesecloth sack and squeeze the ginger liquid into a pot of hot water kept just below the boiling point. Dip a towel into the ginger water, wring it out tightly and apply, hot, directly to the affected area. Another towel, dry, can be placed on top to minimize heat loss. Apply a fresh hot towel every two or three minutes until the skin becomes red. For additional uses of the ginger compress, please see *Natural Healing through Macrobiotics* by Michio Kushi, published by Japan Publications, Inc.

[3] Mr. Kushi once kept a large jar which contained perhaps several hundred stones of various types which macrobiotic friends had naturally discharged over the last ten years. In some cases, these discharges occurred several years after the person had begun to eat macrobiotically, and the person was unaware of the stone until it actually came out.

[4] In regard to the health problems often experienced by Western students who live in Japan, Philip Kapleau, a leading American interpreter of Zen, once stated: "Of the three or four Americans I knew who have lived in a Japanese monastery for six months or more and who ate the standard diet (high in refined, polished rice, and frequently including sugar and chemically processed foods), not one escaped either anemia, beriberi, chronic constipation, or all three." (*Zen Bow*, January, 1969.)

in Lisa's case, had she gone to Japan to study a hundred years ago, there is a good possibility that she would have been able to have cured her condition through her involvement with Zen.

As with many other spiritual and religious teachings, at one time, proper dietary practice formed an integral part of the Zen way of life. Traditionally, Zen monks underwent a rigorous program that included plenty of physical activity, meditation, and experiencing extremes of both hot and cold weather. Their way of cooking, known as *shojin ryori,* or "cuisine for spiritual development," emphasized the proper preparation of locally available, vegetable quality foods such as whole brown rice, pickled vegetables, seaweeds, fresh garden vegetables and processed foods like *miso, umeboshi,* and *tofu.*

The purpose of this way of life is to bring an individual into a state of physical, mental and spiritual health as the base upon which an intuitive grasp of the order of the universe can be realized. The awareness of the eternal and universal order of life and nature is referred to in Zen as *satori,* and was called by Jesus the awareness of the *kingdom of heaven.*[5] As the example of Zen illustrates, proper food forms an integral part of a way of life for the development of spirituality and consciousness. At the same time, Buddhist monks were traditionally noted for their robust health and longevity, testifying to the value of their way of eating in maintaining physical health and vitality. In recent times, however, the tradition of shojin ryori has been modified, due to the influence of modern techniques of food processing and transportation. Instead of organic, brown rice, many of the temples in Japan now serve refined, white rice, while white sugar, once unknown in that part of the world, has found its way into some shojin recipes.[6]

In order to achieve the development of spirituality and consciousness, we need to achieve what I term our *biological grounding.* This is based on the recognition that the achievement of a sound physical condition is synonymous with the achievement of mental and spiritual development. As Lisa and many others have discovered, it is difficult to practice meditation or other spiritual exercises if we

---

[5] His disciples said to him: "When will the kingdom come?" Jesus said: "It will not come by expectation; they will not say, 'See; here,' or 'See, there.' But the Kingdom of the Father is spread upon the earth and men do not see it." From *The Gospel According to Thomas.*

[6] "One of the few crises that occurred in the monastery where I stayed involved brown *gohan,* the Japanese word for rice and a meal. One day, the Roshi surprised everyone by having brown *gohan* served instead of the customary white. Then a rare thing happened: the monks deliberately violated the stringent rule against wasting food by eating a couple of mouthfuls of the rice and then leaving the rest. The next day the brown *gohan* was again served and the same silent drama played out. On the third morning, white and brown rice were placed on the table. All except the Roshi and me reached for the white, which was consumed with the usual speed and gusto. Even so, there is much sickness among the Japanese population as a whole (Japan has the highest incidence of stomach cancer in the world), and TB and other pulmonary diseases are rampant among the Japanese, Buddhist monks included."—Philip Kapleau, *Zen Bow,* January, 1969

have kidney stones, if we are constipated, developing cancer, or are constantly sneezing and coughing.

Many students of Zen have especially discovered that it is very difficult to sit for any length of time in the cross-legged lotus position or in the *seiza* meditation posture if they are troubled by arthritis or if their joints are stiff and swollen. Our good physical health is obviously necessary for activities such as these, but what is the best and most sure way to achieve this? The answer is so obvious that it is often overlooked or neglected. Simply by selecting, preparing, serving and eating our daily food in accordance with the order of the universe and nature. When properly applied, this approach to food, known as macrobiotics, will create the necessary conditions for *cellular satori*, through the purification of our blood, cells (including our billions of brain cells), bodily fluids, and over all internal condition. As each cell and our organism as a whole begins to function in harmony with the solar system, the galaxy, neighboring planets and distant constellations, as well as with the immediate natural cycles of weather and planetary motion, we achieve, along with our physical health, the realization that we are always within the *kingdom of heaven*. This is the aim of Zen and all other great religious and spiritual teachings. Health, peace, happiness and freedom begin at home in the kitchen and at the dinner table. The macrobiotic way of eating is the most fundamental way to achieve this biological grounding in nature and the universe, as the basis for our endless development.

In the West: An Economical Way to Health and Beauty

In the spring of 1974, I met a woman in Philadelphia by the name of Mona. She was about 40 years old, and was somewhat different from the other young people who were staying at the macrobiotic study house there. For one thing, she was quite ill. I noticed that she was having trouble walking, and she could not hold her head in an upright position for any length of time. However, even with these difficulties, she tried as much as possible to participate in the classes and activities that were taking place. During this, our first meeting, I noticed that she had what seemed to be a tremendous amount of courage and determination to cure herself.

Mona had been ill for most of her adult life, beginning with the birth of her first child in 1953. At that time, she had been diagnosed as having a thyroid condition as well as toxemia and problems with fluid retention. Following the birth of her second child, several years later, she developed chronic colds, which led to the removal of her tonsils. From this point, her health spiraled steadily downward. Prior to beginning macrobiotics, she had been suffering from idiopathic edema, a condition in which excess fluid is stored internally, either in a specific localized area, or generally throughout the body. Mona had suffered from the more generalized type, and her abdomen and mid-section had become grotesquely swollen. In medical terminology, the word *idiopathic* means that a disease has started "by itself," and Mona was told that her problems were from "an unknown cause."

Mona had been treated by a number of internists, specialists, and other physicians in the Philadelphia area, but her condition continued to worsen. She began to take an enormous quantity and variety of medication, and at one point was taking up to ten water pills per day, along with vitamin and potassium supplements. During this time, she developed a number of related problems, including fluid in the lungs, kidney infection, a continual low-grade fever, and mononucleosis. She had two biopsies done on her neck in two consecutive years, and was a borderline leukemia case with a white cell count of between 14,000 and 18,000 (a normal count is 5,000–6,000 per cubic mm.). She also began to wear a neck brace, and was developing an arthritic condition with a spur growth on the base of her spine. She was bloated, hunched over, and, at one point, needed a cane to walk. Doses of keflex, along with vibramycin, one of the strongest antibiotics on the market, were unable to restore her condition.

She later described her condition in the following words: "My blood was exhausted. I had nothing in my body but pills and medicine. My face was drawn and haggard, my heart was swollen, my lungs were filled with fluid, and my whole body was sore from being stretched. I had had a liver biopsy, as well as several bone marrow biopsies. My liver and kidneys were swollen, and I had diarrhea for three years. I had my gall bladder removed because it was thought that the gallstones were causing the diarrhea. Also, because of my poor blood, I did not heal after surgery. I had a raw wound that would not come together. I also had my appendix removed and could not stop bleeding when I would cut myself. I would also bruise from the slightest touch. I was told that I could go on for perhaps another six months. I had no hope to live."

Then, just as her spiral of declining health reached its limit, she was introduced to macrobiotics, and soon afterward began to practice it, beginning a new spiral of improving health and regeneration. This process of regeneration is often based on the following realizations:

1. Regardless of our circumstances, we are responsible for any sickness or unhappiness that we experience.
2. Everything has an understandable cause, and the most basic, fundamental cause of any sickness or unhappiness is the food that we eat each day.
3. By changing our diet toward a more natural one in harmony with the universe, we can change our sickness, difficulties, or unhappiness into their opposite conditions.

With this new attitude, in combination with a balanced, natural diet, and the help and support of her friends, Mona began a steady, month-to-month process of improvement. After ten days she was able to remove her neck brace, and she gradually began to lose water weight in her abdomen. Her white cell count returned to normal, and for the first time she experienced days when she actually began to feel well. Naturally, as her health improved, her physical appearance began to change. During her illness, her hair had begun to fall out, and after macrobiotics it began to grow in again, stronger and more beautiful than ever before. Her skin became softer and smoother, and for the first time in many years her nails became stronger and more attractive. Her overall appearance became much more smart, slim, and youthful, while her attitude changed from one of despair to one of new hope.

Inspired with the dream of helping others just as she had been helped, Mona moved to Boston to deepen her understanding of macrobiotics. Following a period of intensive study there, she went to Miami to organize an educational center in association with the East West Foundation. She is presently managing and conducting such activities as macrobiotic cooking classes, seminars on the natural way of health and beauty, special weight-loss classes for women, nutritional counseling and others, along with appearing frequently on television and radio to promote the macrobiotic approach to health and beauty.

Mona's case is not unusual. There are now more than four hundred macrobiotic educational centers throughout the world, located in most of the major cities in the United States and Canada, as well as throughout Europe, South America and the Far East. Although precise figures are unavailable, we can estimate that as many as several million people around the world have received health benefits over the last fifty years through macrobiotics. As a result, a number of medical practitioners and associations throughout the world have begun to incorporate macrobiotic methods in their treatment of sickness. I have personally met thousands of such people from all walks of life who have experienced the relief of many different physical, mental and spiritual ailments through this simple, common sense approach.

Since 1975 the East West Foundation in Boston, the Community Health Foundation in London, the East West Center in Amsterdam, and other international centers have begun compiling and publishing macrobiotic case histories for the medical profession and the general public. In this short time, substantial improvements have been reported with a wide variety of illnesses, some of which are listed below:

1. A variety of cancers, including cancer of the pancreas, prostate, uterus, ovaries, breast, skin, brain, lung and others, as well as related blood disorders such as Hodgkin's disease and leukemia.[7]
2. Disorders of the nervous system including multiple sclerosis, epilepsy, Parkinson's disease, and others.

---

[7] Two of the more outstanding examples of what appear to be the relief of cancer through the macrobiotic dietary approach are the well-publicized cases of Jean Kohler, a professor of music at Ball State University in Muncie, Indiana; and that of Dr. Anthony Sattilaro, President of the Methodist Hospital in Philadelphia. Professor Kohler was diagnosed as having cancer of the pancreas and small intestine in 1973, at which time he began the practice of macrobiotics. To the surprise of his family, physicians, and associates, this normally terminal variety of cancer began to diminish, and ultimately disappeared. Professor Kohler has since recounted the details of his experience and has presented a number of other cases in his book, *Healing Miracles from Macrobiotics*, published in 1979 by the Parker Publishing Company. In June, 1978 Dr. Sattilaro was diagnosed with Stage IV prostatic cancer, which had spread ▶

3. Heart and circulatory disorders including high blood pressure, thrombosis, heart murmur, hardening of the arteries, and others. In order to aid in documenting the connection between diet and heart disease, the East West Foundation worked along with a research team from the Harvard University Medical School in several Boston area studies which demonstrated that persons generally observing the standard macrobiotic way of eating had blood pressure and blood fat levels which were much lower than the normally high average in the United States.[8] These are two of the leading risk factors associated with the development of heart disease.

4. Various cyst, stone, and tumor formations, including breast, ovarian, and uterine cysts, kidneys stones, gallstones, and others.

5. Various psychological and emotional disorders including fear, depression, tension, nightmares, rootlessness, worry, anger, and others, as well as drug abuse, alcoholism and other psycho-social disorders.

As practically everyone who begins to eat macrobiotically has discovered, this approach offers a simple, natural and inexpensive way to restore one's health and happiness, as well as prevent the development of future illnesses and unhappiness. As everyone is aware, the cost of medical treatment has increased tremendously throughout the world over the last decade, reflecting primarily the rapidly declining health of many modern people. In 1979, total payments to doctors and hospitals averaged about $3,500 for a family of four in the United States, while the total cost of medicine in this country is expected to reach $206 billion in 1979, an increase of about 42% over the approximately $38.9 billion spent in 1965. This represents approximately 9.1% of the gross national product. At the present rate of increase, it is estimated that medical costs will increase geometri-

Fig. 12   Medical Expenses in the United States
(Fiscal Years 1979 estimated)

Year	Per Capita	National Total (In billions of dollars)	Percentage of GNP
1965	$198	$38.9	5.9
1970	334	69.2	7.2
1975	588	127.7	8.6
1979	920	206.0	9.1

▶ to the ribs, skull, right shoulder, sternum, and several vertebrae. In the autumn of the same year, he began to practice macrobiotics. Pain diminished within several weeks of beginning the diet, and by the spring of 1979, there was no laboratory evidence of cancer. A subsequent bone-scan in September also revealed no signs of the disease. More detailed accounts of Professor Kohler's and Dr. Sattilaro's experiences are presented in the report, *Cancer and Diet*, available from the East West Foundation, 240 Washington Street, Brookline, Mass. 02146.

[8] For a detailed report on these studies, please see *Blood Pressure in Vegetarians, American Journal of Epidemiology*, Volume 100, No. 5, and *Plasma Lipids and Lipoprotiens in Vegetarians and Controls, New England Journal of Medicine*, May 29, 1975. (Reprints of these articles are contained in the report, *Cancer and Diet*, published by the East West Foundation.)

cally every five years, reaching over $400 billion by 1984. An estimate of the progressive increase in medical costs is presented above in Figure 12.

It is obvious that medical spending is spiralling out of control with no end in sight. When considered along with increases in the major degenerative diseases over the last sixty years, we can envision a time in the near future when everyone in America is a patient and the entire economy must be channelled into paying for it. Where does the problem lie? Is the answer to be found in cost curtailment programs and national health insurance, or does the solution lie at a much deeper and more fundamental level?

At the same time that medical costs have been rapidly rising, food prices have also increased tremendously in the United States, reflecting largely the increasing cost of maintaining an artificial, unecological way of eating. According to the Consumer Price Index, the average cost of eating at home increased by approximately 13.9% between February, 1978 and February, 1979, while the cost of eating out rose by about 10.9% during the same period. In 1978, Americans with average incomes were spending approximately 31% of their earnings on food.

Since it is more ecologically based, a way of eating which emphasizes organically grown whole grains, beans, local vegetables, sea vegetables and naturally-fermented soy products like miso and tamari, periodically supplemented with such foods as seasonal fruits and fish, is actually less expensive than the modern diet. Monthly savings of up to 50% are not uncommon, due in part to such practices as starting a small vegetable garden, purchasing food in bulk at a reduced price, including naturally available wild vegetables such as burdock and dandelion in the menu, and by milling flour and making foods such as tofu, sauerkraut, pickles, etc. at home. In the future, as more and more people begin shifting toward natural, organically produced foods, and as our food supply becomes more regionally based, we can expect the price gap between more naturally processed foods and more artificial, unecological foods to widen even further.

In the June, 1979 issue of the *East West Journal* a survey was published comparing the average cost of feeding a family of four in the Boston area from a natural food store and the cost of feeding them from a supermarket. The natural foods listed in the survey were those which are, according to macrobiotic principles, generally standard for consumption in New England during spring and early summer, while the standard American pattern of eating was compiled according to USDA statistics and material presented in the McGovern committee's report, *Dietary Goals for the United States*. At full retail price, a one-week supply of natural foods was found to average 40 to 50% less than supermarket foods, and, surprisingly enough, the cost of some organic items, especially produce, was found to be the same as or less than their non-organic counterparts.

The relationship between food and health is basic, not only to the practice of macrobiotics, but to the traditional common sense of all cultures. We have all heard the familiar proverbs, "Food is your best medicine" and "You are what you eat." This native wisdom evolved out of our universal dietary heritage, based on whole grains and vegetables as principal foods, practiced throughout the world for countless generations. At the same time, folk medicine, which was often centered in the home, usually consisted of simple dietary adjustments and the occasional use of certain medicinal plants.

At the same time, many of the great personalities throughout history were keenly aware of the importance of proper diet. Thomas Edison, the great American inventor, once stated, "The doctor of the future will give no medicine but will interest his patients in the care of the human frame, in diet, and in the cause and prevention of disease," while several of the leading personalities involved in the founding of the United States, especially Benjamin Franklin and Thomas Jefferson, practiced a semi-vegetarian way of eating which emphasized whole grains. Franklin's dietary experiments are well documented in his autobiography, while the story of his arrival in Philadelphia while eating whole-wheat rolls is well known by every student of American history.[9]

Jefferson once wrote that he used animal products only occasionally, and only as a "condiment" to his principal diet of grains and vegetables. It was their simple, wholesome diet that gave these men the strength, vitality and clear judgment to overcome the many difficulties involved in establishing a new nation. Similar examples are common in the histories of practically every country.

Jefferson also believed that a sound native agriculture was vital for the future of the United States, especially the proper cultivation of cereal grains. He was particularly interested in the cultivation of rice. During one of his visits to France, he noticed that rice was used by many people as a principal food, especially during religious holidays such as Lent, when meat was not eaten. Most of the rice consumed in France came from Italy, so Jefferson went to that country for the purpose of obtaining rice seed to send back to America. However, the Italian government had laws forbidding rice seed to be taken out of the country; but Jefferson was so determined to introduce this valuable food item in North America that he

---

[9] Sayings of Benjamin Franklin on Diet and Health:
  "To lengthen thy life, lessen thy meals."
  "Eat to live, and not live to eat."
  "God heals and the doctor takes the fee."
  "He's the best physician that knows the worthlessness of most medicines."
  "A full belly makes a full brain."
  "Hunger is the best pickle"
  "I saw few die of hunger—of eating, 100,000."

Other Traditional Wisdom on Food and Health:
  "We never repent of having eaten too little." Thomas Jefferson.
  "Much meat much maladies." English proverb, 17th Century.
  "Over-feeding breeds ferocity." Erasmus, 1523.
  "Chew well and you will feel it in your heels." Babylonian Talmud.
  "Feed sparingly and defy the physician." English Proverb, 17th Century.
  "It's a very odd thing—as odd as it can be, That whatever Miss T eats turns into Miss T."
Walter DeLa Mare, *Miss T*, 1913.

risked a possible death penalty by hiring an Italian mule driver to illegally cross the border with several large sacks of seed. The shipment was stopped at the border and turned back. Undaunted, Jefferson decided to fill the large pockets of his coat with seed and carry it across the border himself.

The seed had come from the best rice-growing district in Italy, and upon arriving back in France, Jefferson sent it to Charleston, South Carolina. Here, ten to fifteen of the grains were distributed to each of a select group of Carolina farmers who in turn took personal charge of the planting, cultivation, and harvest of this initial rice crop. Jefferson was so pleased with the outcome of this project that he later arranged for seeds to be sent to the Carolinas from other places such as Egypt and China.

If Jefferson and Franklin could return today, they would probably not recognize many of the modern, processed foods which are eaten widely in America. They would probably also be alarmed at the epidemic increases in major degenerative diseases such as cancer, heart disease, diabetes, arthritis, multiple sclerosis, mental illness, and others, as well as by the rapidly increasing trend toward social decline and disorder. Practically everyday, we read of further reports which document the rapidly declining physical, psychological and spiritual health of many modern people. For example, in this country alone, the cancer rate has jumped from approximately one out of fifteen to one out of four in the thirty-five years since World War II. Today it is estimated that at least fifty-two million Americans will eventually develop this disease. At the same time, about twenty-five million Americans suffer from high blood pressure, one of the leading risk factors in cardiovascular diseases such as heart attack and stroke, which are now the leading causes of death in the United States, resulting in over one million deaths per year. It is estimated that more than ten million people suffer from diabetes, and if the incidence of this disease continues to increase at the present rate, an estimated 20% of the American population will eventually develop it. Also in the last several years, the number of Ceasarian births has increased from 5% to 25% of all live births. About fifteen million Americans suffer from arthritis, while about eight hundred thousand people in the United States develop gallstones every year. There are approximately ten million people who suffer from emphysema in this country, while between six and ten million from severe bronchial asthma. Interestingly enough, about 30% of the adult men and 40% of the adult women in this country are chronically overweight, and a large number of these are obese.

Meanwhile, scientific and medical evidence continues to mount which traces most, if not all, of these problems directly to the foods we eat, especially to the rising consumption of meat and animal protein, saturated fat, sugar, dairy food, artificial and industrialized foods, and chemical additives and preservatives.[10]

---

[10] As mentioned earlier, much of the evidence documenting this connection was summarized in the U.S. Government Report, *Dietary Goals for the United States*, published by the Senate Select Committee on Nutrition and Human Needs in 1977 and 1978.

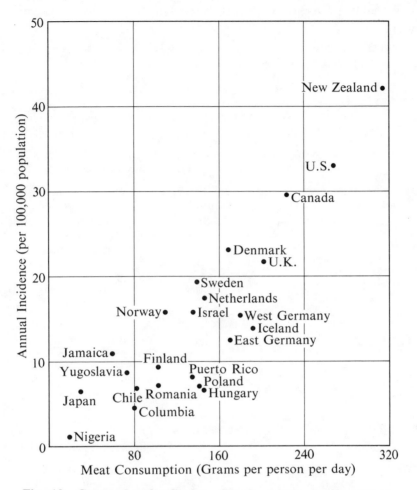

**Fig. 13   Geography of a Cancer—The Correlation between Meat
Consumption and Cancer of the Colon in Women**

The incidence of cancer of the large intestine among women in the countries
listed above is closely related to per capita meat consumption. Another factor
which influences the development of this disease is a low consumption of cereal
grains, which tends to go hand in hand with a large meat consumption. A similar
relationship has also been found between breast cancer and a large intake of
saturated fat.

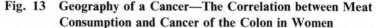

 Within this downward trend, however, an increasing number of people in this
and other countries have begun a shift toward a more natural and ecologically
sound way of eating, more in line with traditional dietary experience over centuries in both East and West. Just as we, as individuals, can experience through
proper food and cooking, the purification of our blood and cells, resulting in the
restoration of a sound physical and mental condition, this simple method is the
most fundamental way of changing our modern worldwide society's spiral of

decline and degeneration into a new spiral of health, peace, freedom and endless development. This peaceful biological revolution has its origin nowhere else but in the kitchen of every home, and whether or not it is successful depends entirely on those who care for the preparation of daily food.

Appendix: Self-Diagnosis

When we apply yin and yang to the understanding of the human body, we gain a whole new way of seeing ourselves and our relationship to our environment. For example, when we look at our face in the mirror, our entire biological history, our present condition, and our future destiny all reveal themselves. Please evaluate yourself according to the following examples, some of which have been used for thousands of years as a part of traditional Oriental diagnosis.

Hair/Sex organs

Forehead/Bladder

Under Eyes/Kidneys

Mouth/
Digestive system,

Between Eyebrows/
Liver

Ears/Kidneys,
Overall constitution

Cheeks/Lungs

Tip of Nose/Heart

Fig. 14   Self-Diagnosis

1.   Does your hair break easily or have many split ends? If so, your sexual organs may be becoming weaker, mostly as a result of consuming sugar, soft-drinks, fruit juice, ice cream, and other very yin items.

2.   Do you frequently perspire from the forehead? If so, you bladder is over-working due to the intake of too much liquid.

3.   Do you have discolored areas under eyes, or are you developing eye-bags? If you have eyebags, your kidneys may be swollen and waterlogged from an excessive intake of liquid. If you have bluish or purplish discoloration under the eyes, your kidneys probably contain deposits of mucus and fat, and you may be developing kidney stones.

4.   Do you have one or several vertical lines between the eyebrows above the nose? If so, your liver is not functioning properly. This condition often results from chronic overeating, as well as from long-term intake of extremes of both more yin and more yang items.

5.   Do you have large, well developed ears with a detached lobe? If you do,

give thanks to your mother. Her moderate eating and hard work during the time you were in the womb resulted in your being born with a strong and well-balanced constitution. Large, well-developed ears indicate that your mother ate a diet comprised of a fairly good balance of minerals, protein and carbohydrates. Small ears, with an attached lobe or no lobe, indicate that a person's overall constitution is weaker, and that animal protein comprised a major part of his or her mother's diet during pregnancy. When you observe people on the street, you may notice that many older people usually have larger and more developed ears, while younger people, especially those born after World War II, often have smaller and less developed ears. This is almost entirely due to the changes in dietary habits which have occurred over the last century, especially the shift from consumption of more grain and vegetable quality foods towards more meat, animal products, sugar and processed foods. Along with revealing a person's overall constitution, the ears also correspond to the kidneys.

6.   Do you have reddish or "rosy" colored cheeks? If so, your lungs are probably expanded and may contain deposits of fat and mucus. The reddish color reflects expansion of blood capillaries, and is an indication of an overly yin condition in the lungs.

7.   Please see the tip of your nose. Is it somewhat expanded? Does it have a slightly reddish color? If so, your heart is probably enlarged, and there is a good possibility that your blood pressure is abnormal. This more yin condition is caused by the repeated overconsumption of sugar, fruit, fatty or oily foods, fruit juice, soda, alcohol and other more yin items.

8.   The mouth is actually the most central part of the face. In it we can read the condition of several of the body's most central functions—the digestive system and the reproductive organs. The upper lip reveals the condition of the upper section of the digestive system, especially the stomach, while the intestines are mirrored in the lower lip. If your lips are swollen beyond their normal size and thickness, your digestive organs have probably become loose and swollen, and your powers of digestion and absorption have become weak. At the same time, your sexual vitality may be declining. An expanded upper lip means that the trouble is primarily located in the stomach, while a swollen or protruding lower lip means that your intestines may not be functioning properly. A puffy or expanded lower lip is often a sign of chronic constipation or diarrhea.

9.   Please look at your facial color. A reddish or pinkish complexion is caused by capillary expansion resulting from the overconsumption of sugar, liquid and other yin items. This color indicates that your heart and circulatory system may be overworking and that your blood pressure may be abnormal. A milky, white complexion results from the overconsumption of milk and other dairy products, and is an indication that mucus and fat deposits are beginning to accumulate throughout the body.

10.   Are your fingernails chipped at the tips? This condition is similar to split hairs, and indicates that the sexual organs are probably becoming weaker. The fingernails should be pink in color. If, when you stretch your fingers, your nails

begin to turn white, you may be developing anemia, largely as a result of consuming too many overly yin items.

11.   Are your hands moist, or dry? If moist, your heart and kidneys are probably overworking from the consumption of too much fluid. Drier hands are normal. If your hands are very warm, you are most likely consuming too many yin foods, and the same is true for overly cold hands. However, cold hands can also result from the intake of too much salt.

12.   Grip your left shoulder with your right hand. Do the same with your left hand on the opposite shoulder. Are your shoulders hard, expanded, or painful when pressed? If so, your intestines are probably expanded and not functioning well. At the same time, you may be suffering from hardening of the arteries and circulatory vessels. This condition results from the chronic overconsumption of animal fats, liquid, sugar, protein, and from overeating in general.

13.   Have you been angry even once in the past year? If so, your liver is not functioning properly. In the Orient, the word for anger is *Kan-Shaku*, which means "liver pain." Anger is a symptom of excess, and is not a sign of good health. This condition results from the repeated overconsumption of extremes of yin and yang, especially animal protein. It can also result from overeating in general.

14.   How many times do you urinate every day? Three or four times per day is normal. If you urinate more than this, your heart and kidneys are overworking from the intake of too much liquid. If you urinate less than three times per day, then you are not drinking enough liquid or you may be eating too much salt.

15.   If you are a woman, do you menstruate regularly in accord with the cycle of the moon? If your menstruation occurs in a cycle which is shorter than the normal twenty-eight day period, your condition is overly yang, probably as a result of consuming too many animal foods. A longer cycle indicates that your condition is overly yin. If your menstrual flow is excessive and prolonged, you are probably eating too many extreme foods. If the flow is thicker than normal, this is usually the result of eating too many animal products. A thinner menstrual flow results from the overconsumption of more yin foods. Menstrual cramps are usually the result of a diet which contains too many animal products.

16.   If you are a woman, do you have some type of vaginal discharge? If so, this is an indication that your diet contains too many excessive factors. Vaginal discharges are often caused by foods such as sugar, dairy, animal fats, and others which cause deposits of mucus and fat to develop within the body, and especially in the sexual organs. A yellowish discharge may indicate that cysts or tumors are developing in the ovaries or uterus, while a greenish discharge may indicate the development of cancer.

For a more comprehensive outline of the above and other traditional methods of diagnosis, please refer to several books by Michio Kushi, including *How to See Your Health: The Book of Oriental Diagnosis* and *Natural Healing through Macrobiotics*, both published by Japan Publications, Inc., and *Oriental Diagnosis*, published by Sunwheel Ltd., London, England.

3. Food for the Past, Present, and Future

> "Tell me what you eat, and I will tell you what you are."
> —Brillat-Savarin, 1825

The Standard Macrobiotic Way of Eating

At the present time, hundreds of thousands of people throughout the world have begun to establish their health and happiness as a result of basing their daily diet on foods such as whole grains, locally grown vegetables, sea vegetables and beans, supplemented with occasional fish or shellfish, seasonal fruits, seeds and nuts. When prepared in the proper way, foods such as these generally comprise an optimally balanced diet in a temperate climate and form the basis of a dietary approach that can be readily adapted to almost any environment. As explained in an earlier chapter, this standard macrobiotic approach fulfills the following criteria:

1. It offers a moderate balance of yin and yang, resulting in an overall harmonization with the average ratio of centripetal ($\triangle$) to cetrifugal ($\triangledown$) forces existing on the earth at present.

2. It accords with our universal dietary heritage based on whole grains and local vegetables as principal foods. (The relationship between whole grains and human evolutionary development is discussed in the Chapter "Cooking with Whole Grains.") At the same time, the tradition of eating primarily cooked food is fundamental to almost every culture and can be traced back to the very origins of civilization.[1]

---

[1] The macrobiotic approach is based largely on maintaining our evolutionary status through proper food. When we begin basing our diet on foods which do not accord with the evolutionary order, we often begin a process of biological degeneration back through more primitive stages of life. For example, while in Japan I met a young Irishman who had been living in Kyoto for about ten years. Along with a number of health problems, he had very strange hands, which were nearly orange in color, somewhat arthritic, and very wrinkled. They were beginning to resemble those of a chimpanzee or an orangutan. I asked him whether he ate many *mikan*, the small oranges grown in Japan throughout the year. He replied that, over the last ten years, he probably ate an average of one *mikan* per day. I told him that *mikan* were a more suitable food for monkeys, and that if he wanted to cure his condition he would have to stop eating so many of them and begin eating whole grains and vegetables. After several weeks of eating this way, the orange color started to fade and his hands began to develop a more normal degree of flexibility.

More specific recommendations for applying this standard macrobiotic way of eating are presented below, and it is our hope that you will be able to use these guidelines as the basis for the establishment of your health and happiness:[2]

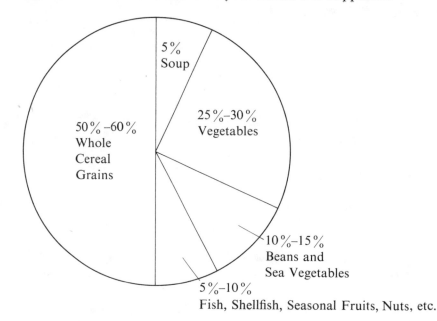

Fig. 15   The Standard Macrobiotic Way of Eating
Standard proportions of daily food items are presented in the above chart. These broad guidelines should be flexibly adapted to harmonize with various climatic, seasonal, and individual differences.

1.   Whole Grains
At least 50% by volume of every meal should be whole cereal grains prepared in a variety of ways. Whole grains include brown rice, millet, barley, whole wheat, whole wheat bread, chapatis and noodles, oats, oatmeal, corn, cornmeal, buckwheat noodles and groats, rye, rye bread, etc. The majority of our whole grain intake should usually be in the form of whole grains themselves, rather than as flour products such as bread, crackers, pasta, noodles and cracked grains. Grains in their whole form should comprise about 80% of the daily intake, while the daily consumption of flour should usually not go beyond 20%. Also, for the improvement of health, it is generally advisable to avoid the use of creamy or floury cereals such as rice cream, buckwheat cream, etc. even if they are made from

---

[2] Copies of these standard dietary recommendations are available from the East West Foundation.   The stand ard dietary and way of life recommendations presented here are adapted from the *Book of Macrobiotics* and *Natural Healing through Macrobiotics* by Michio Kushi.

whole grains. These products, which are made by crushing the grains into flour and cooking them with water, have a tendency to create mucus in the body.

2. Soup
Approximately 5%–10% of daily food intake by volume should include soup (about one or two cups or small bowls). One of these should be seasoned with miso or tamari soy sauce, and the taste should not be overly salty. The stock can be made with a variety of vegetables, beans, grains and other ingredients, and the recipe should be changed often. However, it is recommended that *wakame* seaweed be included in the soup on a daily basis. Persons who have been consuming too much liquid should generally limit themselves to one bowl of soup per day, while those who are in fairly good health may have two. This optional second cup of soup can include any of the many varieties listed in the chapter "Soups and Soup Stocks."

3. Vegetables
About 20 to 30% of each meal may include vegetables. At least two thirds of these should be cooked, and up to one third may be eaten in the form of raw or pressed salad, sprouts, or pickles. During the winter season, salad may not be desirable, so lightly cooked vegetables may be substituted, or a lightly boiled salad may be eaten, while persons with overly yin sicknesses may also need to avoid salad for some period. The various methods for preparing vegetables, such as sautéing, steaming, boiling, baking, and deep-frying are presented in the chapter on vegetable cooking, along with a number of recipe suggestions. Persons who have been consuming too many oily or greasy foods, which produce mucus, may wish to avoid or limit the intake of *tempura* (deep-fried) vegetables.

Among root vegetables, carrots, daikon, turnip, radish, burdock, lotus root, *jinenjo* (mountain potato) and rutabaga are fine for daily use. Among the more round shaped or ground vegetables, cabbage, onions, fall and winter squashes, cauliflower, broccoli, Chinese cabbage, Brussels sprouts, bok choy, and pumpkins are all quite good. Suitable leafy green vegetables include watercress, kale, parsley, dandelion, collards, Swiss chard, mustard greens, carrot, turnip, daikon and radish greens, scallions, leeks, and others.

Vegetables such as cucumber, mushroom, lettuce, parsnips, string beans, yellow squash and celery should be used only on occasion, generally, while, unless you live in the tropics, you should generally avoid vegetables such as potatoes (including sweet potatoes and yams), eggplant, tomatoes, asparagus, spinach, green pepper, beets, zucchini, avocado and the like which have a very high potassium content or which have originated in the tropics.

4. Beans and Sea Vegetables
From 10 to 15% of the daily intake should include cooked beans and seaweeds. The most suitable beans for daily use are *azuki* beans, chickpeas, lentils, and black beans. Other beans, including pinto and kidney beans, as well as split peas, should

be used only occasionally. Seaweeds should also become a part of your daily diet, and these include varieties like *hijiki*, *arame*, *kombu*, wakame, *nori*, dulse, agar agar (*kanten*), and Irish moss. Beans and seaweed can be cooked separately, or, since they complement each other very well, in the same dish. When cooked together, the minerals contained in seaweed have a tendency to balance or neutralize the fat and protein contained in beans, creating a well balanced dish. Suggestions for preparing these foods are presented in the recipe section of this book.

5. Supplemental Foods (Animal Food, Seasonal Fruits, Seeds and Nuts)

A. Animal Foods. Once or twice a week, a small volume of white meat fish can be eaten. In general, the quantity of fish should not go beyond 10 to 15% of the meal in which it is being served. (Red meat or blue-skinned fish should generally be avoided.) Shellfish, including shrimp, lobster, clams, etc. may be used in place of white meat fish. A variety of fish and shellfish recipes are presented later in this book.

    B. Seasonal Fruits and Desserts. Natural desserts may be eaten about two to three times per week, and can be made from ingredients such as squash, pumpkin, and other naturally sweet vegetables, sweet brown rice, azuki beans, chestnuts and other such items, while fruits which are naturally available in your climate can also be used in dessert cooking. It is generally better to eat fruit in a cooked form, although dried or raw fruits can be eaten from time to time. In a temperate climate, such as that in most of the United States, Canada, and Western Europe, the best types of fruit for regular use are apples, cherries, strawberries, blueberries and other berries, raisins, peaches, apricots, nectarines, pears, cantaloupes, watermelon, honeydew and other local melons, currants, and grapes. If necessary, desserts can be occasionally sweetened by adding small quantities of rice honey or barley malt.

    C. Seeds and Nuts. Roasted seeds or nuts, preferably moderately seasoned with tamari soy sauce, may be used from time to time as snacks. Among edible seeds, sunflower, sesame, squash and pumpkin are fine for this purpose, while nuts such as almonds, walnuts and chestnuts are also suitable. (More oily nuts such as peanuts, cashews, Brazil nuts and others should generally be avoided.) Nut butters should be used only occasionally and in very moderate quantities. Among these, sesame butter is the most preferable. Others snacks can be made from roasted beans and grains, and may include items such as rice cakes, crackers, and popcorn.

6. Beverages

If possible, try to use spring or well water for your cooking and drinking. (Distilled water should be avoided.) The most ideal beverages for daily use are bancha twig tea (also known as *kukicha*), *Mu* tea, dandelion tea or coffee, unsweetened grain coffee, roasted barley tea (*mugicha*), rice or other grain teas, or any other traditional tea which does not have an aromatic fragrance or a stimulant effect.

    Alcoholic and carbonated beverages should generally be avoided, although small quantities of high quality beer, *sake*, or mineral water may be enjoyed on special occasions. Fruit juice should also be generally avoided, although moderate amounts may be used in hot weather. (Among these, apple juice is probably the most suitable.) Since many of us tend to drink excessively, it is generally advisable to drink only when thirsty. If you need to urinate more than three or four times per day, or if the palms of your hands or your feet perspire during normal activity, you are drinking too much and should reduce your liquid intake.

7. Oil, Seasoning, and Condiments

Only vegetable quality oils should be used in cooking, preferably those which are unrefined and naturally pressed. For the improvement of health, it is recommended that only high-quality sesame or corn oils be used, and only in moderate quantities. The best seasonings are unrefined white sea salt, tamari soy sauce, miso, and umeboshi, and these should be used moderately, so that your food does not have a salty taste. Naturally processed *kuzu* and arrowroot may also be used from time to time as thickening agents.

The following condiments are especially good for regular use (please refer to the chapter on condiments for more specific recipes):

1. Gomashio (Sesame Salt): This condiment should be freshly prepared every few days. The standard proportion of sesame seeds to sea salt is ten or twelve to one.

2. Roasted Seaweed Powder: This condiment can be made simply by roasting seaweed in the oven until it is burnt and then crushing it into a powder. Wakame, kelp (kombu), dulse, and other seaweeds are fine for use in this way. For those who have been consuming too much salt, this condiment can be used in place of gomashio.

3. Umeboshi Plum: The uses of this effective blood purifier are described throughout this book.

4. Tekka: This more yang condiment is made from finely chopped carrot, lotus root, and burdock which are sautéed and roasted in miso. It should generally be used only on occasion and in moderate quantities.

5. Tamari Soy Sauce: Tamari should be used only moderately as a condiment and should not be used on rice at the table.

8. Foods Which Should be Generally Avoided for the Improvement of Health

1)   All red meat, including beef, lamb, pork, and their by-products, as well as poultry and commercial, unfertilized eggs.

2)   Milk, powdered milk, cheese, butter, yogurt, ice cream, and other dairy products, as well as soy and other margarines.[3]

---

[3] Once promoted as "nature's perfect food," milk is now associated with an increasingly wide spectrum of illnesses, including digestive ailments, allergies, childhood anemia, calcification of the joints, cardiovascular disorders, multiple sclerosis, and others. For example, one ▶

62

3)   Sugar, and any products containing it; honey, syrups, and synthetic or artificial sweeteners such as saccharine.

4)   Tropical and semi-tropical fruits and fruit juices, including citrus (oranges, grapefruits, etc.), bananas, coconuts, mangoes, papayas, dates and date sugar, figs, and others, as well as tomatoes, and other similar vegetables mentioned earlier.

5)   All artificial sodas, colas, soft drinks and beverages, as well as coffee, commercial tea, ginseng tea, and all aromatic, stimulant teas or beverages.

6)   All refined, polished grains and their by-products, including white rice, white bread, rolls, spaghetti, noodles, etc.

7)   All chemicalized food that is colored, preserved, sprayed, dyed or otherwise artificially treated as well as mass-produced, industrialized, synthetic foods, including canned, instant, and frozen food.

8)   All hot spices and any aromatic, stimulating foods or condiments such as pepper, red pepper, mustard, garlic, curry and vinegar.

9)   All artificially synthesized or even naturally produced vitamin, mineral or protein supplements including vitamin tablets, yeast, protein concentrates, etc., as well as artificial infant formulas.

10)   All cottonseed, palm, or coconut oils, vegetable or animal shortenings, and commercial mayonnaise or salad dressings.

11)   Ice cubes and ice-cold drinks.

12)   All drugs and medications, including prescription drugs, sedatives, tranquilizers, and others, along with marijuana, cocaine, LSD and other similar products.

Of equal importance to the balanced selection and preparation of daily food is the practice of good chewing. Since cereals and other vegetable quality foods are digested primarily in the mouth through interaction with saliva, good chewing guarantees that they will be properly digested, and helps create a calm and peaceful attitude during meals. This is especially important if you are seeking relief from any type of sickness. Depending on your condition, you may need to chew each mouthful anywhere from fifty to two hundred times.

You may eat two or three times per day, preferably at regular intervals, and may eat as much as you want provided the proportion is correct and the chewing thorough. Generally, one should not eat for several hours before sleeping, since food eaten just before going to bed cannot be discharged through activity and, therefore, accumulates throughout the body.

▶ widely publicized study recently associated milk drinking with juvenile delinquency, while researchers at the University of Michigan found that the incidence of multiple sclerosis correlates very closely with per capita milk consumption in the United States and twenty-one other countries. At the same time, the majority of the world's population—including a large number of people in Asia, Africa, Southern Europe, and South America—have been found to be *lactose intolerant*, which means that their digestive systems are simply not equipped to handle cow's milk.

The following additional practices are recommended for a more harmonious and healthy way of life:

1) Let us enjoy a physically, mentally, and socially active life without being preoccupied by our condition.

2) Let us be grateful for everything—this wonderful universe, nature, food, society, difficulties, and all people—and let us offer a short prayer of gratitude before and after each meal.

3) If possible, try to go to bed before midnight and get up early every morning.

4) Try to avoid any synthetic or woolen clothing worn directly on the skin. Use natural, vegetable quality materials such as cotton for daily clothing as much as possible, especially for undergarments, socks, and sheets.

5) Try to avoid wearing excessive metallic or synthetic accessories on your fingers, wrists and neck, keeping such ornaments as simple and elegant as possible.

6) Go outdoors often in simple clothing regardless of season. If the weather permits, try to walk barefoot on the grass, soil, or beach for at least half an hour every day.

7) Try to keep your home and surrounding environment orderly, clean, quiet, and as natural as possible. Try to avoid the use of synthetic rugs and furniture, color television, electric blankets and fluorescent lighting. If possible, keep one or several green plants in every room of the house, and, whenever possible, open your windows to allow fresh air to circulate. Please make your home temperature as natural as possible without depending on air conditioning or excessive heating.

8) Initiate and maintain active correspondence, extending your greeting, friendship, and warmest wishes to your parents, brothers and sisters, relatives, friends, teachers, and associates.

9) Avoid taking long, hot baths or showers, as they drain minerals from the body, unless you have been taking too much salt or animal food. Pools should generally be avoided since they are often heavily chemicalized. Swimming in freshwater lakes, ponds, or streams, or in the ocean, is preferable.

10) Please rub and massage your whole body with either a hot, damp towel or a dry one every morning and evening to stimulate circulation and relieve energy stagnation or blockage. If time does not permit, at least do the hands, fingers, feet and toes.

11) Please avoid using chemically perfumed or dyed toilet tissues, cosmetics and toiletries. For care of the teeth use *dentie*, sea salt, or natural toothpaste to brush in the morning and evening.

12) If possible, try to do active physical exercise such as scrubbing floors, cleaning windows, washing clothes, etc. If suitable space is available, begin a small vegetable garden and spend time whenever you can in the planting, harvesting, and care of your vegetables. Systematic exercise such as yoga, sports, *Dō-In* (self-

---

[4] For further information regarding the practice of *Dō-In*, please refer to the *Book of Dō-In: Exercise for Physical and Spritual Development* by Michio Kushi. Further information on the practice of massage can be found in *Barefoot Shiatsu* by Shizuko Yamamoto. Both books are available through Japan Publications, Inc.

64

massage), and martial arts can also be helpful. If possible, learn the art of Shiatsu massage, and frequently give massages to your friends and family members.[4]

Adopting the Standard Diet

The suggestions presented above represent broad guidelines for a way of eating and living which is more in harmony with our natural environment. However, keep in mind that these guidelines should always be flexibly adapted to each individual circumstance, with consideration of the following additional factors:

1. Our Diet should be Ecologically and Climatically Based

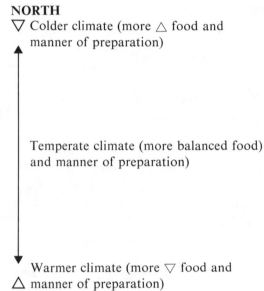

NORTH
▽ Colder climate (more △ food and manner of preparation)

Temperate climate (more balanced food) and manner of preparation)

Warmer climate (more ▽ food and △ manner of preparation)
SOUTH

Fig. 16 Climatic Variations in Diet
Guidelines for adapting dietary practice to environmental and climatic differences are presented above. In general, persons living in a temperate climate, which alternates between a hot summer and cold winter season, can embrace almost the entire scope of dietary variation during the course of a year—relying on more yin foods and cooking methods during the summer and changing to more yang foods and cooking methods during the winter. This is one of the primary reasons why culture and civilization have developed most actively in these regions.

If we live in a more yin, colder climate, it often is necessary to create balance by selecting slightly more yang food items, for example grains such as millet, short-grain rice or buckwheat; root vegetables, and a higher percentage of animal food, while including fewer yin items like fruit and salads in the diet. At the same time, our style of cooking should generally be more yang, with increased emphasis on factors like fire, salt, pressure, and time. In other words, our food can have a slightly saltier taste and be more heavily cooked. In warmer climates, which are more yang, balance is naturally achieved through the selection of slightly more yin items such as medium or long grain rice, corn, leafy vegetables, fruits and salad, while reducing our intake of animal food and salt. Naturally, we would try to emphasize fresher or more lightly cooked foods in this type of climate.

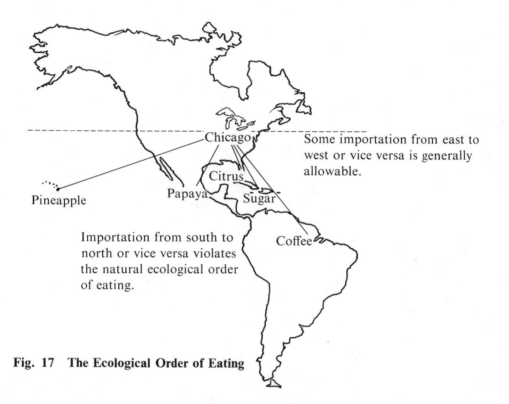

Fig. 17   The Ecological Order of Eating

Ideally, our food should come from the same general area in which we are living. In North America, for example, foods which are grown within a radius of about several hundred miles are the most ideal, while this area would be slightly less in places such as Europe and Japan, due to their greater diversity in climate and environment within a smaller space. Therefore, in order to maintain maximum adaptability to the climate in which they are living, people in more temperate or cool climates should try to avoid foods which are imported from warmer or more tropical climates. For example if, while living in Chicago, we eat large quantities of bananas, pineapples, citrus fruits, coffee, dates, sugar and other products originating far to the south, we will begin to lose our adaptability to the climate in the northern United States, and a variety of sicknesses will result. However, although not ideal, it is possible to maintain overall health by including some daily food items which have been imported from climates similar to those in which we are living. To summarize, we should generally avoid foods which have been imported from south to north or vice-versa, while we will not necessarily damage our health if we include in our diet some foods that have been imported from east to west or vice-versa.

If we move from one climatic zone to another, our selection and manner of preparing our food should also change. However, modifications such as those discussed above should generally be made within the context of the standard diet. The recipes presented in this book are generally suitable for use in a temperate climate such as that of the greater Boston or New England areas. If you live in a different climate, please feel free to adapt or modify these suggestions when necessary.

2.   Our Diet Should Vary with Daily, Monthly, and Seasonal Changes

In order to maintain health, we need to harmonize ourselves with the natural changes occurring in our environment. The basic principle for achieving this is very simple: during the more yin winter season, we should emphasize more yang foods and cooking methods, while in the hot summer months, our diet should generally become more yin. During the more balanced seasons—autumn and spring—our diet should generally be more balanced and central.

The ancient Oriental concept of the *five transformations*, or *Go-Gyo* (五行), is also very helpful when adapting our diet to these changes. This concept is simply a further elaboration of the universal process of change resulting from the continual cycling of yin and yang, and it forms one of the most basic principles underlying the entire spectrum of Far Eastern philosophy and culture. A similar concept has also been expressed at varying times in the West, most notably by

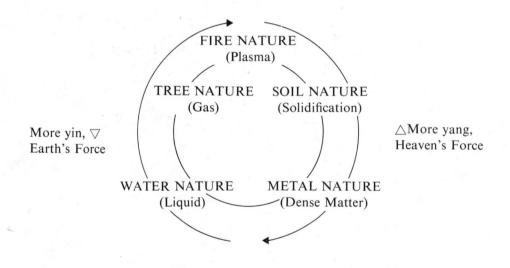

Fig. 18   The Five Transformations—Go-Gyo (五行)

Jesus who, in *The Gospel According to Thomas*, referred to these stages of change as "five trees in paradise."[5]

To better understand this process which occurs throughout the universe, let us consider it in the world of physical matter.

In its most diffused, or yin, state, matter exists in the form of plasma, or highly charged pre-atomic particles. Upon reaching this stage, a process of yangization begins, in which these pre-atomic particles begin to fuse and condense, causing matter to become progressively more dense or solid. Upon reaching its most condensed form, it begins to expand through the stages of liquid and gas, ultimately returning to plasma, at which time the process begins again. In the ancient Far East, the plasmic stage was named "fire nature"; the stage of solidification, "soil nature"; the stage of dense matter, "metal nature"; the liquid stage, "water nature"; and the gaseous state, "tree nature."

Generally, the more yin transformations—water, tree, and fire—are accelerated through an external increase in more yang factors, such as temperature, while the more yang transformations—soil and metal natures—are produced from an increase in yin factors, for example a lowering of temperature. This can be more clearly understood when we consider the relationship between the five transformations and the seasons of the year.

---

[5] During our stay in Japan, we had a number of opportunities to observe the fundamental influence that this concept has had on Japanese culture and way of life in general. For example, during a visit with Mr. Kushi's father, Keizo, at his home in Tokyo, we were introduced to the ornamental stone lantern in the garden. Known in Japanese as *Ishi-No-Tōro* or *Ishi-Dōro*, the lantern resembles a miniature pagoda, with each of its five tiers representing one of the five transformation. Mr. Kushi also explained that five-storied pagodas, of which there are now many in Japan, have a similar correspondence.

This concept has also influenced the Japanese language. For example, the days of the week are named after yin and yang and the five transformations, as are the sun, the moon, and a number of planets in the solar system. These correspondences are as follows:

WEEKDAYS			PLANETS		
Sunday	*Nichiyōbi*	Sun day	Sun	*Tai-Yō*	Great Yang
Monday	*Getsuyōbi*	Moon day	Moon	*Tai-In*	Great Yin
Tuesday	*Kayōbi*	Fire day	Mars	*Ka-Sei*	Fire Star
Wednesday	*Suiyōbi*	Water day	Mercury	*Sui-Sei*	Water Star
Thursday	*Mokuyōbi*	Wood day	Jupiter	*Moku-Sei*	Wood Star
Friday	*Kinyōbi*	Metal day	Venus	*Kin-Sei*	Metal Star
Saturday	*Doyōbi*	Soil day	Saturn	*Do-Sei*	Soil Star

The five transformations are also fundamental to the understanding and practice of traditional forms of Oriental medicine including acupuncture, *shiatsu*, herbal medicine, and others, as well as to a number of astrological systems such as the nine-planetary *ki* study, which is known as *Kyu-Sei-Ki-Gaku*. At the same time, governmental affairs were often conducted in accord with this universal order. The *Tai-Ho* code of A.D. 701–2 records that a department of yin-yang (*Inyoryo*) was established within the government to advise on various policy issues. Further information about the live-transformations is presented by Michio Kushi in all of his Japan Publications titles.

A. The Seasonal Cycle

1. Summer. During the summer, the atmospheric energy of the earth becomes very active and highly charged, while many varieties of vegetation reach their most yin or expanded peak of growth. The more yin process of evaporation is very active in the heat of the summer. The summer season corresponds to the state of "fire nature," which is the most yin, or actively expanding of the five transformations. Among vegetables, those which primarily reflect the more yin, expanding force of the earth, such as leafy greens, are classified in this category, while corn, the most yin of the cereal grains, is harvested at this time and is associated with this season.

2. Late Summer. During this season, the atmosphere usually becomes cooler and drier, and in the plant world the energy which reached its peak during the summer begins to be focused in a more yang, or inward, direction in the seeds and fruit which begin to ripen. The late summer season corresponds to the transformation "soil nature," and of the grains, millet is classified in this category, as are pumpkins, squash, and other more round-shaped vegetables which have a more even balance of heaven's and earth's forces.

3. Autumn. As temperatures continue to become colder, energy enters its most yang, or condensed, phase. Many plants enter a phase of dormancy during this season, while energy which has been accumulated during the previous seasons is concentrated and stored in the form of seeds and grains. Rice is usually harvested in the autumn, while more yang, hard, leafy vegetables like watercress and kale are also classified in this category. The autumn season corresponds to the transformation "soil nature."

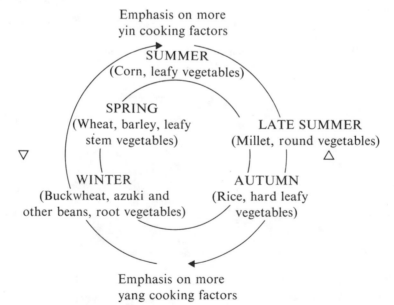

Fig. 19   Guidelines for Seasonal Adjustments in Diet and Cooking Methods

4. Winter. In this season, which corresponds to the transformation "water nature," dormant energies stir as the yearly cycle begins to enter a phase of expansion and forthcoming growth. In the vegetable world, plants and seeds lie dormant, ready to burst forth with the coming of spring. Among grains, buckwheat is classified in this category, as are beans such as azuki. These more yang beans were traditionally harvested in the late autumn. Among vegetables, more yang root vegetables are classified with this season which corresponds to the transformation "water nature."

5. Spring. As temperatures become warmer, the more yin processes of expansion and growth get fully underway. Seeds begin to push forth sprouts and roots, while a variety of winter wheats and barleys are harvested. Vegetables which have a leafy stem shape, such as broccoli, are classified in this category, which corresponds to the transformation "tree nature."

Regardless of season, the standard diet should generally form the basis of our way of eating, since it reflects an overall balance between the forces of heaven and earth which remain relatively constant throughout the year. At the same time, foods such as grains, beans, sea vegetables, and others which are included in the standard diet can be naturally stored throughout the year without artificial methods such as canning, freezing, or chemical preservation.

Among the cereal grains, whole brown rice has the most ideal overall balance of yin and yang components, reflected in the general 1:7 ratio of minerals to proteins to carbohydrates, and should generally be eaten as a principal grain throughout the year. It is also the easiest of the grains to eat in its whole form without being crushed into flour. Secondary grains such as whole wheat, millet, buckwheat and others can also be used on a year-round basis, and can be particularly emphasized during their corresponding season. For example, a more yang grain such as buckwheat is very good as a secondary grain during the cold winter months, while a more yin grain like corn is ideal as a supplement during the summer.

The understanding of the five transformations can also be very helpful in the selection of vegetables and other side dishes. For example, pumpkins and hard squashes are usually harvested during the late summer and early fall, and are ideal for use during these seasons. During the hot summer months, when leafy greens proliferate, they should be more frequently included in the diet, and can be eaten in the more yin form of salad. In the late fall and winter, many varieties of green vegetables are not readily available, so hard, round vegetables like onions, fall squashes, etc., as well as root vegetables like burdock and carrots, can be eaten more frequently. These vegetables can also be naturally stored during these seasons by keeping them in a root cellar or some other cool, dry place.

Our cooking methods should also harmonize with the changing seasons. For example, during the autmn and winter seasons, more yang cooking factors should be emphasized. Therefore, winter meals should have a slightly saltier taste and can include more sautéed, pressure cooked or baked dishes as well as a slightly higher percentage of animal food. In general, we should try to emphasize heaven's more yang, consolidating force during these seasons by serving more cooked, highly energized foods. In the spring and summer, more yin factors should be emphasized so that summer meals may include more steamed, lightly sautéed or boiled vegetable dishes, more salad, a higher percentage of desserts, including some raw fruits, and occasional chilled dishes such as cold *soba*, kanten, or cool beverages. Generally speaking, we should try to emphasize earth's more yin, expansive force during these warmer seasons.

B.   Daily and Monthly Cycles

During the course of a day, the natural flow of life energy also fluctuates in accord with these five stages of change. The transformations of tree, fire, and soil nature generally correspond to the times of morning, midday, and afternoon, respectively; while the transformations of metal and water nature correspond to evening and nighttime.

In the plant and animal worlds, studies of *circadian* rhythms (from the Latin *circa*, meaning "about," and *dies*, "day") have revealed that many plant functions reach a peak of activity during the early morning and daylight hours, while slowing down during the evening and night time hours. For example, in one species of marine algae, the more yin function of cell division was found to occur almost entirely in the early morning, which generally corresponds to the stage of tree nature, a more actively expanding or yin transformation. In this same species, the active process of photosynthesis was found to reach its peak during the middle of the day, around the time generally corresponding to the transformation of fire.

In animals, metabolic activities also fluctuate according to this cycle, generally becoming more active during the day and slowing down at night. For example, our body temperature fluctuates as much as two degrees Fahrenheit during the course of the day, usually reaching a high around midday, and a low during the middle of the night. Functions such as hormone secretion, heart rate, blood pressure, urinary excretion of potassium, sodium and calcium, etc. generally fluctuate in accord with this cycle.[6]

Our diet should also reflect these daily energy fluctuations. For example, in the morning, which corresponds to the more expansive, tree nature of energy, we should usually eat a simpler or more lightly cooked meal. Miso soup is an ideal dish for this time of day, since it is made from wheat and barley (which correspond to the transformation tree nature) and is a fermented food product (fer-

---

[6] It is interesting to note that, just as modern science is studying the cyclical nature of various biochemical and physiological functions, ancient Oriental scientists sought to understand these cycles in terms of vibrational energy or *ki*. For example, the five transformations were understood to govern the cyclic flow of electromagnetic energy through the major organs and their corresponding energy pathways, or meridians. The major organs were classified according to their type of energy and were associated with the five transformations as follows: *Fire nature*, heart and small intestine; *Soil nature*, spleen/pancreas and stomach; *Metal nature*, lungs and large intestine; *Water nature*, kidneys and bladder; *Tree nature*, liver and gall bladder.

mentation is a more yin biological process). Naturally-fermented vegetable pickles, such as those described in this book, are also very good to eat at breakfast. Therefore, a simple breakfast consisting of rice or some other grain, miso soup, and pickles, and perhaps a lightly sautéed or steamed vegetable dish, would be in accord with this natural cycle.

Lunch should also consist of a more lightly cooked or simple meal, while the largest meal of the day should generally be eaten at dinner, around the time corresponding to the transformation metal nature. Therefore, the evening meal can include a wider variety of side dishes such as fish or shellfish, fruit desserts, beans, sea vegetables, and others, and may include more heavily cooked foods.

Another of the natural processes that should be considered is the twenty-eight day cycle of the moon, which alternates between a more yin phase around the time of the new moon and a more yang phase during the full moon. As we approach the new moon, we should emphasize slightly more yang factors in our diet and method of cooking, while more yin factors help to balance the conditions resulting from the full moon.

C.   We Should Eat According to Personal Need

Since everyone is unique, a wide variety of individual differences should be considered when determining the most appropriate diet. For example, infants and children are more yang (small, compact, and active) than adults, and should, therefore, have a somewhat more yin diet, with little or no salt and more sweet tasting foods, including occasional snacks like rice honey or barley malt candies, apple juice, etc. Adults, on the other hand, require more salt in their diets and can generally eat a larger volume of animal food.

Men and women also have differing needs. Men, for example, can usually include a slightly higher percentage of fish or other animal foods in their diets, while women should generally rely more on vegetable quality foods. Our dietary needs are also determined by the type of activity that we are involved in. For example, persons who are very active physically can generally include a higher percentage of animal food in their diets than those who are more sedentary. Active people can also generally consume a slightly larger volume of food without becoming overweight or out of balance.

Previous eating habits also play a large role in determining what a balanced diet should be, as does a person's overall constitution. For example, Japanese and other Asians have traditionally eaten far fewer animal products—especially meat and dairy—than many people in the West.[7] Since animal products generally contain a high concentration of mineral salts, Japanese and other semi-vegetarian

---

[7] In his latest book, *The Japanese*, Professor Edwin O. Reischauer of Harvard University estimates that at present, people in Japan eat about one-fifth of the volume of meat consumed in the United States. He also states that the traditional Japanese diet of whole rice, vegetables, fish, etc. would probably be a "perfect health diet" if people in Japan weren't so intent on refining their rice.

peoples can usually tolerate a somewhat larger quantity of salt in their diets than can people in the West. It is for this reason that many of the recipes in earlier macrobiotic cookbooks, some of which were originally developed in Japan, required modification before being comfortably adopted by people in America and Europe.

At the same time, there are an almost infinite variety of motivations for wanting to eat a more natural diet. For example, some people may be interested in restoring their health, or losing weight, or developing their spirituality, while others may be concerned about nutritional balance or economic considerations. In terms of the macrobiotic approach, however, we can generally classify the varieties of eating as follows:

1. Eating to Restore Health. When we eat for this purpose, it is usually necessary to carefully observe a way of eating that will restore one's condition to a state of equilibrium with the surrounding environment. The period of careful attention to diet can be anywhere from several months to several years, depending on the type of illness that we wish to relieve.[8]

2. Eating to Maintain a Healthy Level of Activity. Once our health has been generally established, we may want to broaden our diet somewhat in order to pursue various activities. For example, persons who are involved in business may want to include a slightly higher percentage of animal food in their diets, as would those who are doing active, physical work. At the same time, social events such as parties, holidays, or celebrations may require that we eat more widely; while in the pursuit of our activities or for enjoyment, we may want to eat in restaurants. However, when eating in this manner, it is generally advisable to avoid the extreme foods listed earlier and to select only the highest quality items. At the same time, the standard diet should be kept as the central basis of our way of eating, and, when necessary, we should return to it entirely.

3. Eating to Realize Our Dream. At this level we begin to freely use our diet as a means to both formulate and realize our dream, based on a developing understanding of the profound physical, psychological, and spiritual effects of food. For example, if we wish to develop our power to insight or our universal consciousness, we may decide to forego the use of animal food or to fast for a certain period. Or, if we go to a foreign country, we may wish to naturally adapt our way of eating to the traditional dietary customs and natural surroundings of our new environment.

At this level, the standard diet effortlessly and naturally forms the basis of our way of eating, and is not viewed as a "diet," but simply as the most natural and normal way for human beings to eat. When we cook at this level, we intuitively adjust our menu and style of preparation as our environment changes, and begin to intuitively prepare foods that will automatically benefit the health and well-being of all those who eat our cooking.

---

[8] General dietary and way of life recommendations for a variety of conditions are presented in *Natural Healing through Macrobiotics* and in the *Book of Macrobiotics* by Michio Kushi.

Nutrition and Macrobiotics

"I will single out what for me are the three most significant ways in which macrobiotics differs from conventional nutritional science:

1. Macrobiotics appreciates and emphasizes the crucial importance of societal, cultural, and familial background in determining proper dietary patterns.

2. Macrobiotics appreciates and emphasizes the crucial importance of prenatal nutrition and breastfeeding in determining the future development of each individual.

3. Macrobiotics appreciates and emphasizes the crucial importance of incorporating diet in a universal system of thought and behavior. Macrobiotics does not get caught in the trap of singling out cholesterol or vitamins, or trace minerals or proteins. Macrobiotics is a synthesizing system. Modern nutrition, in contrast, depends on analysis . . . . This often leads, as everyone knows, to paralysis by analysis."

Robert S. Mendelsohn, M.D. (author of *Confessions of a Medical Heretic*) in the publication "Cancer & Diet."

1. The Cycle of Nutritional Energy

Nutrition is generally defined as the sum of the processes by which an organism obtains, takes in, and utilizes food. These processes initially involve the transformation of inorganic elements such as carbon, hydrogen, oxygen, nitrogen, phosphorus, and iron into the organic material of plants. The organic matter of plants—carbohydrates, proteins, and fats—is then converted by man and animals into both energy and physical substance. These processes depend to a large extent on the energy of the sun, and, like everything else, the mechanism whereby this energy is converted into the energy of life occurs according to yin and yang and the cycle of the five transformations.

In the biological energy cycle, solar energy is stored in green plants and then converted by man and animals into cellular energy. This cycle is also generally known as the carbon cycle, since it involves the alternating extraction of carbon (in the form of carbon dioxide) from, and its subsequent release back into the atmosphere.

We can generally trace the transformation of solar energy through the following stages which correlate with the five transformations:

1. Solar Energy: It is generally estimated that each square yard of the earth receives about a thousand watts of solar energy per minute, mostly in the form of light and heat. Most of this enormous quantity of energy is either reflected back into space or absorbed by the planet's surface and re-radiated as heat. Solar energy corresponds in this cycle to the stage of plasma, or *fire nature*.

74

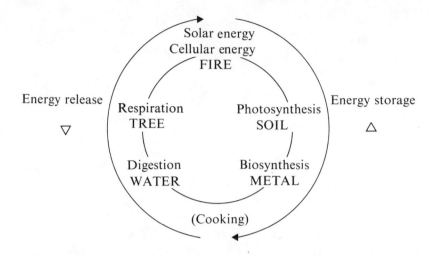

Fig. 20   The Cycle of Nutritional Energy (The Carbon Cycle)
Photosynthesis and biosynthesis are the stages in the energy cycle in which free energy is stored and condensed, while digestion and respiration are the processes through which this energy is broken down and released. In terms of the circulation of energy, the first two processes are more yang, and the second two are more yin.

2.   *Photosynthesis*:   In this process, solar energy is absorbed by plants and combined with water and atmospheric carbon dioxide to produce carbohydrates. Even though this process utilizes less than one percent of the solar energy which reaches the earth, the annual production of fixed carbon (carbon that has been converted to organic form through photosynthesis) by both land and water vegetation is estimated to be about 150 billion tons.

Chemically, the process of photosynthesis can be stated as follows:

$$6CO_2 6H_2O + \text{solar energy} \longrightarrow C_6H_{12}O_6 + 6O_2,$$

or, carbon dioxide plus water plus solar energy changes into carbohydrate (glucose) plus free oxygen. Since this process is one of yangization, in which free energy is captured and stored in the form of carbohydrate, oxygen, which is yin, is released. This comes about as a result of the influence of sunlight on the water molecules which are used in this process. Sunlight, which is more yang, is readily attracted to and absorbed by the more yin oxygen atom, causing it to become more yang and therefore less attracted to the more yang atoms of hydrogen which comprise the water molecule. This causes the water molecule to separate, with the oxygen being released into the atmosphere, and the hydrogen combining with the carbon dioxide to form *glucose*, or simple sugar.

Glucose is the most primary food made by green plants, and the other living forms of vegetable matter, such as protein, are the result of chemical alterations of this basic compound. All living organisms, including man also depend upon chemical derivatives of this basic compound, both for their energy needs and in the creation of their physical structures. The potential energy stored in glucose is the primary source of the bilogical energy which nourishes all things. Our modern civilization is also dependent on this energy, since most of the power used to drive our automobiles, heat our homes and power our appliances can be traced back to this source.

The process whereby the sun's energy is stored in the form of glucose is *endo-thermic*, which means that the glucose contains more energy than the original elements out of which it was created. In this cycle, photosynthesis corresponds to the stage of solidification, or *soil nature*.

3. *Biosynthesis*: In this process, the free energy of the sun reaches its most yang or condensed state as the glucose, or "simple sugar" produced during photosynthesis is used to create more complex carbohydrates. These larger carbohydrate molecules are formed by the condensation and combination of many smaller glucose molecules, and exist in higher plants in the form of starch. In the rice plant, for example, each grain is composed primarily of starch in the form of *polysaccharide glucose*, or "complex carbohydrate," while the proteins, minerals and fats that it contains are built around this basic substance.[9] This process corresponds to the stage of dense matter, or *metal nature*, in which energy enters its most yang, condensed phase.

4. *Digestion*: With digestion, a reverse process begins, as the nutritional factors created by biosynthesis are broken down into their more basic compounds. For example, polysaccharides, or complex sugars, are reduced during digestion to their original form of glucose. This process begins as food enters the mouth and continues along the digestive tract through the activity of enzymes secreted by the salivary glands, the stomach, pancreas, and small intestine.

In the case of polysaccharide glucose, such as that of cereal grains, digestion takes place largely in the mouth through the interaction with *pytalin*, an enzyme contained in saliva. Therefore, proper chewing is an essential first step in securing the smooth release of the energy which these foods contain. Polysaccharide glucose is further broken down in the stomach, and then completely digested in the duodenum and small intestine. Digestion corresponds in this cycle to the stage of *water nature*, or liquid matter, since it is the initial process leading to the eventual breakdown and release of the energy stored in plants.

Man is unique among the animals in that, in between the stages of biosynthesis and digestion, an additional process has been added. This process, cooking, can be considered as a form of "predigestion," since it allows for a more efficient breakdown and release of the potential energy stored in plants. Cooked foods can be considered to be far more "energized" than those which are not cooked.

---

[9] There are several main varieties of carbohydrate: simple sugars, or *monosaccharides*, such as those found in fruits and honey; double sugars, or *disaccharides*, which are found in sugar and milk; and more complex sugars, or *polysaccharides*, which are found in grains, beans and vegetables. Among these, *polysaccharide glucose*, such as that found in whole grains, beans and vegetables, should comprise the mainstay of the human diet. Many recent health reports such as *Dietary Goals for the United States* and the Surgeon General's report on Health Promotion have also recommended re-establishing complex carbohydrates as the basis of our diet.

5. *Respiration*: Once the digested foodstuffs have been broken down into their most basic forms—for example, carbohydrates into glucose, proteins into amino acids, and fats into fatty acids and glycerol—they pass through the villi of the small intestine and into the bloodstream. (However, not all foods undergo this normal process. Extremely unbalanced items such as refined sugar enter the bloodstream almost immediately after being eaten, causing an imbalance in the blood and a variety of compensatory mechanisms.) Here the process of metabolism begins, which involves two simultaneous phases. The more yang phase, *anabolism*, consists of the various processes that nutrients undergo in the building up of the body's chemical or physical substance, while the more yin process, *catabolism*, involves the breakdown of nutritional substances in order to provide energy. Catabolism occurs at the cellular level through the process of respiration, in which the energy stored in glucose is released or converted back into free energy. This process requires oxygen which is provided through breathing, while carbon dioxide and water, which are the elements used in photosynthesis, are given off as waste products. This process corresponds to the stage of *tree nature*, or gaseous matter, since the end product of respiration is conversion of glucose into free energy which is in turn used by each of the body's cells.

The processes of photosynthesis and biosynthesis, which occur in plants, represent stages in the biological energy cycle in which free energy is condensed or stored, and are governed by the centripetal force of heaven. The complementary processes of digestion and respiration, which occur in animals, represent the stages in this cycle where this stored energy is broken down and released, and are governed more by the centrifugal force of the earth. However, as we saw in Chapter I the vegetable kingdom is structurally more yin, and is produced more as a result of earth's force, while the structurally more yang animal kingdom is generally governed more by heaven's force. However, since they are structurally more yin, vegetables tend to attract more yang factors in the form of carbon dioxide and solar energy, while tending to repel oxygen, which is also more yin. Animals, on the other hand, tend to attract yin in the form of oxygen, while giving off carbon dioxide and energy.

2. Nutritional Comparisons

In the *Book of Macrobiotics*, Michio Kushi introduced the importance of maintaining a ratio of about one to seven (between 1:5 and 1:10) between the more yang and more yin factors in our daily diet. This ratio is reflected nutritionally in the proportion of minerals to proteins and proteins to carbohydrates, and when our diet is based on foods that genrally maintain a one to seven ratio between these factors, it is much easier to establish and maintain a harmonious balance with our surroundings.

Among vegetable foods, the cereal grains most closely approach this ratio. In this species, which is the most highly developed within the vegetable kingdom, the process of biosynthesis has reached its most evolutionarily advanced form. The biosynthetic functions of the cereal grains, which are responsible for the synthesis of complex carbohydrates as well as for the arrangement of minerals, proteins, and carbohydrates in an overall ratio of one to seven, most closely complements the digestive processes found in man, which are the most highly developed within the animal kingdom.

Mineral to Protein to Carbohydrate Ratios

	Minerals	Protein	Carbohydrates
Short grain brown rice	1.2 g.	7.5 g.	77.4 g.
Whole grain wheat	1.7	14.0	69.1
Whole millet	2.5	9.9	72.9
Pearl barley	0.9	8.2	78.8
Broccoli	1.1	3.6	5.9
Apples	0.3	0.2	14.5
White sugar	Trace	—	99.5
Beef	0.8	16.9	—
Eggs	1.0	12.9	0.9

In the chart presented above, which is taken from food composition tables compiled by the United States Department of Agriculture and the Japan Nutritionists Association, the cereal grains, represented here by brown rice, whole wheat, millet and barley, most closely approach a one to seven ratio of minerals to protein to carbohydrate, while other vegetable foods such as broccoli or apples are not so close to this ratio.[10] As we can also see, refined sugar is an extremely unbalanced item, consisting of nearly 100% refined carbohydrate, with practically no minerals or proteins. On the other hand, beef and eggs are also very unbalanced since they contain mostly protein with only a small percentage of minerals and practically no carbohydrate.

Since eggs and beef (which is representative of meat in general) are so heavily weighted in favor of protein, most people try to supply the missing minerals by cooking them with plenty of salt or by adding it at the table. Also, since these foods lack carbohydrate, they are often eaten along with foods such as potatoes or starchy white bread, or are followed by an alcoholic beverage or a sugary dessert. A diet such as this requires the intake of a larger than normal volume of water along with an acceleration of breathing and respiration, since two additional factors—water and air—must also be taken in a one-to-seven ratio above and beyond our intake of carbohydrates. Obviously, a diet such as this is based on a more extreme balance which taxes and often overloads the body's metabolism and powers of elimination.

---

[10] All of the food composition figures quoted in this section are taken from these sources and are based on the nutrients contained in 100 grams of the edible portion of the given food. More complete nutritional composition tables are presented in the *Book of Macrobiotics*.

Another food which naturally maintains an almost perfect 1:7 ratio is breast milk, with about 0.2 grams of mineral ash, 1.4 grams of protein and 7.1 grams of carbohydrate. Comparing this to cow's milk, which contains roughly 0.7 grams of mineral, 3.5 grams of protein and 4.9 grams of carbohydrate in a ratio of about 1:1.4 to 1:1.5, we can see that breast milk is the most suitable food for human infants, while cow's milk is more ideally suited for calves.

A way of eating which is based on whole grains, beans, cooked vegetables and sea vegetables with occasional salad, fish, seasonal fruits and other supplements contains sufficient quantities of all the essential nutritional factors and provides them in their highest quality and most naturally balanced form.[11]

In the case of protein, for example, 100 grams of brown rice contains 7.5 grams; whole wheat, 14.0 grams; Hatcho miso, 16.8 grams; *mugi* miso, 14.0 grams; azuki beans, 21.5 grams; chickpeas, 20.5 grams; lentils, 24.7 grams; and soybeans, 34.1 grams, while animal products such as cow's milk contain 3.5 grams; eggs, 12.9 grams, and beef, 16.9 grams. As we can see, whole wheat contains more protein than eggs, as do the varieties of miso and beans listed above, while all of the representative beans have a higher quantity of protein than beef. At the same time, many varieties of fish and shellfish are rich sources of protein, and these can be included in the standard way of eating from time to time.

Vegetable quality proteins are usually of a higher quality than proteins derived from animal sources, mostly because they lack the large quantities of saturated fat and oil which exist in animal foods. Egg yolks, for instance, contain roughly 30.6 grams of saturated fat per 100 grams; butter contains 81.1 grams, and cheddar cheese contains about 32.2 grams. Compare this to brown rice, which contains about 1.9 grams; whole wheat, which contains 1.9 grams; whole wheat flour, which contains 2.0 grams, or azuki beans and lentils which contain 1.6 and 1.1 grams respectively. It is now widely known that the unsaturated fats and oils contained in these vegetable foods are of superior quality to the saturated variety found in animal products.

Some people may have the impression that dairy products are necessary to supply a sufficient daily amount of calcium. However, many vegetable foods, especially beans, seaweeds, and leafy green vegetables, are far richer in calcium than are dairy products. Soybeans, for example, contain 226 mg., while tofu contains 128 mg. and Hatcho miso, 140 mg.; while cow's milk contains only 118 mg. and yogurt, 120 mg. Among the leafy green vegetables, collard greens contain 203 mg.; daikon greens, 190 mg.; dandelion greens, 187 mg.; kale, 179 mg.; mustard greens, 183 mg. and parsley, 203 mg. Among seaweeds, arame contains 1,170 mg.; hijiki, 1,400 mg.; kelp, 1,093 mg. and wakame, 1,300 mg. There are also a number of other items which are frequently used in macrobiotics and which contain plenty

---

[11] For a more detailed review of considerations such as the importance of eating complex carbohydrates, the superiority of vegetable quality proteins, and a variety of questions relating to the fat, mineral, vitamin and caloric contents of natural foods, please refer to the *Book of Macrobiotics* by Michio Kushi.

of calcium. Two of these, for example, bancha tea and sesame seeds, contain 720 mg. and 1,160 mg. respectively.

A diet based on macrobiotic principles should also contain ample amounts of iron. Whole millet, for instance, contains 6.8 mg.; buckwheat noodles, 5.0 mg.; azuki beans, 4.8 mg.; chickpeas, 6.9 mg.; lentils, 6.8 mg.; Hacho miso, 6.5 mg.; mugi miso; 4.0 mg.; pumpkin seeds, 11.2 mg.; sesame seeds, 10.5 mg.; arame, 12 mg. and hijiki, 29 mg. Interestingly enough, all of these vegetable foods contain more iron per hundred grams than beef, which contains 2.5 mg; eggs, which contain 2.3 mg. and cow's milk, which contains only a slight trace of this element.

The standard macrobiotic way of eating also provides a proper balance of all of the necessary vitamins, including vitamins C and B_{12}. Many green leafy vegtables contain plenty of vitamin C, for example kale which contains 125 mg., and parsley at 172 mg. Bancha twig tea also contains plenty of vitamin C, with 130 mg. per 100 grams. Interestingly, oranges and orange juice each contain about 50 mg. of vitamin C. In regard to vitamin B_{12}, recent studies have demonstrated that this vitamin exists in suitable quantities in fermented foods like miso, as well as in seaweed. Therefore, a dish such as miso soup, which contains seaweed, provides ample quantities of vitamin B_{12}. Contrary to popular belief, it is not necessary to eat animal foods such as meat or eggs to obtain the proper quantities of this vitamin.

Appendix: The Spiral of Cooking

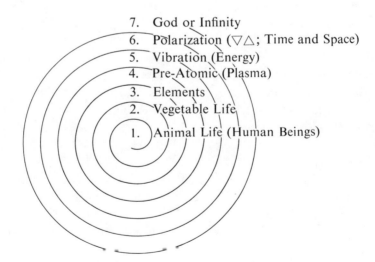

Fig. 21 The Spiral of Cooking
This spiral of creation or materialization corresponds to the process described in the *Book of Genesis*, in which God or Infinity manifests through progressive stages arriving ultimately in the form of human life. All of these forms of our huge macrocòsmic environment are utilized in the process of cooking.

Macrobiotic cooking is the art of balancing the myriad factors which make up our total environment. All of the various levels of existence, which form a vast, logarithmic spiral extending from each of us to infinity itself, are called into play when we cook.

From the world of animals, of which we are a part, we select a variety of species, especially fish, shellfish and other more primitive species which are further removed from us on the evolutionary scale.

From the vegetable world, out of which all animal life has arisen, we select a wide variety of species from the land and sea, in harmony with the changing of the seasons, the conditions of our environment and our evolutionary heritage.

From the world of elements—soil, air and water—which gives birth to the vegetable kingdom, we moderately season our meals with salt and minerals so as to maintain the quality of our blood, which reflects our origin in the primordial ocean. We also use the pressure of the atmosphere to consolidate the energy in our foods and add the proper amount of water to prepare them for digestion.

From the world of plasma, or the pre-atomic energy fields which give birth to the elements, we use fire to energize our foods in harmony with the season and environment.

From the world of vibration, which is the origin of the visible universe, comes energy in the forms of the fire, water, vegetables, minerals, animals and other factors that we transform into our daily meals. We also cook with a peaceful, happy thankful and harmonious spirit, and transfer this vibration to all who eat our cooking.

From the primary polarization of the universe, yin and yang, come the worlds of space and time that we seek to balance in our cooking. In the realm of space, we balance the universal forces of centripetality and centrifugality which govern the whole universe, and which appear on our planet as the forces of heaven and earth, creating all forms of life. Out of the world of time arises the evolutionary order of eating, based on billions of years of biological development, culminating in the appearance of cereal grains in the vegetable world and man in the world of animals. We seek to encompass this entire evolutionary process in the range of foods that we cook, from the most primitive, single-celled enzymes and bacteria, such as those in fermented foods, to the most highly developed cereal grains.

From the world of God, or the Oneness of the Infinite Universe, comes the primary intuition that we use to judge and create balance in our cooking, synthesizing all of the complementary factors of these previous worlds into an harmonious whole. It is this endless and beginningless realm of perfect balance that we seek to recreate when we cook.

The art of cooking is truly the art of life, and the spiral of cooking is nothing but the spiral of life itself.

Part Two

Cooking for Health, Happiness, and Freedom

1. Cooking with Whole Grains

The main shrine at Ise. The shrine buildings at Ise are modelled after ancient grain storehouses in the prehistoric *azekura* style of architecture.

"The man-made countryside was draped with a wide variety of crops. There were rivet or cone wheats for cold, retentive and rank soil, and bread wheats for ordinary crops. These were all winter wheats. Spring varieties did exist, but were not often grown. Conversely, spring barleys were much more usual than winter ones. Bigg, or "beer," the chief variety of winter barley was hardly met with outside the northerly parts of England. Rye, too, was known in both winter and spring types, but it was the winter ones that were most often sown. There were naked oats, which made porridge without any milling; black oats and "skegs" for poor lands; and red, white, and reed oats for good ones."

Eric Kerridge, *The Farmers of Old England*

"A meal without rice is no meal." Japanese Proverb

In both East and West, North and South, since the dawn of the human race, we have looked to the cereal grains as our main source of food. The majority of the world's agriculture still centers on their production, and a large number of people throughout the world continue to eat them directly as their principal food.

Whenever scientific historians attempt to trace the origins of the cereal grains, they inevitably enter into the realms of legend and mythology. For example, the Greeks believed that the birth of agriculture was synonymous with the birth of cereal grains, and credited both to their Goddess, Demeter. According to legend,

Demeter gave the first seeds of wheat to her priest, Triptolemus, and instructed him to drive around the earth in his chariot drawn by dragons and serpents, bringing the belssings of agriculture and civilization to all people. The Romans renamed Demeter into Ceres, and the modern word *cereal* is derived from her name.

In the Far East, the cereal grains, especially rice, are also associated with the Gods. For example, while in Japan, we had the opportunity to visit a place known as the Ise Shrine, which is, perhaps, the most well known spiritual center in that country. Dating back to the birth of Christ, this group of shrines consists of an inner shrine known as *naigu* and an outer shrine known as *gegu*, as well as more than 120 related shrine buildings. The shrine complex is located in a beautiful natural setting not far from the Pacific coast in the mountains of Mie prefecture. All of the shrine buildings are constructed of cypress wood which, when freshly cut, gives off a rich golden glow. Interestingly enough, the main shrine buildings are completely rebuilt every twenty years, according to the original plan which dates back nearly two thousand years.

The inner shrine is dedicated to Amaterasu-Ōmikami, who is one of the most central deities of the Shinto faith and who represents both the sun and the brilliant radiance of the infinite universe. Of almost equal importance is Toyo-Uke-no-Oo-Kami, or the "rich blossoming Goddess," who is enshrined in the outer building and who presides over agriculture and life-giving food, especially rice.

The Ise Shrine is perhaps the most important of the many thousands of shrines in Japan, and millions of people visit it every year to offer their thanks and expressions of gratitude. A special rice field is also kept within the shrine grounds, along with facilities for making sea salt according to ancient methods. These were originally established, along with examples of pure, natural water, as quality standards for use in judging these essential items.

The shrine buildings at Ise represent the most ancient style of architecture found in Japan, and according to legend are modelled after buildings which were used in ancient times to store brown rice and other whole grains. It is difficult to describe the impression that seeing the Shrine left on us. Perhaps it was similar to the sense of beauty and wonder that we all experience from the magic of nature, or the sense of wholeness that I experience when I enter a natural food store and see gleaming barrels of whole grains, or when I cook with them in my kitchen.

Most archaeologists believe that grains were first used as food about 10,000 years ago when the ancestors of wheat were first cultivated in ancient Sumer. It is generally believed that prior to this no agriculture existed and that man lived primarily as a hunter and gatherer, relying heavily on the use of various animal products. However, this view does not take into account our biological constitution, and is usually based on prehistoric evidence gathered mostly in Europe—which at that time may have been under an ice sheet—without considering that people in other parts of the world with more moderate climates may have had different dietary customs. When we examine our teeth, for example, we discover that we have twenty molars, which are perfect for crushing and grinding grains and other hard, fibrous foods. Our eight front incisors seem best suited for cutting vegetables, while only the four front canine teeth seem to be useful for eating animal food. Based on the structure of the teeth, we can probably assume that human beings have evolved primarily as a result of following a diet based generally on five parts whole grain and two parts vegetable food to about one part animal food. Also, our digestive systems are too long to be suitable for a diet based on animal foods, which decompose very rapidly. Because of its length, the human digestive tract seems much more naturally suited to a diet based more on whole grains and vegetables.

When George Ohsawa first visited this country more than twenty years ago, he was surprised to discover that America was possibly the first nation in the history of the world to have almost completely abandoned cereal grains, which have traditionally been humanity's most important staple food. Is it not interesting that as we have gotten further away from humanity's traditional food, what are known as the "degenerative diseases"—cancer, heart disease, mental illness and others— have all increased?

Fortunately, a growing number of individuals and families in this and other countries throughout the world have regained their dietary common sense, and are now basing their daily diets around whole grains. Whole grains are thoroughly nutritious, economical, and delicious, and are very easy to prepare. I sincerely hope that you will begin to cook them every day as the foundation of your health and happiness.

BROWN RICE

Rice is one of the oldest of the cultivated grains. Historically, it is known to have been cultivated for at least five thousand years in Japan, while it is still a staple food throughout the Far East, China, India, Indonesia, Mexico, and other parts of the world.

As we saw in the Part One, whole, natural rice closely approaches the most ideal ratio of basic nutrients, and closely corresponds to the 1:7 ratio of the human form. Besides being the most ideally balanced, brown rice also contains most of the essential amino acids and is high in protein, calcium, iron, vitamin B, and other minerals.

While in Japan, I had many opportunities to see rice growing at various stages in the fields. It is such a delicate and flexible plant. Most people in Japan now eat refined, white rice, but a growing number are starting to return to the more traditional brown rice or are eating partially refined rice. In Japanese, brown rice is called *genmai* and white rice is called *hakumai*. *Gen* means "original" and *haku* means "white." In general, the rice in Japan is somewhat richer in minerals due to the volcanic soil in which it is grown, while American rice is generally larger and somewhat sweeter in taste. There are three main varieties of rice now available in most natural food stores: *short grain*, which is sweeter and more glutinous; *medium grain*, which is more soft and moist; and *long grain*, which is light and fluffy when cooked.

Some of the many uses of rice include eating it as a cereal, using it it soups, salads, desserts, breads, beverages, *sushi*, *nori-maki*, vegetable pies, croquettes, casseroles, pilaf, paella, stuffings, and in many other ways. The possibilities are almost endless.

Rice can be prepared in a variety of ways, including pressure-cooking, boiling, baking, roasting, and frying. In Japan, rice was traditionally cooked in a heavy cast-iron pot with a heavy wooden lid which rested on top. This utensil is similar to a pressure cooker with a loose-fitting lid, and it allows steam to slowly and gradually escape around the edges. Based on my experience, pressure-cooking is by far the best way to prepare brown rice. Pressure-cooked rice is easier to digest, sweeter, more nutritious, more thoroughly cooked, and is usually not watery. Before cooking, rice may also be soaked for several hours or overnight in the pressure-cooker with the appropriate amount of water and salt. Never wash the rice and allow it to sit in a colander before placing it in the pressure-cooker, since if it is allowed to sit for too long after it is washed, it will absorb the water remaining on it and will begin to expand. This will usually cause the rice to turn out to be very wet.

Rice can be cooked at different temperatures to produce different vibrational qualities, tastes, or yin and yang qualities. For example, one method is to begin pressure-cooking with a low flame and allow the pressure to come up very gradually. This more yin method produces a very peaceful, harmonious feeling in the rice as well as a sweeter flavor, since the grains are allowed to adapt slowly to the high temperature. A second method is to begin cooking with a low flame and gradually increase the temperature to high over a span of several minutes. A third way is to begin with a high flame, waiting until the pressure is up to reduce the flame to low and allow the grain to finish cooking. This method produces a more yang effect. Of course, the differences in quality, taste, and feeling produced by these methods are very subtle. It may take some time until you are able to notice the difference. With the first method, your rice will take longer to cook, while the last method is the quickest.

A fourth method is to wash the rice, place it in a pressure-cooker with water and salt, cover it, and let it soak for several hours or overnight before cooking. With this method, the rice has a chance to soften and thus is very well-cooked and easy to digest. This method can be used occasionally along with others mentioned above.

Short, medium and long grain rice can be used interchangeably, although in a colder climate, such as that of New England or the northern United States, more yang, short grain rice is probably the most suitable; the other varieties can be used from time to time as supplements, ideally during the warmer seasons. On the other hand, in a warmer climate, such as that in Florida, more yin, long grain rice may be more appropriate for regular use, while the other varieties can be occasionally cooked together with it or used as supplements. As a general rule, however, short grain rice can usually be eaten in almost any type of climate. Please experiment and discover which variety is more suitable for your condition and environment. We have relied mostly on short grain rice both while living in Boston and during our stay in Japan. We find it to be the sweetest, most glutinous, and most delicious of the different varieties of rice.

When preparing a small amount of rice, for example one or two cups, you may need to use slightly more water, lower temperature, and slightly less time in cooking so that the rice does not burn or turn out too dry. When making a larger quantity of rice, you may need to reduce the amount of water that you add for each cup of grain while increasing the cooking time up to 50 or 55 minutes, so that your rice does not turn out too soft or wet.

You should not fill your pressure-cooker to more than 70% of its capacity with grain and water; more than this may clog the pressure valve and interfere with the cooking process.

After your rice has finished cooking, try to allow the pressure to gradually come down by itself. This creates a more peaceful quality in the rice, and your rice will have a more delicious flavor. Also, the moisture from the rice will loosen any scorched or burnt grains that may be left on the bottom of the pot, thus making them easier to remove without wasting any rice. Occasionally, if you are in a hurry, or if you want a lighter, fluffier rice, you may bring the pressure down quickly by lifting the pressure valve. However, if your rice happens to stick to the bottom of the pot, it can be removed quite easily by adding a little water and allowing it to sit until it becomes soft. Then, drain off the water and set the rice aside for use in making soft rice, bread, etc.

When removing rice from the pressure-cooker, first wet your rice paddle with water to prevent the grains from sticking to it. Then, press the paddle down around the sides of the pot to loosen the grains which are off to the sides. Remove the grain one scoop at a time, digging deeply into the pot so that each scoop includes both the more yang grains at the bottom and the more yin grains at the top. Place each scoop in a wooden bowl and, with gentle cutting strokes, smooth it out into the bowl. This insures an even mixture of the more yin (top) and more yang (bottom) grains throughout the bowl, creating a more balanced condition in those who eat the rice. If you have a scorched, hard, bottom layer of rice in your pot, gently push each piece of this down into the center or at the edges of the bowl, and cover them with the softer grains. The heat and moisture from these softer grains will cause the harder rice to soften. Or you may place the burnt layers on a bamboo mat and allow them to dry for two or three days, and then deep-fry them for a crispy, crunchy snack.

Never leave your pressure-cooker on the burner once you have finished cooking, even if you have turned off the flame. Your rice will still continue to cook from the heat of the metal flame deflector and the burner.

Always remove your rice from the pressure-cooker or pot as soon as the pressure has come down. If rice is allowed to sit in the pot, the moisture that it contains will cause the grains to expand, thus producing a very wet and often tasteless bowl of rice. By placing your rice immediately into a wooden bowl and covering it with a bamboo mat, you allow it to cool slowly, permitting air to circulate and moisture to escape.

For additional information on the selection and preparation of brown rice, please refer to my first cookbook, *Introducing Macrobiotic Cooking*.

Pressure-Cooked Brown Rice
>**1 cup brown rice**
>**1 1/4 to 1 1/2 cups cold water per cup of rice**
>**pinch of sea salt per cup of rice**

Quickly, but gently, wash rice. Place rice in pressure-cooker. Smooth out the surface of the rice so that it is evenly distributed in the pressure-cooker. Slowly pour water down the side of the pressure-cooker so that the surface remains undisturbed and even. Add salt. Place cover on pressure-cooker and turn flame to the desired temperature as explained earlier in this chapter. The amount of time it takes for the pressure to build up will depend on the temperature you have adjusted your flame to. As soon as the pressure gauge begins to hiss loudly or jiggle, remove pot from flame and place a flame-deflector on the burner. Place pressure-cooker on flame deflector. Reduce flame to low and cook for 45–50 minutes. When rice is done, remove from flame and allow pressure to come down. Remove cover. Remove rice from pressure-cooker with bamboo rice paddle as explained previously.

Boiled Brown Rice
>**1 cup brown rice**
>**approximately 2 cups cold water per cup of rice**
>**pinch of sea salt per cup of rice**

Wash rice and place in pot. When boiling rice, your pot should be heavy and have a heavy lid which fits tightly on the pot. Smooth rice evenly. Add water and sea salt. Cover and place on flame. Bring rice to a boil, turn flame to low or medium-low, and simmer for approximately an hour or until all water has been absorbed. Remove rice with wooden paddle and place in serving bowl.

Roasted Rice
>**1 cup brown rice**
>**approximately 1 cup of water per cup of rice**
>**pinch of sea salt per cup of rice**

Wash rice and roast in a dry skillet until golden brown. Place rice in a pressure-cooker. Add water and sea salt. Cover; place on flame. When pressure is up, place flame-deflector under pressure-cooker and reduce flame to low. Cook for 40–50 minutes. Allow pressure to come down and remove from pot as for pressure-cooked rice. This rice will have a slightly nutty flavor.

Pressure-Cooked Brown Rice with Bancha

    1 cup brown rice
    1-1/4 to 1-1/2 cups bancha tea per cup of rice
    pinch of sea salt and 1/8 to 1/4 tsp. tamari per cup of rice

Wash rice and place in pressure-cooker as for regular pressure-cooked rice. Add bancha, salt, and tamari. Cover and cook as for regular pressure-cooked rice. Remove rice and place in serving bowl.

    This method is a little more yang than regular pressure-cooking, but is very delicious because of the unique flavor obtained from the bancha and tamari. It produces a slightly more golden brown color than regular cooked rice. This method can be used occasionally for variety but is not recommended for everyday use.

Fried Rice

    4 cups of cooked rice
    1 Tbsp. sesame oil
    1/2 cup daikon cut into 1-1/2″ rectangular shapes
    1/4–1/2 cup diced daikon greens
    1–2 Tbsp. tamari or to taste

Lightly brush skillet with sesame oil. Heat skillet but do not allow oil to smoke. Add daikon and greens. Place rice on top of vegetables and cover skillet. If rice is dry, add a few drops of water. Cook the rice on a low flame for approximately 10–15 minutes. Add tamari and cook about 5 minutes more. Mix and place in serving bowl.

    There are many combinations of vegetables that can be used for variety. For suggestions please refer to my first book, *Introducing Macrobiotic Cooking*.

Shrimp Fried Rice

    1 cup cooked brown rice
    1/2 cup shrimp; cleaned, deveined and finely diced
    1/4 cup diced onion
    1–2 Tbsp. tamari or to taste

Lightly brush skillet with sesame oil. Heat skillet. Add onions and shrimp. Place rice on top of shrimp and onions. Cook for approximately 10 minutes, then add tamari to taste. Continue to cook on a low flame for another 5 minutes or so. Mix shrimp and onions in with rice, remove and place in serving bowl.

Black Bean Rice

    1 cup brown rice
    1/4 cup or approximately 10% Japanese black beans (black soybeans)
    pinch of sea salt per cup of rice
    1-1/4 to 1-1/2 cups of water per cup of rice

Wash beans and roast in a dry skillet until the bean skins begin to crack slightly. Remove from skillet. Wash rice, place in pressure-cooker along with beans, and mix. Smooth surface of rice and beans evenly. Add water and salt. Cover. Place on desired flame and allow to come to pressure. Cook 45–50 minutes. Remove from flame and allow pressure to come down. Remove rice as explained previously and place in a serving bowl.

Brown Rice and Soybeans

    1 cup brown rice
    1/4 cup soybeans, soaked overnight or for several hours
    1-1/4 to 1-1/2 cups of water per cup of rice
    pinch of sea salt per cup of rice

Wash and soak soybeans overnight or roast in a dry skillet until the skins begin to crack slightly. These beans are quite yin and burn easily if the flame is too high. If you roast them, make sure that you stir constantly to prevent burning. Wash rice, add to pressure-cooker along with beans, and mix. Add water and salt. Cover and place on flame. Bring to pressure. Reduce flame to low and place flame-deflector under pot. Cook for 45–50 minutes. Allow pressure to come down. Remove with wooden paddle and place in a serving bowl.

Brown Rice and Kidney Beans

    1 cup brown rice
    1/4 cup kidney beans (you may also use azuki or pinto beans in the same way)
    1-1/4 to 1-1/2 cups of water per cup of rice
    pinch of sea salt per cup of rice

Wash beans, place in a small saucepan, and cover with water. Cover and bring to a boil. Reduce flame to medium-low and simmer for half an hour. Remove from flame and allow to cool. This cooling may take about one hour. Wash rice, place in pressure-cooker along with beans, and cooking water. (The water used for cooking the beans should be included in the water that you would normally add to the rice. Do not add bean water plus 1-1/4 to 1-1/2 cups of plain water or your dish will turn out too soft.) Mix beans and rice and add salt. Cover. Place on flame and cook as for regular pressure-cooked rice.

    Chickpeas should be soaked overnight or for a few hours and then added to the rice and cooking water.

    Beans such as mung beans and lentils may also be cooked with rice. These beans do not require soaking, roasting, or boiling before adding to the rice.

Brown Rice and Whole Corn

    1 cup brown rice
    1/4 cup dried whole corn kernels, soaked overnight
    1-1/4 to 1-1/2 cups water per cup of grains
    pinch of salt per cup of grains

Soak corn overnight. Wash rice and place in pressure cooker. Add corn, water, and salt. Cover. Place on flame. Allow pressure to come up. Place flame-deflector under pot and reduce flame to low. Cook as for pressure-cooked brown rice.

Brown Rice and Wheat Berries

    1 cup brown rice

1/4 cup whole wheat berries
1-1/4 to 1-1/2 cups water per cup of grains
pinch of salt per cup of grains

Soak wheat berries overnight. Wash rice and place in pressure-cooker. Add wheat berries, water, and salt. Cover and place on flame. Allow pressure to come up. Place flame-deflector under pot and reduce flame to low. Cook for approximately 50–60 minutes. Allow pressure to come down. Remove cover and place rice in a serving bowl with wooden paddle.

Brown Rice and Barley

1 cup brown rice
1/4 to 1/2 cup barley
1-1/4 to 1-1/2 cups water per cup of grains
pinch of sea salt per cup of grains

Wash rice and barley separately. Place in pressure-cooker and mix. Smooth surface of grain evenly. Add water and salt; cover. Place on flame. Allow pressure to come up. Reduce flame to low, place flame-deflector under pot, and cook as for pressure-cooked rice. Allow pressure to come down, remove cover, and place in serving bowl.

This combination is quite delicious, especially in the hot summer months as it is very light.

Barley belongs to the rice family and so these grains blend very well.

Brown Rice and Millet

1 cup brown rice
1/4 cup millet
1-1/4 to 1-1/2 cups water per cup of grains
pinch of sea salt per cup of grains

Wash rice and millet separately. Place in pressure-cooker and add water and salt. Cook as for above recipe.

This combination is very delicious. It is slightly drier than plain pressure-cooked rice or rice and other grains, because millet is one of the more yang grains.

If these proportions are too dry for you, simply add more water or less millet.

Rice and Vegetables

1 cup brown rice
1/4 cup diced onion
1/4 cup finely diced carrot or small matchsticks
1/8 cup burdock, finely diced or small matchsticks
1-1/4 to 1-1/2 cups water per cup of rice
pinch of sea salt per cup of rice

Wash rice and place in pressure-cooker. Add vegetables and mix with rice, or layer the vegetables on top of the rice in this order: onions, carrots, burdock. Add water and salt; cover. Cook as for regular pressure-cooked rice.

You may also add a small amount of tamari along with salt before cooking.

Other vegetable combinations which are delicious when cooked with rice are: sweet corn and onions; deep-fried strips of tofu, onions, burdock, and carrot; onions and sliced green beans; onions and fresh green peas; onions, green peas, and carrot; and others.

Brown Rice and Shiitake (Dried Japanese Mushrooms)

    1 cup brown rice
    2 *shiitake*
    1-1/4 to 1-1/2 cups water per cup of rice
    pinch of salt per cup of rice
    small amount of tamari (1 or 2 drops per cup of rice)

Soak shiitake in 1/2 cup water for about 15 minutes. Remove hard stem with knife. Slice shiitake and then cut into small pieces. Wash rice and add to pressure-cooker with shiitake, water, and salt. The shiitake water should be included in the water for cooking rice. Add salt and tamari. Cover and cook as for regular pressure-cooked rice.

Brown Rice and Chirimen Iriko

    1 cup brown rice
    1/8 cup *chirimen iriko* (very small dried fish)
    1-1/4 to 1-1/2 cups water per cup of rice
    pinch of salt per cup of rice

Wash rice and place in pressure-cooker. Add iriko, water, and salt. Cover, place on flame, and cook as for regular pressure-cooked rice.

Another very delicious combination can be made with rice, diced onions, and shrimp. Clean shrimp and devein. Dice onion and shrimp. Add to rice and mix. Add water and salt and cook as above. Another variation is to cook rice, and after it is done, mix it together with sautéed diced onion and shrimp or diced onion and diced clams which have been sautéed.

Brown Rice and Seitan

    1 cup brown rice
    1/4 cup diced *seitan* (see next section for instructions on preparation)
    1-1/4 to 1-1/2 cups water per cup of rice
    pinch of sea salt per cup of rice

Prepare seitan, dice, and allow to cool. Wash rice, place in pressure-cooker and mix in seitan. Add water and salt. Cover and cook as for regular pressure-cooked rice.

Nori-Maki and Sushi

Before going to Japan, I had always thought that sushi and nori-maki were the same thing. As I quickly discovered, however, nori-maki is a type of sushi but is not usually referrred to as such. *Su* in Japanese means *vinegar*. One type of sushi is made by mixing rice with vinegar and a variety of vegetables, fish, shiitake and other ingredients, and is more like a rice-salad. Another type is made by mixing rice with vinegar and molding it into an oblong patty. Then Japanese green mustard, called *wasabi*, is placed on top. Slices of raw fish, cooked or uncooked shrimp, etc. are then placed on top of the patty and served.

When making sushi according to macrobiotic principles, we usually use lemon juice instead of vinegar. Vinegar made from brown rice can be used on special occasions, while regular vinegar is very yin and is usually avoided. Since it is made from a fermented grain, brown rice vinegar is somewhat more suitable for health, although those who are trying to cure a serious illness should generally avoid using it.

Nori-maki are made by combining rice with any number of ingredients and rolling them together inside sheets of toasted *nori*. The following are only a few of the almost infinite variety of combinations that can be used in making nori-maki: rice and raw fish; rice and strips of steamed or boiled vegetables; rice, vegetables, and strips of deep-fried tofu; rice and pickles; rice and *shiso* leaves; rice, scallions, and *natto*; etc. In addition, nori-maki are usually seasoned with either umeboshi, umeboshi paste, lemon juice, vinegar, wasabi, pickles, or shiso leaves. The ingredients in nori-maki are then rolled into a cylinder and sliced into 1–1-1/2 inch-thick rounds and arranged on a serving platter or in a special wooden box.

> **nori**
> **cooked rice (slightly cooled)**
> **carrot cut into strips 1/4″ thick and steamed or boiled with a pinch of sea salt**
> **watercress—boil one minute and rinse under cold water**
> **deep-fried tofu strips (see tofu section)**
> **umeboshi or umeboshi paste or shiso leaves**

Toast nori by holding the smooth, shiny side facing up about 10 inches above the flame. Rotate the nori so that it is evenly toasted, taking about five seconds. The nori will change color from black to green.

There are several varieties of nori presently available. Some are very thin, and when used to make nori-maki, will often split or tear. Thicker sheets are much better for making nori-maki, since they usually don't split when rolling and are easy to slice. Each sheet of nori will yield approximately 7 to 8 rounds of nori-maki.

To prepare, place nori on a bamboo sushi mat. Prepare vegetables as described above and rinse under cold water so they will retain their bright color. Deep-fry tofu as explained in the chapter on tofu. Place a small bowl of water near the sushi mat. Wet your fingers occasionally to keep the rice from sticking to them. Spread the cooked rice evenly on the sheet of nori. Don't cover the entire sheets; leave about 1/2 inch at the bottom and 1-1/2–2 inches at the top uncovered.

Press the carrot strips and two or three pieces of the watercress (in a row) gently into the rice about 1-1/2 to 2 inches from the bottom of the sheet of nori. Then, lay the strips of deep-fried tofu on top of the vegetables. Using your fingers, evenly spread a very thin layer of umeboshi or umeboshi paste, or lay shiso leaves lengthwise, along the row of vegetables. The vegetables, tofu, and umeboshi should be placed so that they form a continuous row from one side of the nori to the other.

Pick up the bottom part of the sushi mat with your fingers and begin to roll it by pressing it firmly against the nori and rice. While rolling, slowly pull the mat back so that you don't roll it up into the nori and rice. Continue rolling and pulling the mat back until you reach the uncovered area. To seal, wet the edge of the nori with a little water and finish rolling.

Wet a very sharp knife and slice the roll in half so that you have two rolls of equal length, then slice each half into four equal rounds. Make sure that you wet your knife before you slice. This makes the cutting very easy and smooth and prevents the rice from sticking to the knife.

Arrange each round on a serving plate or tray and place sprigs of parsley, watercress, pine stems, or leaves attractively on the plate for decoration.

Sushi (Rice-Salad)

4 cups pressure-cooked rice

1 cup deep-fried tofu (*age*) cut into very thin matchstick slices (1-1/2″ long) and boil in water to remove excess oil. Then boil in a small amount of water and tamari for 5–6 minutes.

1/2 cup carrot, finely shaved or cut in thin matchsticks. Sauté in a small amount of sesame oil until done. Add small amount of tamari while sautéing.

1/4 cup burdock, shaved or cut into thin matchsticks. Sauté in a small amount of sesame oil for several minutes, add a small amount of water and sauté until almost done. Add tamari to taste and cook until water is absorbed.

1/4 cup chirimen iriko which have been soaked in water until soft.

2 shiitake which have been soaked for about 10 minutes. Remove stem, and slice very thin. Boil in soaking water for several minutes with a small amount of tamari until liquid evaporates or is absorbed.

1/2 cup green beans, cut into matchsticks 1-1/2 inches long and lightly steamed with a pinch of sea salt

lemon juice

Pressure-cook the rice, remove, and place in a shallow wooden bowl. Add a little lemon juice and mix evenly into rice. Use a bamboo paddle to mix with gentle but quick cutting motions and continue until the rice is cool.

At this point you can do one of several things: (1) you can mix in all of the ingredients with the rice; (2) you can sprinkle the ingredients on top of the rice; (3) you can mix half of the ingredients into the rice and arrange the rest very attractively on top; or (4) you can arrange all of the ingredients very attractively on top of the rice.

Sushi No. 2

3 cups cooked rice

1/2 tsp. lemon juice

fish such as fresh raw tuna, sea bass, stripped bass, red snapper or shrimp (see fish section for instructions on cutting raw fish)

wasabi (optional)

Cook rice as explained previously. Mix lemon juice in with a bamboo paddle until rice becomes cool. Wet hands with water and roll rice into small balls. Place a piece of sliced raw fish in the palm of your hand. Very thinly spread wasabi on the slice of fish. Do not put too much on as it is very spicy. Place one of the riceballs on top of the raw fish. Cup your hand and press the rice with your index and middle fingers to pack firmly. The patty should be slightly oblong in shape (about 2″ long and about 1″–1-1/2″ wide) with a piece of fish or shellfish on top. Repeat until rice is used up. Arrange attractively on a plate or tray and decorate with sprigs of parsley, watercress, etc.

Tri-Colored Rice
    3 cups cooked rice (cooled)
    1/3 to 1/2 cup boiled green peas
    1/3 to 1/2 cup fresh sweet corn removed from the cob and boiled
    1/3 to 1/2 cup diced carrot, boiled
Pressure-cook rice, place in a small wooden bowl, and allow to cool. Place cooked vegetables one at a time evenly in rows or as three equal triangles on top of the rice. Arrange so that the colors are balanced in the bowl, for instance a row of peas, then a row of carrots, and then a row of corn.

Other variations: broccoli, deep fried tofu strips and carrots; watercress (sliced), daikon, and carrots; diced seitan, green beans, and carrots; etc.

This dish is very attractive at parties, or for picnics or holiday meals.

Rice Kayu
    1 cup brown rice
    5 cups cold water
    1–1-1/2 umeboshi plums
Wash rice and place in pressure-cooker with water and umeboshi plums. You can break the umeboshi into pieces if you want. You may also omit the umeboshi and add salt instead. Cover the pressure-cooker. Place on flame and bring to pressure. Reduce flame to low, and place flame-deflector under the pressure-cooker for one hour. Remove from flame, allow pressure to come down, and remove cover. Place rice in serving bowls and garnish with sliced scallions and strips of toasted nori.

This dish is very easy to digest and makes a very good breakfast cereal. It is especially good for children or sick people.

For a slightly different flavor, cook the rice with bancha tea, vegetable stock, or seaweed water. As another variation, add vegetables such as Chinese cabbage or daikon to the rice after the pressure comes down, and simmer until the vegetables are soft.

Ojiya
    3 cups cooked rice
    1/2 cup daikon, cut into matchsticks
    1/2 cup carrot, cut into matchsticks
    1/4 cup diced onion

1/4 cup diced daikon greens or any other hard green
season with either sea salt, tamari or miso to taste
3–3-1/2 cups cold water

Place rice in a cooking pot with water. Place on flame and bring to a boil. Reduce flame to medium-low, cover, and simmer for about 30 minutes. Then, you can either sauté the vegetables first in a small amount of sesame oil and add them to the rice, or omit the sautéing and add them directly. Continue cooking until the vegetables are soft. You may want to wait until the last few minutes before adding the greens so that they retain their bright color. Reduce flame to low and season with sea salt, tamari, or miso to taste.

There are many different combinations of vegetables, fish, beans, deep-fried tofu, and other ingredients that can be used in this dish. You can garnish the *ojiya* with chopped parsley, scallions, gomashio, or strips of toasted nori. If you are adding shellfish such as clams, oysters, or shrimp, make sure to either add them during the last few minutes of cooking, or cook them lightly in the rice for a few minutes at the beginning, remove them, and then add them again toward the end. This prevents the shellfish from becoming too hard or rubbery.

Ojiya is also very good for children or sick persons. It is especially good on a cold winter morning, but is also delicious any time of the year.

Miso Soft Rice

This dish is made basically the same way as rice kayu or ojiya. You may add various combinations of vegetables. Simply season with miso at the very end of cooking, garnish, and serve. This dish is more yang because of the miso and is often eaten on cold winter mornings for breakfast. The taste should not be too salty.

Pumpkin Rice Kayu

Prepare as you would regular rice kayu, only add cubed Hokkaido pumpkin or buttercup squash at the beginning. Season with sea salt. The rice will have a golden color and a very sweet, delicious flavor. It can be served as a breakfast cereal or as porridge for dinner. Garnish with chopped parsley, scallions, nori strips, etc.

Riceballs

A riceball is a small ball of rice which contains either umeboshi, shiso, pickles, fish, or vegetables at the center. It is shaped into a ball or into small rectangles, and then wrapped in toasted nori. Riceballs make great lunch items and are great when you are travelling, for picnics, or as snacks.

A riceball is actually a complete meal in itself. After eating them, I always feel very clean and balanced. I have also found them especially appealing during pregnancy. Riceballs are very soothing to the stomach.

Riceballs can also be made without using nori. Simply mold the rice into balls, triangles or other shapes, and roll them in toasted sesame seeds. Riceballs can also be made from fried rice. Or you can deep-fry your riceballs by adding a small amount of sesame oil to a skillet and frying until golden brown. Old rice-balls which are slightly sour or dry can be sliced and deep-fried for a crunchy snack. The sour taste should disappear entirely.

Details on making riceballs are presented in *Introducing Macrobiotic Cooking*.

OTHER GRAINS

Sweet Rice

Sweet rice was traditionally cultivated in Japan and China and is now grown in the United States and is available in most natural food stores. It is more glutinous than regular rice, and in Japan is used in making *mochi*, a sticky rice cake that is traditionally served during New Years, at weddings, and on other festive occasions. Because of its sticky quality, it is believed that mochi will help keep a newly married couple closely united and will help to strengthen family ties. Japanese wrestlers, known as *Sumo*, also consume large amounts of mochi, which because of its high fat content, helps them to gain weight. It is also used in making *sake* and a sweet drink called *amazake*. Amazake is traditionally used as a sweetener in desserts.

The residue left over from making sake, called *lees*, tastes and smells very much like cheese and is used in making soups, vegetable dishes, and pickles that are all deliciously sweet.

Sweet rice can also be eaten plain, mixed with other grains, or used in making desserts, breads, etc. It is high in protein, vitamin B (niacin) and fat, and contains a number of other nutrients. I am sure that you will find it very delicious.

It can also be used in making soft rice kayu, soups, and dumplings for soups and stews.

Mochi is very good for women to eat when they are breastfeeding because it gives both mother and baby added strength and helps the baby gain weight by increasing the fat content of breast milk. However, too much mochi may cause your milk to become overly thick or sticky, so be careful to eat a reasonable quantity of it.

Pressure-Cooked Sweet Rice
 1 cup sweet rice
 1–1-1/4 cups water
 pinch of salt

Wash rice, place in pressure-cooker, add water and salt and place on flame. When pressure comes up, reduce flame to low and cook as for regular rice.

Sweet Rice and Azuki Beans
 1–1-1/4 cups water
 1 cup sweet rice
 1/4 cup azuki beans (boiled in water for 1/2 hour and allowed to cool)
 pinch of sea salt

Prepare azuki beans as mentioned above and cool. Wash rice and place in pressure-cooker with azuki beans, azuki bean water, sea salt, and additional water if necessary. Cover, place on flame and allow pressure to come up. Reduce flame to low and cook as for regular rice.

Sweet Rice and Regular Brown Rice
2 cups sweet rice
1 cup brown rice
3-1/2–3/4 cups water
pinch of sea salt

Prepare as for regular rice.

Mochi
2 cups sweet rice
1–1-1/4 cups water per cup of rice
pinch of sea salt per cup of rice

Pressure-cook as for regular rice. Allow pressure to come down. Place rice in a large, heavy wooden bowl. With a large wooden pestle, such as the *surikogi* which comes with a *suribachi* or a larger, heavier pestle, pound the rice vigorously until all the grains are broken and the rice becomes very sticky. This will take about an hour or more of vigorous pounding. Occasionally, wet your pestle with water and sprinkle a few drops of water on the rice to prevent it from sticking.

The Japanese prepare a variety of mochis, such as millet mochi, black bean mochi and mugwort mochi. In Japan they grow a sweet, glutinous millet which is combined with sweet rice and used in making mochi. I have never seen it in the United States, but a North American version can be made by using 2 cups of sweet rice and half a cup of regular, hulled millet. Prepare in the same way as the above recipe. Black bean mochi can be made by adding dry-roasted Japanese black beans to the rice during the final minutes of pounding. This is my favorite type of mochi and I'm sure you will enjoy it very much too. Mugwort is a wild grass which is very high in Vitamin A, niacin, Vitamin C and calcium. We use it occasionally as a tea, and it is also used in making *moxa*. When using it in mochi, it is pounded fresh into the sweet rice. It is considered to be very good for pregnant and breastfeeding women, though it does have a bitter flavor that may take some time to adjust to.

After your mochi has been sufficiently pounded, wet your hands and form the mochi dough into small cakes and place them on a cookie sheet that has been dusted with rice flour or oiled. You may also form the dough into oblong loaves about 10 inches long, four inches wide and 1/2″–1″ thick. Dust the mochi with rice flour. You may eat it fresh as is, slice it and bake it until it puffs up, or allow it to dry by leaving it exposed to the air and store it for later use. You may also store it in the refrigerator to prevent mold formation. If mold does form, simply cut it off and eat the remaining part. You can also pan-fry it over a low flame in a dry skillet. When cooking it in this way, cover the skillet and occasionally turn mochi over to avoid burning. Cook until each piece expands and puffs up. You may eat as is or season it with tamari and eat it wrapped with strips of toasted nori. You may also add it to miso soup at the very end of cooking.

Deep-Fried Mochi
10 pieces of dried mochi
tamari
grated daikon

Deep-fry mochi in hot sesame oil, occasionally turning, until golden brown. Remove and allow to drain on a paper towel. Serve with tamari and grated daikon. The mochi will puff up and be very crisp on the outside. The daikon will help to digest the oil.

Wakayama-Style Mochi
During a visit with the Kushi family in Tokyo, we were introduced to this wonderful way of serving mochi. Wakayama is a prefecture in the southern part of Honshu, the main island in Japan, and it is there that the Kushi family originally lived.

To serve, simply place several pieces of mochi in a bowl and present with a dish of very high quality sea salt. Each person should then take a piece of mochi and sprinkle a pinch of salt over it. Then, hot bancha tea should be poured over it as a broth. It is one of the most delicious mochi dishes I have ever eaten, and I am very grateful for the opportunity to have learned of it.

Mochi with Kinako and Ame
10 pieces of mochi
small amount of *kinako* (roasted soybean flour—available in most Oriental food stores)
***ame* (rice syrup), yinnie syrup or barley-corn syrup**

Heat mochi in a dry skillet as explained previously. Place *ame* in a small saucepan and heat. Dip each piece of mochi into the hot ame and roll in *kinako* until evenly coated and serve.

You can omit the ame by simply dipping the mochi into hot water and rolling it in kinako.

Ohagi
Ohagi are basically prepared in the same way as mochi except that the rice is only pounded until the grains are about half broken. This will take approximately 20–30 minutes. The dough is then formed into small balls and coated with a variety of different coatings. Some of these include azuki beans, puréed chestnuts, crushed sesame seeds, kinako, ground walnuts, ground pecans, and squash purée.

Ohagi make wonderful and very attractive party snacks, and should be attractively arranged with several different varieties on a tray. They are also great for picnics.

Walnut Ohagi

1 cup walnuts
tamari

Prepare ohagi dough as explained above. Dry roast walnuts for several minutes in a skillet until a nutty fragrance is released. Sprinkle lightly with tamari. Stir constantly to avoid burning. Remove from skillet and place on a chopping block. Chop the walnuts very finely and place in suribachi. Grind with a pestle until walnuts are very fine but not pasty. You may add several drops of tamari while grinding if desired.

Moisten your hands and roll about 1 tablespoon of ohagi dough into a ball. Roll in ground walnuts and shape into small rounds. Arrange on a tray.

Sesame Ohagi

1 cup sesame seeds
tamari

Prepare ohagi dough. Wash sesame seeds. Using a low flame, roast in a dry skillet until the seeds begin to pop, release a nutty fragrance, and are easily crushed with your thumbnail. Place in a suribachi. Grind until each seed is about half crushed. Add a small amount of tamri to taste. Moisten hands and form cakes as above. Roll cakes in sesame mixture and arrange on a platter.

Azuki Bean Ohagi

1 cup azuki beans
1/8–1/4 cup barley corn syrup or yinnie syrup (optional)
1/4 tsp. sea salt

Wash beans and place in a pot. Add water to cover. Occasionally add more water while cooking as the water begins to be absorbed and the beans expand. Repeat until done. Season with sea salt and syrup if desired. Cook about ten minutes longer. Mash beans with a pestle until thick and smooth.

Prepare the ohagi dough. Wet hands and form dough into small balls. Place approximately 1 tablespoon of azuki bean purée around each ball of dough and shape into rounds. Place on tray.

Chestnut Ohagi

2 cups water
1 cup dried chestnuts
pinch of sea salt

Soak chestnuts overnight or dry roast them in a skillet until they release a sweet fragrance. Pressure-cook for 45 minutes. Mash chestunuts with a pestle until very smooth and creamy.

Prepare ohagi dough. Wet hands and coat with chestnut purée as above.

These are very delicious and quite sweet. Arrange attractively on a tray.

MILLET

Millet was traditionally used as a staple grain in Japan, where it is called *awa*, and in many other Far Eastern countries. Unfortunately, however, millet is not used as much in modern Japan as it was in the past. It is now used mainly as food for the colorful parakeets which Japanese ladies treasure so much. It is also used now and then to make millet mochi, especially during the New Year holiday. The only type of millet that we could find in Japan was the glutinous variety used in making mochi.

Millet is still widely eaten in Africa as a staple food, where it is cooked, pounded, and shaped into cakes or loaves. It is also considered a staple grain in places such as Northern China, India, and Korea, and is often used by the Hunzas.

Millet is one of the more yang of the cereal grains because it is very small, hard, and round, and because it often grows in colder climates and is mainly alkaline in content. Millet is very good for illnesses of the stomach, spleen, or pancreas, and will help to settle an acid stomach very quickly. Millet contains all but one of the essential amino acids and is high in protein, iron, and niacin.

Millet is a very versatile food. It can be used in making soups, vegetable dishes, stuffings, cabbage rolls, croquettes, breads, muffins and pastries, or can be eaten as a cereal.

It also has a very attractive, soft-yellow color which is very soothing and usually appealing, and which complements other foods very well. When lightly toasted in a dry skillet before cooking, it has a very delicious, nutty flavor which I am sure you will like.

Millet and Cauliflower
    2 cups millet
    2 cups cauliflower flowerettes (not too large)
    1 onion, diced or sliced diagonally
    6 cups boiling water
    sesame oil (optional)
    pinch of sea salt per cup of millet

Wash millet. Lightly brush a very small amount of sesame oil in the bottom of pot. Sauté onions 2–3 minutes, add cauliflower and sauté another 4–5 minutes. Add millet and sauté for 2–3 minutes, stirring to avoid burning. Add boiling water and sea salt. Bring to a boil. Cover, reduce flame to low and simmer 30–35 minutes.

If you wish to have a softer millet, simply add 4 cups of boiling water instead of 3 cups. If you want drier millet, add a little less water. Also, if you wish to reduce your oil intake, eliminate the sautéeing procedure and simply toast the millet in a dry pot.

Millet Loaf
    2 cups millet

Sauce
    1/2 cup whole wheat pastry flour

1 carrot, diced	3 cups water or vegetable stock
1 onion, diced	1 onion, diced very finely
1/4 cup burdock, quartered and sliced	1/4 lb. mushrooms, sliced
6 cups boiling water	3 Tbsp. tamari
pinch of sea salt per cup of millet	sesame oil (optional)
sesame oil (optional)	

Wash millet and cook as above. When done, place in a loaf pan or casserole dish. Press down so that surface is even.

Brush skillet lightly with sesame oil. Heat pan. Add mushrooms, onions, and pinch of sea salt and sauté until onions are translucent. Add flour to vegetables. Mix evenly with a wooden spoon so that vegetables are coated with flour. Slowly add water and stir constantly to avoid lumping. Bring to a boil. Reduce flame to low, cover, and simmer 5–7 minutes. Add tamari, cover and simmer for an additional 10–15 minutes. Stir occasionally to prevent sticking or burning. If you have a flame-deflector, place it under pot to prevent burning and sticking.

Pour sauce over millet to cover surface. With a chopstick, poke several small holes in the millet so that sauce can be absorbed into the millet. Bake at 350° F. for 30–35 minutes. If loaf becomes too dry, add a little more sauce to cover. Slice and serve or scoop with spoon and serve. Garnish with chopped parsley.

If you wish to omit the sauce, simply add a little more water to the millet when cooking. Slice, garnish and serve.

You may add different combinations of vegetables to the millet for variety.

Millet Croquettes

  2 cups cooked millet
  1/2 cup diced onion
  1/2 cup diced celery and leaves
  1/4 cup chopped parsley
  1/4 cup finely diced carrots
  1/2 cup water
  1/2 cup pastry flour
  sea salt or tamari

Mix millet and vegetables. Add salt and/or tamari and mix well. Add flour and mix. Add water and mix again.

Heat sesame oil in a tempura pot. To test oil, place a small morsel of the croquette in the oil. If it rises to the surface immediately, the oil is hot enough. The oil should not smoke. If it does, it is too hot, so reduce the flame.

Place batter in the hot oil with a tablespoon. Place 4 or 5 tablespoons of batter at a time in the oil. (If you add too much batter it will lower the temperature of the oil and thus cause the croquettes to be oily and soggy.) Deep-fry until golden brown. Serve with dipping sauce made from grated daikon and tamari. This will help dissolve the oil and make it easier to digest.

You may omit deep-frying and form the batter into patties and pan-fry with a small amount of oil, or bake for 25 minutes or so at 350° F.

Cornmeal

Since cornmeal is basically a flour product, it should be used mostly as a supplemental grain. It can be used in making desserts, breads, muffins, sauces, gravies, corn fritters, tempura batter, and in a variety of other ways.

When I was a small child, my mother and grandmother made cornmeal for us as a breakfast cereal. They would often prepare it for supper by placing the cooked meal in a bowl and allowing it to chill, and then slicing and frying it in a skillet.

It was a very delicious treat.

Corn was the staple food of most of the Indian tribes in both North and South America, including the Hopi, Aztec, and Maya, and is also eaten throughout Asia. In Japan it is called *tōmorokoshi*.

Fried Cornmeal

1 cup cornmeal
3–3-1/2 cups boiling water
pinch of sea salt per cup of cornmeal

Toast cornmeal in a dry pot on a medium-low flame until it starts to release a nutty fragrance. Allow to cool slightly. Slowly add boiling water and sea salt. Mix constantly to prevent lumping. Bring to a boil, cover, reduce flame to low and simmer for 30–35 minutes.

Place cornmeal in a loaf pan or shallow bowl. Place in refrigerator or in cool place and allow to cool. It will become hard. Remove from pan or bowl by turning dish upside-down on chopping board or plate. Slice into pieces about 1/4″ thick, 3″ long and 2″ wide.

Place a small amount of sesame oil in a skillet or on a cast iron griddle. Heat skillet. Place several slices on the skillet and fry each side until golden brown. Garnish with sliced scallions and serve with a small amount of tamari.

Barley

Barley is believed to be one of the oldest of the cultivated grains. It is a relative of the rice plant, and is believed to have originated around Syria. In Japan, it is called *mugi*.

Barley is a very adaptable grain and it grows in many different climatic areas. It is considered a staple grain in many countries in the Far East, Asia, Middle East, Europe, and South America, and people in Tibet consider it to be their most important food. It is also grown in North America, but is presently used mostly in making beer and other alcoholic beverages and for feeding livestock.

Barley has somewhat of a bland flavor when cooked by itself, but when combined with other grains, it is very delicious. My children love it in soups, combined with rice, or in bread. It is especially good during the hot summer months when combined with rice. It makes the grain seem lighter and gives it more of a cooling effect.

Barley can be used in making soups, vegetable-grain dishes, vegetable-grain pies, stuffings, breads, etc. It can also be used in its whole form to make muffins or other breads, and it can be toasted and ground into flour to make breads and pastries. It also makes a very delicious tea when it is roasted with the hulls on and boiled in water. In Japan, barley tea is called *mugicha*.

Barley and Vegetables
    1 cup barley
    1/2 cup diced onion
    1/4 cup diced carrot
    1/8 cup diced shiitake (soaked in water 10–15 minutes)
    3 cups water
    pinch of sea salt

Wash barley. Place vegetables and barley in a pot. Add water and sea salt. Bring to a boil, cover, reduce flame to low and simmer 40 minutes or so. Place in a serving bowl. It can also be pressure-cooked if desired.

You may sauté the vegetables in a small amount of sesame oil before cooking with barley for a slightly different flavor. You can also lightly toast the barley before cooking to change the flavor somewhat.

Soft Barley Cereal
    1 cup barley
    4–5 cups water
    pinch of sea salt

Wash barley and cook as above, but increase cooking time to 1-1/4–1-1/2 hours. Serve hot and garnish with scallions, chopped parsley, nori or gomashio.

OATS

Oats are the highest of the grains in protein and fat. They are also rich in iron and calcium. For centuries, oats have served as a staple food for the people of Scotland, Ireland and the British Isles, as well as in other European countries. In America, oats were consumed much more in the past than they are today, mostly in the form of hot morning cereal. Perhaps the decline of this valuable food item is due in part to the introduction of quick, packaged and sugar-coated breakfast cereals.

Unfortunately, the majority of the oats produced in the United States today are consumed by livestock or are used as filler for various ground meat products.

I have found that almost all children love to eat oats for breakfast, either in their whole form or in the form of rolled oats. Occasionally, a few raisins or a small amount of rice honey can be cooked in with the oats for variety and as a special treat.

Oats and oatmeal can be used in many ways, such as for cereals, soups, puddings, breads, desserts, etc. Oat-milk is very delicious when used in making desserts.

There are many varieties of oats, but the three main types are whole, rolled, and steel-cut.

Whole Oats
1 cup whole oats
5–6 cups water
pinch of sea salt per cup of oats

Wash oats and place in a heated skillet. Toast until golden brown. Stir constantly to prevent burning. Remove and place in pot. Add water and sea salt and bring to a boil. Reduce flame to very low, cover, and place a flame-deflector under the pot to prevent scorching. Simmer overnight or for 2–3 hours on a higher flame, until soft and creamy.

Oatmeal and Rice Cereal
2 cups oatmeal (rolled oats)
1–1-1/2 cups cooked rice
5 cups water
pinch of sea salt

Place rice, oatmeal, water and sea salt in a pot. Stir to mix. Bring to a boil, reduce flame to low, cover and place flame-deflector under pot. Simmer for 25–30 minutes until creamy.

I have found this to be a delicous breakfast combination. Oatmeal and millet can also be combined in this way, and are also very delicious. This cereal is very good when served with scallions and toasted sesame seeds or gomashio sprinkled on top.

It is also good when cooked with a small amount of dulse seaweed.

BUCKWHEAT (KASHA)

Before the advent of fast-food breakfast items, buckwheat was often eaten for breakfast, either as a morning cereal or in the form of pancakes. Recently, there has been a tremendous increase in the popularity of buckwheat pancakes in many restaurants. Unfortunately, though, the batter is often pre-packaged and contains sugar. Today, buckwheat is used largely in the production of honey by beekeepers.

It is still a staple grain in parts of Europe, Poland and Russia, where it is eaten in its whole form, and in Japan, where it has been used for centuries in the production of many kinds of noodles called *soba*.

Many Jewish people throughout the world still use buckwheat in making *knishes* or in a fried buckwheat and noodle dish known as *kasha varnitchkes*. It is also used by some people in making stuffed cabbage rolls.

Buckwheat is the most yang of the grains. The buckwheat plant grows in very cold climates and requires a very short growing season, while the grains it produces are very small, hard and compact. Because it is so yang, insects do not attack it. I have also heard that when it is sprayed or chemically fertilized, the plant often refuses to grow. So, buckwheat is not usually grown with many chemicals.

With the exception of soba, which can be eaten year-round, buckwheat should mainly be eaten during the fall and winter months. It is very yang and should usually not be eaten daily or as a main grain in this climate. Children also should not eat large amounts of buckwheat, as they are already very yang.

Buckwheat generates body heat and is known for its ability to give a person strength. It is very good for the lungs, kidneys, bladder and for water or fluid retention.

Buckwheat is usually available in a roasted and unroasted form. The roasted variety should be re-roasted for only 3–5 minutes before use, while the unroasted variety should be roasted in a dry skillet for 10–15 minutes. Stir constantly to avoid burning.

The hulls of buckwheat make great filler for pillows and are very comfortable to sleep on.

Buckwheat is very high in protein, calcium, iron, vitamin B (niacin) and other minerals. Some of its many uses include as a cereal, in soups, casseroles, vegetable-grain pies or dishes, noodles, pancakes, breads, desserts and pastries, as well as in medicinal preparations.

Kasha and Parsley

    1 cup buckwheat groats (roasted)
    2 cups boiling water
    1 onion, diced
    1/4 cup chopped parsley
    sesame oil (optional)
    pinch of sea salt per cup of groats

Lightly brush a small pot with oil. Add onions and sauté until translucent. Add chopped parsley and buckwheat. Sauté 3–4 minutes, stirring occasionally. Add boiling water and sea salt. Cover, reduce flame to low and simmer for 25–30 minutes or until water is absorbed.

Kasha Cereal

    1 cup buckwheat groats
    4–5 cups boiling water
    1 onion, diced
    pinch of sea salt per cup of groats

Place onion, buckwheat, water and sea salt in pot. Bring to a boil again. Cover, reduce flame to low and simmer for 30 minutes until very soft. Serve with chopped parsley or scallions as a garnish.

Buckwheat Loaf

    2 cups roasted buckwheat groats
    1 onion diced
    1 cup cabbage, cut in small squares

1/2 cup carrot, quartered and sliced thin
4 cups boiling water
pinch of sea salt per cup of groats
sesame oil (optional)

Sauté vegetables and cook as above. When done, place in a loaf pan or casserole dish. Place in 350° F. oven and bake 10–15 minutes. Pour sauce (see Millet Loaf Sauce) over the buckwheat. Poke small holes in loaf so sauce drains into it. Bake another 20–25 minutes and garnish with chopped parsley, scallions or chives. You may also omit the sauce and simply bake plain.

Buckwheat Burgers

These can be made by cooking buckwheat and vegetables as above. Add a small amount of pastry flour and form into patties. Pan-fry or bake as you would for the millet patties mentioned previously.

BULGHUR AND CRACKED WHEAT

Bulghur is a form of whole wheat that is partially boiled and then dried, while cracked wheat is not pre-cooked but is simply whole wheat that has been partially milled.

Because they lose some of their nutritional value in these processes, these grains should not be eaten as staples but only as a supplemental food.

Bulghur and cracked wheat are used widely in the Middle East. Since they are more yin, they are somewhat more suitable in a hotter climate and when eaten produce a more light feeling in the stomach.

Bulghur can be cooked together with vegetables or used in dishes such as pies, salads, cookies, and pastries.

Bulghur and Vegetables

    1 cup bulghur
    2–2-1/2 cups boiling water
    1 small onion, diced
    1/2 cup diced carrot
    1/4 cup diced celery
    1 Tbsp. chopped parsley
    pinch of sea salt per cup of bulghur

Place onion, carrot, celery, and bulghur in a pot. Add boiling water and sea salt. Bring to a boil again. Cover, reduce flame to low and simmer for about 15–20 minutes. Mix lightly and serve with chopped parsley.

Cous-Cous

Cous-cous is not a whole grain and should only be used on occasion. It is made from wheat that is refined, but not bleached, and then cracked. It cooks very quickly simply by steaming it.

It is eaten widely in Morocco, Portugal, parts of Europe, and in the Middle East.

It has many uses, such as for salads, stuffings for squash and fish dishes, fish casseroles, cakes, cookies, etc.

Cous-Cous and Vegetables

> 2 cups cous-cous
> 1 cup cooked chickpeas
> 1 onion, diced
> 1/2 cup carrot, diced
> 1/4 cup finely diced celery
>
> 1/2 cup water
> sesame oil
> pinch of sea salt per cup of cous-cous

Wash cous-cous thoroughly in a fine mesh strainer. Allow to sit for about five minutes or so. Place cous-cous in a steamer and steam for 5–6 minutes. Remove and place in a bowl. Occasionally fluff with a fork or chopsticks.

Lightly brush sesame oil in the bottom of a skillet. Heat and add onions, and sauté until transparent. Add celery and carrots and a pinch of salt. Sauté until carrots and celery are done. They should be a little crisp. Add water and remaining salt. Bring to a boil, lower flame and simmer for 2–3 minutes. Add chickpeas, vegetables and water to cous-cous. Mix with wooden fork or spoon. Cover and allow to sit for 10–15 minutes or until water is absorbed. Toss again with fork and serve with scallions or chopped parsley.

RYE

Rye is a very popular grain in Europe and in some parts of Asia. It is grown mainly for flour to make delicious rye breads and other pastries. Rye grows mostly in the cold, northern regions of the United States and Europe.

In America it is mainly used in making whiskey, some bread, and to feed livestock.

Most people do not eat rye in its whole form and often believe that it has a flavor like caraway seeds, which are sometimes used in making rye bread. It has somewhat of a mild flavor, but is hard and requires some chewing. It is delicious when mixed with rice.

We use it mainly for baking.

WHEAT

Wheat is another grain that is seldom used in its whole form. Its main use is for flour to make breads, pastries, and noodles. Wheat is difficult to digest in its whole form and must be chewed well. It also requires a long cooking time. However, wheat berries are very delicious when combined with rice.

Wheat is grown in much of the United States, especially in the Midwest and Northeast. It is also grown widely in Europe and Asia. In Japan, it is called *komugi*. There are many varieties of wheat available. The main varieties are: *hard red winter wheat*, which is high in gluten and protein and is very suitable for breads and *seitan*; *soft pastry wheat*, which is lower in protein and gluten and is used mainly in making pastries, sauces, etc.; and *durum wheat*, which has almost no gluten and a lower protein content, and which is excellent for making noodles, macaroni and spaghetti.

Please refer to *Introducing Macrobiotic Cooking* for the following additional whole grain recipes: pressure-cooked and boiled rice; soft rice; fried rice; chestnut rice; sushi (including a pictorial description); millet and vegetables; soft millet; kasha stuffed cabbage; mochi.

2. Special Grain Dishes: Seitan, Fu, and Noodles

SEITAN

Seitan is made from whole wheat flour. The harder varieties of wheat, such as hard spring or hard red winter wheat, produce the best quality seitan, as they are higher in gluten and protein and lower in starch than the others. Seitan is very high in protein and may help you to reduce your intake of animal food. It also helps produce strength and vitality. Seitan is still eaten throughout the world as a source of high-quality protein.

There are a number of methods for making seitan which are discussed in most macrobiotic cookbooks. There are both long and short methods of making it. I will explain the short method in the following recipes, as it may be somewhat easier to follow. Either method will produce about the same quantity and quality of seitan, so please experiment to discover which you prefer.

Seitan (Short Method)
 3-1/2 lbs. hard spring wheat flour or hard red winter wheat flour
 8–9 cups warm water
Place whole wheat flour in a large bowl or pot. Add water gradually. Knead for approximately 5 minutes, until all flour is mixed with water. As you knead, the dough may become stiffer and a little more difficult to knead. When this happens, cover the dough with warm water and let it sit for about 5–10 minutes. Knead dough in soaking water for 2–3 minutes. Drain soaking water into a large glass jar or large pot and save. (This water can be used as a thickening agent in gravies, stews, puddings, sauces, sourdough starters for bread, waffles, pancakes, etc.) Place dough in large strainer and place on top of a large pot. Pour cold

water over the gluten and knead. Repeat, alternating between cold and warm water until most of the bran and starch are removed. You will then have a sticky ball of gluten in the strainer.

Then rinse the ball of gluten under the faucet once again with cold water. Remember to save most of the bran and starch water. If you don't have an immediate use for the water, either refrigerate it or allow the starch and bran to separate from the water and settle on the bottom of the jar. Then slowly pour off most of the clear water on top. Place the starch and bran sediment on a cookie sheet or baking dish and place in the sun. Allow the water to evaporate and the starch will become hard like kuzu. Break into pieces and store in a jar for future use. When you are ready to use it, simply dilute it in water as you would with kuzu, and use as a thickening agent.

Separate ball of gluten into 5–6 pieces and place in 6 cups of boiling water. Boil 3–5 minutes or until the pieces float to the surface. If they stick to the bottom of the pot, gently nudge with a chopstick and they will float to the surface. Remove gluten balls and allow them to cool slightly. Slice into bite-sized pieces. Place a 2–3 inches strip of kombu in the 6 cups of water and add 1/4–1/3 cup tamari. Add pieces of gluten. Bring to a boil, reduce flame, cover and simmer for 30–35 minutes. Your seitan is now ready to eat as it is or can be added to soups, salads, stuffings, etc.

Seitan Stew

>**2 taro potato, diced**
>**1 onion, sliced diagonally**
>**2 carrots (irregular or rolling method)**
>**1 cup fresh green peas (When in season. If not available, use celery sliced into small chunks)**
>**all of the above seitan and cooking water**
>**1–2 cups starch water to thicken**
>**tamari to taste**

Prepare gluten as above, but do not boil in water. Separate gluten into bite-sized pieces. Deep-fry in hot sesame oil until golden brown. Remove and drain oil on paper towels. Place a 2–3 inch strip of kombu in the bottom of a pot. Place deep-fried seitan on top. Add 6 cups of water and 1/4–1/3 cup tamari. Bring to a boil. Reduce flame to low, cover and simmer 35/45 minutes.

Add onions, taro, carrots and celery. When carrots are about half-done, add the green peas. Add 1–2 cups of starch water from washing gluten and allow to thicken. Stir occasionally to prevent burning. You may want to add a little more tamari to taste if necessary, but the stew should not have an overly salty taste.

Garnish with chopped parsley, scallions or chives.

Seitan Fried Rice

>**4 cups cooked rice**
>**1-1/2 cups diced cooked seitan**
>**1/2 cup diced daikon greens**

tamari to taste
sesame oil

Lightly brush sesame oil on bottom of skillet. Heat skillet. Add greens and seitan. Place rice on top. Cover and reduce flame to low. When vegetables are almost done, add tamari to taste and cook another 5 minutes or so. Mix and serve.

If you don't have daikon greens, use kale, mustard greens, celery, scallions, chives, etc. Add scallions and chives at the end of cooking so that they retain their dark green color.

Stuffed Mushrooms

    10 large mushrooms (remove stems)
    1-1/4 cups cooked seitan, chopped or finely minced
    1 scallion, finely chopped
    1/2 onion, minced
    1/4 carrot, minced
    sesame oil

Lightly brush oil in skillet and heat. Sauté scallions, onions and carrots on a low flame until done. Remove and place in mixing bowl. Add seitan and mix. Stuff each mushroom cap with about 1 tablespoon of stuffing and place in a baking dish.

Sauce

    1 onion, minced
    1 Tbsp. minced parsley
    2 cups seitan-tamari cooking water
    1/2–1 cup seitan starch water

Place above ingredients in a saucepan, except for the parsley. Bring to a boil, reduce flame to low. Simmer until onions are done. If sauce is too thick, add more tamari-water. If too thin, add more starch water.

Gently pour sauce over stuffed mushrooms. Bake at 350° F. until mushrooms are tender. Occasionally spoon sauce over mushrooms to prevent drying.

Sprinkle minced parsley over mushrooms and serve.

Stuffed Squash or Hokkaido Pumpkin

    1 large buttercup squash or Hokkaido pumpkin
    1-1/2 cups whole wheat bread cubes
    1/2 onion, diced
    1–1-1/2 cups diced seitan (cooked)
    4–5 shiitake mushrooms, soaked, sliced and destemmed
    1/2 cup water
    1/2 stalk celery, diced
    tamari
    sesame oil

Cut off the top of the squash as you would when making a jack-o'lantern. Clean out insides. Save seeds. They are delicious when roasted with tamari.

Toast bread cubes in a dry skillet until golden brown. Sauté onions, shiitake and celery until onions are translucent. Place in mixing bowl.

Add bread cubes and seitan to the sautéed vegetables and mix. Add water and a small amount of tamari. Mix. Place stuffing inside squash and place top back on the squash.

Bake at 450° F. until squash is 80% done. Poke with a bamboo stick or chopstick to test if it is done.

Make a gravy similar to the sauce recipe presented above and spoon inside the squash so that it filters down into the stuffing. Bake until squash is tender. Remaining gravy can be spooned over the stuffing and squash after serving.

FU⁻

Fu is another high-protein food which is made in a similar way to seitan. Several macrobiotic cookbooks have recipes for making fu. It is also available in some natural food stores and Oriental markets in a dried and packaged form.

It is a very delicious food and most children love it, as do many adults.

Fu is usually packaged in either flat sheets, large rounds with a hole in the center, or small rounds with a hole in the center.

Fu and Vegetables
 1 package flat fu
 1 cake tofu, cubed
 4 shiitake mushrooms, soaked, destemmed and quartered
 1/2 bunch of broccoli, cut into small flowerettes
 tamari to taste
 4 cups water

Break fu into small, bite-sized pieces. They expand when they begin to cook. Place fu in pot with water. Add shiitake, tofu and broccoli. Bring to a boil, reduce flame to low, cover and simmer for 5–7 minutes. Season with tamari and cook until broccoli is tender. Serve.

Sautéed Fu
 1/2 package large round fu, or 1 package flat fu, soaked
 1 onion, diced
 4 shiitake mushrooms, soaked, destemmed and sliced
 1 cup carrots, thinly sliced diagonally
 1-1/2 cups sliced green beans
 tamari to taste
 sesame oil

Soak fu several minutes. Squeeze water out and slice rounds into cubes or flat sheets into small strips.

Brush skillet with sesame oil and heat. Add onions and shiitake. Sauté until onions are translucent. Add carrots, green beans, and fu. Sauté until carrots and beans are almost done. Add tamari to taste and cook 5 minutes longer. Serve.

Fu is also delicious when added to tamari broth or miso soup. It is also good when deep-fried and added to soup broth after first draining off the excess oil. If you want a quick snack, simply boil it in water and tamari. Serve with tamari to taste.

NOODLES

Noodles are one of our favorite year-round foods. They can be prepared for breakfast, lunch, dinner or as a snack. They are quick, easy to prepare, and very satisfying, and are great for unexpected company. Noodles can be prepared in a variety of ways so that you will never tire of them, and there are many different kinds of broth that can be served over them. Noodles can also be deep-fried after boiling as a crunchy snack or for *chow mein*. You can also make *soba sushi* or prepare them in a casserole, or eat them fried or in vegetable or fish dishes such as *sukiyaki*.

Noodles are also fun for children to eat and are easy to chew and digest.

I was quite surprised the first time I ate noodles with friends in Japan, as they often make a loud slurping noise which is quite funny. They told me that the louder a person slurps while eating noodles, the better they seem to taste. They were probably just as surprised to see us eat noodles and not make much noise, since this is often considered an indication that the noodles are not so well prepared.

There are many suitable varieties of noodles available in natural food stores and in Oriental markets. Probably the most popular are *soba*, which are Japanese noodles made primarily from buckwheat flour. The many varieties of soba include those made with 100% buckwheat flour; those made with 80% buckwheat and 20% whole wheat flours or 60% buckwheat and 40% whole wheat; *jinenjo soba*, which include a percentage of jinenjo flour (from the root vegetable called *jinenjo*); and *ito soba*, which are very thin and short in comparison to the other varieties. *Ito soba* are good any time of the year, but especially in the summer when served with a cool broth.

The next major category of noodles are known as *udon*, and are made with whole wheat and unbleached white flours. Another variety, *somen*, are like small, thin *udon* and are becoming increasingly popular in this country. Also, some natural food stores sell Chinese-style noodles called *ramen*, which are either *udon* or *soba* which have been deep-fried. However, I don't suggest buying these in an Oriental market, as they are sometimes fried in chicken fat. Another of the Japanese noodles, *saifun*, is a clear cellophane noodle made from mung beans. These are very good for salads or prepared in vegetables dishes.

There are also many European- and American-style whole grain noodles which are fine for regular use, such as spaghetti, shells, rigatoni, ziti, spirals, elbows, flat noodles, lasagna, etc. These are usually made from whole wheat flour or from combinations of whole wheat and other flours. Some are even made from corn or artichoke flour.

American noodle products are usually made without salt being added, and when you cook them you should add a pinch of salt to the water before adding the noodles. On the other hand, Japanese noodles are usually made with salt, so you do not need to add it when cooking them.

There are two basic methods for cooking noodles. With the first method, bring a pot of water to a boil and add the noodles. Bring the water to a boil again and add a small amount of cold water to stop the boiling action. Bring to a boil again and repeat the adding of cold water three times. Then turn off the flame. The noodles are done. You may eat them hot as is with a little tamari and chopped scallion, or, if you wish to add them to another dish or serve them with broth, first rinse them under cold water. If you serve them with broth, simply place the noodles in the hot broth to heat up just before serving.

With the second method, bring a pot of water to a boil and add the noodles. Again bring to a boil, reduce the flame to medium low, and cook until done. To test whether the noodles are cooked, remove one and break it in half. If the center of the noodle is a different color than the outside, it is not done. When the noodle is done, the center and outside should be the same color. When done, remove the noodles and place in a strainer. Rinse under cold water to prevent clumping or or sticking together.

Soba and Broth

  1 package of soba (any variety)
  one 2–3 inch strip of kombu
  4 cups water
  2 dried shiitake mushrooms (soaked, destemmed and sliced)
  2–3 Tbsp. tamari

Broth No. 2

  one 2–3 inch strip kombu
  4 cups water
  2 shiitake mushrooms (soaked, destemmed and sliced)
  1 Tbsp. bonito (dried fish) flakes
  2–3 Tbsp. tamari

Broth No. 3

  4 shiitake mushrooms (soaked, destemmed and sliced)
  2–3 Tbsp. tamari

Broth No. 4

  one 2–3 inch strip of kombu
  4 cups water
  2–3 Tbsp. tamari

Cook noodles as described previously, rinse and drain. Place water in pot. Place kombu and shiitake in water. (If you are using bonito flakes, place in water, bring to a boil, lower flame and simmer for 3–4 minutes. Remove flakes with wire skimmer or pour broth through strainer. Then add kombu and shiitake.) Bring to a boil, reduce flame to low, and simmer for 1–2 minutes. Remove kombu and continue to simmer shiitake for another 5 minutes or so. Remove shiitake and set aside. Since the kombu can be used again for broth, place it on a bamboo mat to dry until you use it again. Add tamari to stock and simmer for about 5–7 minutes. The broth is now ready. Place noodles in the broth to warm up. Do not boil or cook them again as they will become very soggy. Serve immediately. Garnish with slices of shiitake, scallions, chives, strips of toasted nori or any combination of the above.

Noodle cooking water can be saved and used as a tea, in soup stock, or if you allow it to sit and sour slightly for a couple of days, you can use it in making breads, muffins, doughnuts, waffles or pancakes. The sour water acts as a leavening agent. You can also use the sour water as a base for a sourdough starter. Simply mix the sour water with some whole wheat flour and allow it to sit, adding more flour and water when necessary.

Summer Soba
In Japan they have a wonderful tradition of serving cold soba in the summer. It is very cooling and refreshing to eat when nothing else seems appetizing.

Cold soba can be prepared in several ways. The first, and most popular way is to prepare a broth using any of the previous recipes and refrigerate it or place ice cubes around the pot to allow it to chill. Prepare soba as mentioned and rinse under cold water until the noodles are cold. Drain the noodles and ladle the broth into individual serving bowls. Place sliced scallions or raw minced onion in the broth. Serve one bowl of broth to each person. Then, place individual servings of soba on plates, or, if you have them, special bamboo serving boxes which have a bamboo mat in the bottom. To eat, take a chopstickful of soba, dip in the cold broth and eat. You can also serve with strips of toasted nori or a little grated ginger in the broth.

In the second way, cool the broth as above. Place ice cubes in a serving dish and set the cooked, cold soba on top of the ice and allow it to chill slightly. Place cold broth in individual bowls, add a serving of soba and garnish with the above mentioned items. Place the serving dish with remaining cold noodles on the table and each person can replenish their bowls as desired.

Winter Udon or Soba
This dish is very good during the fall and winter months, as it raises the body temperature and makes the cold much much more tolerable. It is somewhat of a yang dish, and should therefore not be eaten daily or during hot weather. It is truly one of the most delicious noodle dishes I have ever eaten. We came across this dish while in Japan. I am sure you will enjoy it.

1 package udon or soba
4 shiitake, soaked, destemmed and sliced
4–5 slices of deep-fried tofu (2″×3″)

one 2–3 inch strip of kombu
1/2 onion, diced
1/4–1/2 Tbsp. grated ginger
scallions
approximately 4 Tbsp. kuzu, diluted in water, to thicken broth
tamari to taste
4–5 cups water

Cook noodles, rinse in cold water and drain. Place shiitake and kombu in water and bring to a boil. Reduce flame to low, cover and simmer for 1–2 minutes. Remove kombu and set aside for later use. Cover and continue to simmer shiitake for an additional 7–8 minutes. You may add bonito flakes to the stock to give a slightly different flavor if you wish.

Deep-fry tofu slices until golden brown. Remove and drain excess oil off onto a paper towel. Slice tofu into strips and place in the shiitake-kombu soup stock and simmer tofu and shiitake for 5–7 minutes.

Dilute kuzu in small amount of water. Add to soup stock and stir. Bring to a boil, reduce flame to low and season with tamari to taste. Cover and simmer for 10–15 minutes.

Place individual servings of noodles in each bowl. Ladle kuzu sauce, shiitake and tofu over the noodles. Garnish with sliced scallions and grated ginger in each bowl. Serve and add tamari to taste.

Udon with Jinenjo

 1 pkg. udon
 5–6 cups of tamari broth
 1 cup grated jinenjo
 sliced scallions

Cook noodles, rinse and drain. Prepare any of the previously mentioned broths. Grate jinenjo (it will be very sticky like egg white). Warm noodles in the broth as explained previously and place in individual serving bowls. Add one or two tablespoons of grated jinenjo and a few sliced scallions to each serving.

This dish is also more yang, due to the addition of jinenjo. It can be eaten once or twice per week and is also very good in the cold seasons.

Noodles with Fish

This dish can be prepared in the same way as you would regular noodles and broth. When it is done, place a small piece of broiled fish and sliced scallions on top of the noodles.

Soba Tempura

 1 pkg. soba
 5–6 cups tamari broth
 scallions
 5–6 mushrooms
 5–6 broccoli flowerettes

Tempura Batter

 3/4 cup whole wheat pastry flour
 1/4 cup corn flour
 1–1-1/4 cups cold water
 1/4 tsp. sea salt

5–6 carrot slices
5–6 onion rounds
5–6 small pieces of white meat fish (if desired)

Cook noodles, rinse and drain. Prepare broth and keep hot.

Mix batter and set aside for a few minutes. Heat sesame oil. Dip vegetables in batter and deep-fry until golden brown. Drain oil on paper towels.

Place noodles in hot broth to heat up. Remove from broth and place in serving bowls. Ladle broth over noodles. Place sliced scallions and one piece of each kind of vegetable on top of noodles. If you tempura fish, do it after you have finished all the vegetables, as it leaves a fishy taste in the oil. Serve. You can also serve a side dish of grated daikon and tamari to help digest the oil from the tempura.

Somen with Deep-Fried Tofu

Somen are very thin, white noodles which are available in some natural food stores and in many Oriental markets. They are very delicious and feel light in the stomach, and are especially good in the spring and summer. They usually come in a package with five small bundles of noodles tied individually. Each bundle will serve one bowl of noodles to about three people.

5–6 cups tamari broth
3 individual bundles of *somen* (about 3/5 of a pkg.)
5–6 slices of deep-fried tofu (2″ × 3″)
1 cup sliced, sautéed mushrooms
sliced scallions

Cook noodles, rinse and drain. These noodles are very thin and require much less time to cook than soba or udon. Be careful not to overcook them or they become soggy.

Slice tofu and allow water to drain. Heat deep-frying oil to correct temperature. Deep-fry tofu until golden brown.

Wash mushrooms, slice and sauté with small amount of oil and tamari.

Heat tamari broth and place noodles in it to warm up. Place noodles in individual serving bowls and ladle hot broth over each. Place one piece of deep-fried tofu, one tablespoon of sautéed mushrooms and a few slices of scallion in each bowl. You can also garnish with toasted nori strips or a few bonito flakes.

Udon with White Clam Sauce

1–1-1/2 pkgs. udon
1 qt. unshucked clams
1-1/2 cups clam juice
2 cups water
1 onion, diced
2 Tbsp. minced parsley
2 tsp. tamari
sesame oil

Cook udon, rinse and drain. Remove clams from shells and wash. Save water that drains from the clams as you are shucking them and strain it through a fine mesh strainer to remove sand. Set aside and allow any remaining sand to settle to the bottom of the bowl. Drain off the clear juice and save for use in the sauce.

Wash clams and place in a bowl. More juice will drain in the bowl. Cut the clams into small pieces. Place about 2 tablespoons of sesame oil in a skillet and heat. Add clams and onions. Sauté until onions are translucent (about 3 minutes). Add all of the clam juice and water and cook for about 5 minutes. Add tamari and parsley. Bring to a boil, reduce flame to very low and simmer for 5–10 minutes longer.

Place noodles in a pot of hot water for about a minute to warm up. Then place noodles in serving bowls. Ladle the clams and clam sauce over the udon and serve hot.

Season with extra tamari and parsley to taste if necessary.

Fried Soba or Udon
   1 package soba
   1/2 cup sliced celery (sliced thinly)
   5 shiitake mushrooms—soaked, destemmed and sliced
   1/2 cup sliced scallions
   1–2 Tbsp. tamari
   sesame oil

Cook soba, rinse and drain. Brush a skillet with sesame oil and heat. Add shiitake and celery. Place soba on top of the vegetables and cover. Reduce flame to low and simmer until the celery is about half cooked. Add scallions and tamari and sauté for another 3–5 minutes. Serve hot. You may garnish with toasted nori strips or roasted sesame seeds, or eat as is.

Fried Udon
   1 package udon
   1 cup shredded cabbage
   1/2 cup diced onion
   4–5 shiitake mushrooms—soaked, destemmed and sliced
   1 cup shrimp, deveined and washed
   2 Tbsp. minced parsley
   sesame oil
   1–2 Tbsp. tamari

Cook udon, rinse and drain. Remove shells and blue veins from shrimp and slice into small pieces.

Brush skillet with oil and heat. Place onions and mushrooms in skillet. Sauté on a low flame for 2–3 minutes. Add cabbage, cover and sauté until cabbage is just about cooked. Add shrimp, cover, and sauté for 2 minutes. Add udon and tamari and sauté for another 5–7 minutes, stirring occasionally. Add parsley during the last 2–3 minutes. Serve.

Chinese Style Noodles
   1 package udon or 3/5 of a package of somen

Sauce

  4 shiitake mushrooms, soaked, destemmed and sliced
  1 small onion sliced in half moons
  1/2 lb. snow peas
  1 cup celery, thinly sliced on the diagonal
  1–1-1/2 cups thinly sliced Chinese cabbage
  sesame oil
  4–5 cups water
  approximately 4 Tbsp. kuzu diluted in water
  tamari to taste (not enough to make sauce taste salty or appear brown in color—
    You may season with sea salt and tamari to retain clear color)

Cook, rinse, and drain noodles. Set aside.

Brush a small amount of sesame oil in a skillet and heat. Add onions and shiitake. Sauté until onions are translucent. Add celery and sauté for 2–3 minutes. Add Chinese cabbage and snow peas. Sauté for 1–2 minutes. Add water and diluted kuzu. Bring to a boil, reduce flame to very low, cover and simmer until kuzu thickens. Season to taste with tamari and simmer 1–2 minutes. Remove from flame.

Place noodles in individual serving bowls and ladle the vegetable sauce over each bowl. Garnish with sliced scallions and serve.

Chow Mein
  1 package udon

Sauce

  2 mustard green leaves, sliced
  2 cups mung bean sprouts
  1 cup celery, thinly sliced diagonally
  1 onion, diced
  5 shiitake mushrooms, soaked, destemmed and sliced
  1 cup Chinese cabbage, thinly sliced
  3 cups cooked seitan cut into small cubes
  5 cups seitan-tamari broth water
  1–2 cups starch water from making seitan, or approximately 1/3 cup diluted
    kuzu to thicken

Cook, rinse and drain noodles. Slice noodles in half. Heat a pot of sesame oil and deep-fry noodles until golden brown. Remove and drain on paper towels. Break crispy noodles into smaller pieces.

Place seitan-tamari broth in a pot and bring to a boil. Reduce flame to low and add onions and mushrooms. Simmer about 7 minutes. Add seitan and starch water or kuzu to thicken. Bring to a boil, reduce flame and simmer about 10 minutes. Add celery, bean sprouts, and Chinese cabbage. Simmer about 5 minutes. If necessary, season to taste with tamari, but taste should not be salty.

Place deep-fried noodles in individual serving bowls and ladle the sauce over the noodles. Serve.

Baked Noodles with Tempura
    1 package udon or soba
    5–6 fresh mushrooms
    5–6 slices of carrot
    5–6 broccoli flowerettes
    5–6 thin slices of burdock
    1 medium onion, halved then quartered
    2 cups tamari broth
    tempura batter
    tamari

Cook, rinse and drain noodles.

Heat oil in a tempura pot. Mix tempura batter using previous recipe. When oil is hot, dip vegetables in batter and place in hot oil. Deep-fry until golden brown. Remove and drain on paper towels.

Layer the cooked noodles and vegetables in a casserole dish until all ingredients are used up. Add tamari broth and, if desired, a little extra tamari to taste. Cover and bake at 375° F. for 30–35 minutes. Remove cover and bake 5–10 minutes longer. Serve.

The batter on the vegetables will become soft and melt in with the noodles, giving this dish a very delicious flavor.

Stuffed Shells
    1/2 cup fresh green peas
    1 cup string beans, diced
    1 ear corn (remove kernels with knife)
    1/2 onion, diced
    2 blocks tofu, mashed in suribachi
    1 tsp. tamari
    1 dozen large whole wheat stuffing shells
    sesame oil

Sauté vegetables until done. Mix vegetables with mashed tofu. Add tamari.

Cook, rinse and drain shells. Stuff shells with vegetable and tofu mixture and place in a baking dish. Cover dish and bake for 20–25 minutes. Remove and serve.

You can make a light kuzu-tamari sauce to serve over each shell if desired. You can also stuff with seitan, *okara*, or vegetables instead of tofu.

Saifun with Bonito
    1 package saifun (mung bean noodles)
    bonito flakes (small flakes; not the large ones for soup stock)
    tamari

Place several cups of water in a pot and bring to a boil. Turn off and drop in saifun. Leave for several minutes. Remove and rinse under cold water and allow to drain.

Place in an attractive serving bowl and garnish with bonito flakes and tamari in the center. Serve.

These noodles can be used in vegetable dishes, soups, and salads. They are especially good in the summer.

For additional *Seitan*, *Fu* and *Noodle* dishes including seitan stew, seitan-barley soup, seitan stuffed cabbage, seitan croquettes, fried noodles and noodles in broth, please refer to *Introducing Macrobiotic Cooking*.

3. Soups and Soup Stocks

Soups are one of my favorite dishes. They can be made with just about any of the grains and all kinds of noodles, vegetables, beans, tofu, and seitan and can be seasoned with miso, tamari, sea salt, kombu and other seaweeds, shiitake, bonito flakes, chirimen iriko, umeboshi, and other ingredients. Kuzu, arrowroot, seitan starch water, and flours can also be used in soups and stews, as thickening agents.

Soups and stews are often eaten at the beginning of the meal, as they help prepare the digestive system for the other foods which follow. Certain soups can produce a cooling effect on the body in the hot months, while others can be used to help generate heat in the winter. Certain soups are also beneficial for certain types of illnesses or weaknesses. It is very interesting to observe how certain soups and combinations of ingredients affect our physical, mental, and spiritual well-being.

There are many ways to prepare soups. For example, you can start with a variety of soup stocks as a base, or sauté all or part of the ingredients before adding to soup, or roast the grains first. You can also start with hot or cold water as a base.

In my first cookbook *Introducing Macrobiotic Cooking*—I introduced a technique for preparing soups that I learned from Aveline Kushi. This method is called the *layer method* because all of the ingredients are layered according to their yin and yang properties. For instance, if you were making a soup with onions, carrots, burdock, celery, and millet, you would first place the onions, which are the most yin of these vegetables, on the botton of the pot closest to the flame. A layer of carrots would then go on top of the onions, while the burdock, which is the most yang of these vegetables, would go on top of the carrots. The celery should be left out until the soup is almost done, as its bright green color will become very dull if it is cooked too long. Millet, being a grain which is more yang than these vegetables, would be placed on the top layer, farthest from the flame, in the most yin position.

Yin flavors tend to expand upward during cooking, while more yang flavors tend to go downward. With the layering method, the ingredients mix and complement each other naturally without interference from the cook. Therefore, do not stir or mix the ingredients until the very end. When you add water, pour it very slowly down the sides of the pot so that the layers are not disturbed. Only add enough water to barely cover. As the grain and other ingredients absorb the water and expand, continue to add just enough to cover. Repeat this until the grain is thoroughly cooked. Add only a pinch of salt at the beginning to bring out the sweetness of the ingredients. The remaining seasoning should be added after the millet is done. Additional water should also be added after the millet is done in order to make the soup as thick or as thin as you wish. The soup should be cooked on a low flame so that it does not boil rapidly and disturb the layers.

This soup requires very little attention from the cook, except to add water when necessary, and pretty much cooks itself.

This cooking method creates a very calm and peaceful vibration in your soup, and, therefore, in those who eat it. I am sure you will enjoy it very much. Of course, you should use all of the other methods as well as this one. If you use only one method, your cooking may become overly one-sided or rigid. All tastes and senses should be stimulated daily, and this can be accomplished by using various cooking techniques, ingredients, garnishes, and condiments. For instance, when making a soup such as the one above, change the ingredients often or occasionally sauté the vegetables and roast the grain. You can also use rice, barley, or other grains in place of millet.

Please be flexible in your approach to cooking, and the rewards of creating a happy, healthy, and peaceful family will be tremendous.

GRAIN SOUPS

Ten-don

Ten-don is a one-dish meal which includes rice, soup, and vegetables. I discovered this wonderful dish in Japan, and it has since become a favorite in our house. I'm sure you will enjoy it also.

> **5 cups freshly cooked brown rice**
> **5 cups water**
> **3 shiitake mushrooms, soaked**
> **one 2–3 inch strip of kombu**
> **1 Tbsp. bonito flakes**
> **tamari to taste**
> **batter for making tempura**

1/4 lb. green string beans cut in half lengthwise
1 cup carrot, cut into matchsticks
5 medium shrimp, shelled and deveined
1 stalk celery, cut into 1-1/2″ strips

Place water in pot. Add bonito flakes. Bring to a boil. Reduce flame to low and simmer about 5 minutes. Strain broth to remove bonito flakes and place broth back in pot. Add shiitake and kombu. Bring to a boil, reduce flame to low and simmer for 2 minutes. Remove kombu and save for later use. Continue to simmer the shiitake about 10 minutes. Remove shiitake and use again for other stock or in soup. Add tamari to taste and simmer on very low flame until ready to serve.

Prepare tempura batter using the previous recipe. Heat tempura oil. Dip vegetables in batter and deep-fry until golden brown. Drain on paper towels. Dip shrimp in batter and deep-fry until golden brown. Drain on paper towels.

Place a serving of rice in each individual bowl and place a piece of each kind of tempura on top. Add 1/2 cup of soup broth to each bowl and serve.

Millet-Seitan Soup

1/2 cup millet
1 cup seitan cooked in tamari and water, diced
1 onion, diced
1 small carrot, diced
1/2 cup green beans or other green cut thinly on a diagonal
1/4 tsp. sea salt

Wash millet as discussed previously. Layer the ingredients as follows: onions on the bottom, carrots next, then seitan, burdock, and finally, millet. Add the green beans or other greens toward the end. Do not mix. Add a pinch of salt. Gently pour just enough water to cover the ingredients down the side of the pot. Turn flame to high. Bring to a boil, reduce flame to low, cover and simmer. When the millet begins to expand, add only enough water to barely cover the top. Repeat until the millet is done. Add 4 cups of cold water and the remaining seasoning. Simmer 20 minutes or so. Add green beans during the final 10–15 minutes. Stir and serve. Garnish with sliced scallions, parsley or toasted nori.

Barley Mushroom Soup

1/2 cup barley
1 onion, diced
5 medium shiitake, soaked, destemmed and sliced thin
1 stalk celery, diced
1 small carrot, diced
5–6 cups water
1/4–1/2 tsp. sea salt

Wash barley. Place barley and water in a pot. Bring to a boil, reduce flame to low, cover and simmer about 25 minutes. Add onion, shiitake and carrots. Bring to a boil, reduce flame and simmer another 10–15 minutes. Add sea salt. Add celery and cook for another 5 minutes. Season with a little tamari to taste if necessary. Garnish and serve.

Barley Kidney Bean Soup
   1/2 cup barley
   1/4 cup kidney beans
   1 onion, diced
   1 stalk celery, diced
   3–4 shiitake, soaked, destemmed and sliced
   5–6 cups water
   1/4–1/2 tsp. sea salt

Wash barley and beans. Layer ingredients in the pot in the following order: onions, shiitake, barley, kidney beans. Bring to a boil, reduce flame to low and simmer until beans are almost done. Add celery and sea salt. Cook for another 10–15 minutes. Garnish and serve.

Kasha Soup
   1 cup buckwheat, roasted
   1 onion, diced
   1/4 cup minced parsley
   5–6 cups water
   pinch of sea salt
   tamari to taste

Brush a small amount of sesame oil in a pot. Heat and sauté onions until they are translucent. Add buckwheat and sauté 5 minutes. Add pinch of sea salt and water. Bring to a boil, cover, reduce flame to low and simmer 25–30 minutes. Add parsley. Season with tamari to taste and simmer 10 minutes more. Serve.

Rice Soup
   1/2 cup rice, uncooked
   1 onion, diced
   1 cup butternut or buttercup squash or Hokkaido pumpkin, diced, cubed or thinly sliced in small pieces
   1 stalk celery, diced
   5–6 cups water
   1-1/2–2-1/2 Tbsp. tamari
   pinch of sea salt

Wash rice. Layer onion, celery and squash in that order in a pot. Place rice on top. Add water and pinch of sea salt. Bring to a boil, cover, reduce flame to low and simmer until rice is soft. Add tamari and simmer 15–20 minutes more. If you need to add more water, do so when necessary for desired consistency.

   Garnish with sliced scallions or minced parsley. Serve.

Corn Soup
   4 ears of fresh sweet corn
   1 stalk of celery, diced

1 onion, diced
5–6 cups water or kombu stock
1/4 cup navy beans
1/4 tsp. sea salt
tamari to taste if extra seasoning is desired

Wash beans. Remove corn from ears with knife. Place celery, onions, corn and beans in pot. Add water and pinch of sea salt. Bring to a boil, reduce flame to low, cover and simmer until beans are soft. Add remaining sea salt and a small amount of tamari if necessary. Garnish and serve.

Oatmeal/Dulse Soup

1 cup rolled oats
1/4 cup dulse, soaked and finely sliced
1 onion, diced
1/2 cup celery, diced
5–6 cups water
1/4–1/2 tsp. sea salt

Place onions, celery, dulse and rolled oats in that order in a pot. Add water and bring to a boil. Reduce flame to low and simmer 25–30 minutes. Add sea salt and simmer 5–10 minutes more. Garnish and serve.

Shell Soup

2 cups cooked whole wheat shells
one 2″–3″ strip kombu
2 shiitake mushrooms, soaked, destemmed and sliced
1 onion, cut in half-moons
1/4 cup diced celery
5–6 cups water
tamari to taste

Cook shells, rinse and drain. Place kombu and water in a pot. Bring to a boil. Reduce flame to low and simmer 2–3 minutes. Remove kombu and slice in half lengthwise. Then slice kombu diagonally into matchsticks and add back to water. Add shiitake and onions. Simmer 10 minutes. Add shells and celery. Season with tamari to taste and simmer 5–7 minutes more. Serve.

Sweet Rice Soup

5–6 cups water
1 cup sweet rice
3 shiitake mushrooms
1/2 cup carrot, cut in matchsticks
1 onion, diced
1/4 cup celery, diced
1/4–1/2 tsp. sea salt
one 6″ strip kombu
1/8 cup burdock, quartered

Wash rice. Place kombu and water in pot. Bring to boil. Reduce flame and simmer

2 minutes. Remove kombu and save for future use. Add sweet rice and bring to a boil. Reduce flame to low and simmer 35–40 minutes. Purée sweet rice with a Foley food mill and place back in pot. Add onions, carrot, mushrooms, celery and burdock. Simmer 15–20 minutes. Season with sea salt and simmer 5–7 minutes. Garnish and serve.

BEAN SOUPS

Azuki Bean Soup
    1-1/2 cups azuki beans
    1 onion, diced
    1–1-1/2 cups diced buttercup squash
    5–6 cups water
    1/4–1/2 tsp. sea salt
    tamari to taste

Wash beans and place in pot with water. Bring to a boil, reduce flame to low, cover and simmer until beans are about 50%–60% done. Add onions and squash. Add a pinch of salt. Bring to a boil again. Lower flame and simmer until beans are done. Add remaining salt and tamari to taste. Simmer 10–15 minutes. Garnish with scallions or parsley and serve.

Kidney Bean Soup
    2 cups kidney beans
    1 onion, diced
    1/2 cup celery, diced
    5–6 cups water
    4–5 tsp. puréed brown rice miso

Wash beans. Place beans and water in a pot and bring to a boil. Reduce flame to low, cover and simmer until beans are about 80% done. Add onions, celery and miso. Simmer 15–20 minutes. Garnish and serve.

Black Bean Soup
    2 cups black beans
    1 medium onion, diced
    5–6 cups water
    1/2 Tbsp. sea salt

Wash beans and place in pressure-cooker. Add water and cover. When pressure comes up, reduce flame to low and cook 45 minutes. Remove from flame and allow pressure to come down. Remove cover. Add onions and sea salt. Simmer 20–25 minutes. If you add a little less salt and a small amount of tamari during the last 10–15 minutes, your soup will have a nice flavor.

If you wish to add carrots or other colored vegetables to this soup, add them toward the end as they may turn purple from the bean juice.

Garnish with some greens and serve.

Split Pea Soup

    1 cup split peas
    1 medium onion, diced
    1/4 cup jinenjo (mountain potato), diced
    1/4 cup wakame, soaked and sliced
    4–5 cups water
    1/4–1/2 tsp. sea salt

Wash peas. Place peas, onions, wakame and jinenjo in a pot. Add water. Bring to a boil, reduce flame to low and cover. Simmer 45 minutes. Add sea salt and simmer 10–15 minutes or until soup is creamy.

Garnish with toasted bread cubes or minced carrot. Serve.

Split Pea/Seitan Soup

    1 cup split peas
    1 cup cooked seitan (cooked in tamari water and diced)
    1/2 cup diced onion
    1/4 cup diced carrot
    4–5 cups water
    1/4 tsp. sea salt

Cook as above. Garnish and serve.

Lentil Soup

    1 cup lentils
    1 onion, diced
    1/2 cup carrot, diced
    1 cup cooked elbow macaroni
    1 Tbsp. minced parsley
    4–5 cups water
    1/4–1/2 tsp. sea salt

Wash lentils. Cook macaroni, rinse and drain. Set aside. Add lentils, onions, carrots and water to a pot. Bring to a boil. Reduce flame to low, cover and simmer about 45 minutes. Add noodles, parsley and sea salt. Cover and simmer 10 minutes longer. Garnish and serve.

Navy Bean Soup

    1 cup navy beans
    1 onion, diced
    1/2 cup fresh sweet corn
    1/4 cup celery, diced
    4–5 cups water
    1/4–1/2 tsp. sea salt

Wash navy beans. Place beans and water in a pot. Bring to a boil. Reduce flame to low and simmer about 45 minutes. Add onions, corn, celery, and sea salt. Cover and simmer for another 20 minutes or until beans are very soft. Garnish and serve.

Lima Bean Soup
>   1 cup large lima beans
>   1 onion, diced
>   1/2 cup cabbage, chopped very finely
>   1/4 cup diced carrot
>   4–5 cups water
>   lightly season with puréed miso or tamari to taste

Cook as above. Add seasoning during the last 15–20 minutes. Garnish and serve.

Gazpacho
>   3 cups cooked chickpeas
>   3 cups cooking water from chickpeas
>   1/2 carrot, grated
>   1/2 cucumber, cut in small matchsticks
>   1 scallion, sliced diagonally
>   1 cup seasoned toasted bread cubes
>   tamari

Wash chickpeas and cook as described in bean chapter. Purée chickpeas and water in a Foley food mill until creamy. Place the puréed chickpeas in individual serving bowls and chill in the refrigerator.

Toast the bread cubes in a skillet until golden brown and crispy. Season with a little tamari and ground wakame powder.

Garnish each bowl with a small amount of grated carrot, cucumber, scallion, and bread cubes. Add several drops of tamari to the vegetables. Serve cold.

This soup is especially good during the summer.

VEGETABLE SOUPS

Kenchin Soup

Kenchin soup was introduced to Japan from China and is made from the pieces of vegetables that are left over from other dishes. You can season the soup with tamari or miso and add fish to it. It can also be lightly thickened with kuzu if you wish. It is especially good in the winter but can be eaten during other seasons as well.
>   7–8 cups water
>   1/2 cup onion, diced
>   1/4 cup celery, diced
>   1/4 cup carrots, diced
>   1/4 cup burdock, quartered and finely diced
>   1/2 cup daikon, cut in small rectangles
>   1/2 cup Chinese cabbage, finely sliced
>   1 cup deep-fried tofu cubes
>   5 Tbsp. diluted kuzu
>   tamari to taste

Lightly sauté the vegetables or use the layering method method described previously. If you sauté, place vegetables in a pot and add just enough water to cover.

Add a pinch of salt. Bring to a boil, reduce flame to low, cover and simmer about
5 minutes. Add tofu and remaining water and cook until all vegetables are
soft. Dilute 5 tablespoons of kuzu in a small amount of water and add to the
soup. Stir. Add tamari to taste when kuzu begins to thicken. Simmer about 5–10
minutes more. Serve.

French Onion Soup

> 2 large onions, halved and sliced into very thin half-moons
> onion skins (wash before peeling onions)
> 6 cups water
> one 2–3 inch strip kombu
> 5 shiitake mushrooms, soaked, destemmed and sliced
> 1/2 Tbsp. bonito flakes
> tamari to taste
> sesame oil
> toasted bread cubes
> pinch of sea salt

Wash onions, remove skins and save. Place water in a saucepan and add onion
skins. Bring to a boil. Reduce flame and simmer about 3–4 minutes. Remove
onion skins. Add bonito flakes and simmer 5–6 minutes. Remove bonito flakes.
Add kombu and cook 2 minutes. Remove and slice thin. Place back in pot. Lightly
brush sesame oil in a pot. Add onions and sauté until translucent. Add water
and shiitake to the onions. Add a pinch of sea salt. Bring to a boil, reduce flame
to low and simmer 30–45 minutes. Add tamari and simmer 10 minutes more.
Garnish with toasted bread cubes, sliced scallions, or minced parsley.

Pumpkin Soup

> 1 large Hokkaido pumpkin
> 1 onion, diced
> 5–6 cups water
> 1/4–1/2 tsp. sea salt

Wash pumpkin, cut in half and remove seeds (save and roast with tamari for a
snack). Peel off skin and save. (Skins can be cut into matchsticks and used in
miso soup or in making tempura.) Cut pumpkin into cubes. Place onions, pumpkin, a pinch of sea salt, and water in a pot. Bring to a boil, reduce flame to low,
cover and simmer until pumpkin is soft. Then purée in a Foley food mill until
pumpkin is creamy. Add remaining salt. If necessary, add a little more water to
achieve desired consistency. The soup should be a little, but not too thick. Add
remaining sea salt and simmer 15–20 minutes.

Garnish with sliced scallions or minced parsley and a few toasted bread cubes.

Summer Squash Soup

> 4 yellow summer squash
> 5–6 cups water
> 1 onion, diced

1/4 tsp. sea salt
a little tamari if necessary

Cook as above. Garnish with minced parsley or chives.

This soup can also be seasoned with miso or tamari instead of sea salt.

Sake-no-Kasu

Sake-no-kasu is a soup made from *sake lees,* which is the by-product or sediment left over from brewing sake, or Japanese rice wine. Sake lees is similar to cheese in that it is also produced through fermentation; however, it is usually of a much higher quality than cheese because it is made from grains which have been natural-ly fermented. It also contains a small percentage of alcohol which adds a wonderful flavor to whatever it is cooked with.

Sake lees can be used in vegetable dishes to add a delicious white, creamy sauce; in soups; fish dishes; pickles; salad dressings and a variety of other ways. It usually comes in a package containing slices of lees, and is a cream color.

Our family enjoyed it in soup and in other dishes during our stay in Japan. Some of the Japanese markets in America carry it. However, please read the package label or ask if there are chemicals or preservatives added to it before you buy it.

This soup is especially good in the winter as it increases body warmth and circulation.

6 cups water
1/2 cup sake lees
1-1/2 cups daikon, cut into thick matchsticks or triangles
1 cup carrot, cut as above
3 slices of deep-fried tofu (2″ × 3″ × 1/4″)
1 onion, diced
pinch of sea salt
tamari to taste
1/2 cups fresh okara

Drain tofu and deep-fry until golden brown. Slice tofu into thin strips and drain on paper towels. Place onions, tofu, daikon and carrot in a pot. Add water and a pinch of sea salt. Bring to a boil, reduce flame to low, cover and simmer until vegetables are soft.

Break sake lees into small pieces and place in a suribachi. Add a small amount of soup broth and blend in the suribachi.

Add sake lees to the vegetables and broth. Season with tamari or miso to taste. Simmer another 20 minutes on a low flame. Garnish and serve.

The tofu can be omitted from the recipe if you want a less oily soup. You may also add crabmeat, salmon, or other fish to the soup toward the very end. If you add the fish too soon, however, it will become too hard from excessive cooking.

Okara Soup

Okara is the soybean pulp or lees left over from making tofu. In some cookbooks, it is referred to as *unohana*. Please refer to the bean section of this book for additional suggestions on using okara and directions on how to make it.

    5–6 cups water
    1 cup Chinese cabbage, thinly sliced
    1/2 cup carrots, diced or quartered
    1-1/2 cup onion, diced
    1/4 cup burdock, diced or quartered
    tamari to taste
    pinch of sea salt

Layer the vegetables in a pot as explained at the beginning of this chapter. Add water and a pinch of sea salt. Bring to a boil, reduce flame to low, cover and simmer until vegetables are soft. Add okara and tamari to taste. Simmer 3–5 minutes and garnish. This soup should not be too salty.

Jinenjo Soup

Jinenjo is a type of potato that was traditionally harvested in the mountains of Japan. It grows wild and is very difficult to harvest, as it sometimes grows as much as several feet into the rocks and soil. I have heard that it takes up to five years for jinenjo to grow just a few inches. It is now commercially cultivated and there are presently two or three varieties available. I have only seen one kind in this country, and it is sold in many Oriental food shops and natural food stores. It is usually packed in sawdust to keep it fresh and is sold in pieces from about 6 inches to sometimes more than 2 feet in length. It has a very thin, light tan skin with many small dots which have tiny hair-like roots protruding from them. To clean, simply scrub gently with a vegetable brush and leave the skin on.

    Jinenjo is much more yang than regular potatoes, and is suitable for regular use. It was traditionally used to promote strength and vitality. It can be sliced and baked, pan-fried, or boiled, or grated and either cooked or served raw on top of noodles. It can also be grated and mixed with tofu and vegetables and then deep-fried into croquettes.

    5–6 cups kombu stock
    4 shiitake mushrooms, soaked, destemmed and sliced
    1–1-1/2 cups grated jinenjo
    6 sprigs of watercress, boiled less than one minute
    3 slices of lemon, cut in half
    tamari to taste

Prepare kombu stock. Place in a pot and add shiitake. Bring to a boil, reduce flame to low, cover and simmer 10 minutes. Add grated jinenjo and stir to mix well. Season with tamari. Simmer 3 minutes and remove from flame. Place in serving bowls. Garnish each bowl with a sprig of watercress and half a slice of lemon. Serve.

    This soup can also be seasoned with miso instead of tamari.

Taro Potato Soup

Taro is another tuberous plant that grows in Japan, America, Africa and other

countries throughout the world. It is often called by other names, such as albi.
Do not be confused, as it is the same potato. I have seen two or three varieties
sold in this country in Oriental markets, Armenian groceries, natural food stores
and in some supermarkets.

Taro is frequently used by macrobiotic people for its medicinal properties.
A very effective plaster can be made by grating taro or albi and mixing it with
whole wheat flour. This plaster is usually applied over an area where a tumor is
developing. The taro draws toxins from the tumor and helps to reduce its size.

Along with being of value as a natural medicine, it is also very delicious to eat
as a vegetable, in soups, or in a variety of other ways.

It is usually round or egg-shaped and may come in small or large sizes. It has
a very hairy skin which should be peeled before using. Like jinenjo, it is low in
potassium and is a more yang vegetable.

5–6 cups water
1 onion, diced
1/2 cup carrot, quartered
2 cups taro potato, peeled, quartered and sliced into bite-sized pieces
1 cup cooked whole wheat shells or elbows
1/4 cup celery, sliced diagonally
tamari to taste
pinch of sea salt

Cook noodles, rinse and drain. Set aside. Peel skin off taro, wash and slice as
directed.

Place vegetables in a pot with water and a pinch of sea salt. Bring to a boil,
reduce flame to low, cover and simmer until vegetables are soft. Add noodles
and tamari to taste. Simmer 5 minutes. Garnish and serve.

Taro Soup No. 2

5–6 cups kombu-bonito stock
4 shiitake mushrooms, soaked, destemmed and quartered
3 medium taro, peeled and quartered
6 sprigs watercress, boiled less than a minute
6 pieces of carrot, cut in 1/4 inch-thick flower shapes
pinch of sea salt
tamari or yellow miso to taste

Prepare kombu/bonito stock and place in a pot. Cook each vegetable separately in
another small pot until soft, except for the shiitake and watercress. Boil watercress in a small amount of water for about 45–50 seconds, remove and wash under
cold water to retain bright green color.

Place shiitake in pot with kombu/bonito stock. Simmer 10 minutes. Season
with tamari to taste. Add pre-cooked vegetables and heat for a minute or two.
Do not add watercress. Remove from flame. Place one piece of taro, carrot and
shiitake in each serving bowl and almost cover with broth. Garnish with one
sprig of watercress and serve.

Grated Daikon Soup

    5–6 cups kombu stock
    2 cups grated daikon
    1 cake tofu, cut into bite-sized pieces
    1/4 tsp. sea salt
    small amount of tamari to taste

Place kombu stock and grated daikon in a pot with a pinch of sea salt. Bring to a boil, cover, reduce flame to low and simmer 10 minutes. Add tofu and tamari to taste. Simmer 3–4 minutes. Place in serving bowls. Garnish with scallions and serve.

Cream of Mushroom Soup

    1/2 lb. fresh mushrooms, washed and sliced
    5–6 cups bonito flake broth
    1 cup onion, diced
    2 Tbsp. minced parsley
    1/4 cup celery, diced
    1/3 cup brown rice flour
    1/8 tsp. sea salt
    tamari to taste
    sesame oil

Prepare broth by placing 2 tablespoons of bonito flakes in water. Bring to a boil and simmer 5 minutes. Strain to remove flakes and place broth back in pot.

Lightly brush sesame oil in a skillet and heat. Lightly sauté onions, mushrooms and celery. Add flour and mix thoroughly. Gradually add broth to vegetables and mix constantly to prevent lumping. Place back in pot. Bring to a boil, reduce flame to low, add salt and cover. Simmer 10 minutes. Add tamari to taste and simmer 5 minutes. Garnish with parsley.

Cream of Celery Soup

    5–6 cups kombu stock
    2 cups celery, diced
    1 cup onion, diced
    1/3 cup brown rice flour
    1/8 tsp. sea salt
    tamari to taste

Place water, celery and onions in pot. Add a pinch of sea salt. Bring to a boil, reduce flame to low, cover and simmer 15–20 minutes.

Mix flour in a small amount of water in a cup until all flour is dissolved and there are no lumps. Slowly add to vegetables and broth, stirring constantly to prevent lumping. Add remaining sea salt and tamari to taste. Simmer another 15–20 minutes on low flame. Garnish and serve.

Carrot Soup

    5–6 cups water

3 cups grated carrot (use a fine grater)
1 cup minced onion
1/4 tsp. sea salt

Place onions and grated carrot in a pot. Add water and a pinch of sea salt. Bring to a boil, reduce flame to low, cover and simmer 20–25 minutes. Add remaining sea salt and simmer another 10–15 minutes. Garnish and serve.

FISH SOUPS

Tuna and Wakame Soup
  1–2 fillets of fresh tuna
  5–6 cups water
  1 cup wakame, soaked and sliced
  one 2–3 inch strip kombu
  3 shiitake mushrooms
  tamari to taste

Place water, kombu and shiitake in a pot and prepare broth as described previously.

Remove kombu and shiitake and save for future use. Pre-cook tuna in a small amount of water or broil until tender. Do not over-cook. (Tuna cooks very quickly.) Drain off water from cooking tuna and add to broth.

Add wakame to soup broth and bring to a boil. Reduce flame to low, cover and simmer 5 minutes or so. Add tuna and simmer 2–3 minutes. Serve.

Crab Soup
  6 pieces of crab leg (without shell), 2″–3″ long
    (lobster meat or fresh shrimp may also be used)
  5–6 cups kombu stock
  1 cake tofu, cut into 1″ cubes
  tamari to taste
  scallions

Place water and a pinch of salt in pot. Add shellfish. Bring to a boil, reduce flame to low and simmer until fish is tender. Do not overcook. Remove fish from water and set aside.

Lightly season broth with tamari. Add tofu and as the water comes to a boil again, turn off the flame. Place one piece of tofu and crabmeat in each serving bowl and pour hot broth over it. Add a teaspoon of thinly slivered scallions to each bowl and serve.

Fish Stew
  6 small pearl onions
  12 pieces of carrot, cut in irregular shapes
  3 rounds of daikon, quartered (about 1/2″ thick)
  6 scallions, cut diagonally about 2″ long
  1 lb. white meat fish (haddock, cod, etc.)

2 long strips of kombu, soaked to soften
6 cups water
kuzu to very lightly thicken
tamari to taste

Soak kombu and cut into 3″ strips. Tie each piece of kombu into a knot. (The knot should be in the center of each strip.)

Place onions, carrots, daikon, water and kombu in a pot with a pinch of sea salt. Bring to a boil, reduce flame to low, cover and simmer until vegetables are soft. Add fish (cut into 2″ pieces). Simmer 1–2 minutes. Add kuzu to very lightly thicken broth. Season with tamari and simmer 2–3 minutes. Add scallion strips and simmer 1–2 minutes. Serve.

Clam Chowder
5–6 cups water or kombu stock
1 pint freshly-shelled clams
3 taro potatoes, cut into bite-sized pieces
1 carrot, diced (not too small)
1 cup diced onion
parsley
1/8 tsp. sea salt

Cut clams into small pieces. Save clam juice and add to broth water. Add onions, taro and carrot to broth. Add a pinch of sea salt. Bring to a boil, reduce flame to low, cover and simmer until vegetables are soft. Add clams and remaining salt to season if necessary. Simmer 3–4 minutes on a very low flame. Place in serving bowls and garnish with minced parsley or a sprig of parsley in each bowl.

MISO SOUPS

Miso is a fermented food made by combining soybeans with various ingredients such as rice, barley, wheat, white rice, sea salt, water, and a bacterial agent known as *koji*.

Besides being a very versatile seasoning and condiment, miso is extremely beneficial from a health point of view. It strengthens weak intestines by aiding in the production of beneficial bacteria which are necessary for proper digestion. It also helps in the discharge of toxins from the body. It is high in protein, calcium, iron and vitamin B, making it an essential food in every macrobiotic kitchen.

The miso sold in most natural food stores is especially processed from natural ingredients according to traditional methods used for centuries, and contains no chemicals or preservatives. Paradoxically, most of the miso now sold in Japan and in Oriental markets in this country is artificially fermented, the ingredients are usually not organic, and a variety of chemicals (including MSG), preservatives, and sugar are added to it. This type of miso is not beneficial to the body.

The most common types of miso sold in the United States are *mugi* (barley) miso; *genmai* (brown rice) miso; *kome* (white rice) miso; and *Hatcho* (soybean and salt) miso. There are also   number of other "quick" misos, so called because they require less time to ferment. These include yellow, *shiro* (white), and *aka* (red) miso. These are all very delicious when used in fish dishes and they can also be used in vegetable cooking. Another type of miso, known as *natto miso*, is made from soybeans and ginger and can be used occasionally as a condiment. One of the by-products of the miso-making process is called *moromi*, and this can be used as a condiment or as a seasoning.

Mugi miso is used most often by macrobiotic cooks in America and Europe. It is very suitable to this climate and can be used year-round. Hatcho is perhaps used least in this climate, since many people have the impression that it is a very yang form of miso. Actually, it is less salty than brown rice miso, but because it is fermented for over three years under heavy pressure, it still has a more yang nature. Most misos are fermented for one or two years. Brown rice miso and kome miso are generally the lightest of the misos, and are especially good in the summer, while yellow, shiro, and aka miso are a little sweeter than the others.

Due to the rising popularity of miso in this country, several varieties are now being manufactured and processed here, while a number of students from Europe and America have gone to Japan to study traditional miso making. Recently, I received a letter from two of these friends, John and Jan Bellamy, who went to Japan last year to prepare for the future establishment of a miso factory near Asheville, North Carolina. Their letter, which reveals something about the miso making process, and traditional life in rural Japan, reads as follows:

"John and I arrived in Tokyo late in October. After a few days there, we visited the Sendai Miso-Shoyu (Soy Sauce) Company and then went to Yaita (about halfway between Tokyo and Sendai) to meet our miso teacher. This experience has surpassed our wildest dreams. We are living with this family in their 300-year old grass-roofed house in a very traditional part of rural Japan. This family has been on this land for over 500 years.

The miso shop is perfect for our study. It's fairly small and very traditional-most of the work is done by hand, with the aid of just a few simple machines. The Onozakis make no compromises in terms of quality. They make a 1-1/2 year kome miso aged in huge cedar vats held together with braided bamboo. This miso, very mellow, delicious, and unpasteurized, can be eaten every day without becomming tired of it. We work alongside the Onozakis 6-1/2 days a week, so we have gotten a great deal of experience. For the whole month of March, Mr. Onozaki has put John in charge of making the *koji*, which is the most important and difficult part of making miso. He is to make all the decisions regarding temperature, seeding, and ventilation, so by the time we leave we should feel confident enough to do it on our own.

The family consists of the 78 year-old grandmother, her son and his wife, and three daughters. They are a very hard-working, thoughtful, and humble family of samurai descent. The women in the area, and Mrs. Onozaki in particular, are just unbelievable. Mrs. Onozaki does the work of three people and doesn't even know it. She (and most women around here) know everything they need to know, from childcare to gardening, cooking, pickling, natural remedies (both foods and herbs), sewing, flower-arranging, and keeping their husbands happy. I have so much to learn from her. I have never seen her angry, in fact she is usually smiling and has a great sense of humor.

Our schedule is intense. Before breakfast, I must wash our clothes in ice-cold mountain water (they have no hot running water), clean our room, and steam the rice. After a simple breakfast we begin work at 8:00. The work is hard and long and the conditions over the past 2-1/2 months have been either extreme cold or extreme heat (cold in the shop, hot in the *koji* room). After work we have dinner, wash up, and retire to our room for a few hours of studying, writing, taking notes on what we learned during the day, etc.

For the past 2 months the average morning temperature in the house has 0°C (35°F.). The only heat is provided by the *kotatsu*, or the small table with a built-in heating unit. The water in the flower pots often turns to ice during the night and they must put things in the refrigerator to keep them from freezing. Actually, though, we rarely feel cold except for our hands and feet. We also have much more energy than usual and we haven't seen as much as a "common" cold since we've been here. In fact, it's very unusual to see any of our neighbors blowing their nose.

The old people are our favorites-we love to listen to their stories. They're incredibly strong and hard-working; many working well into their 70's and even 80's. For just one of several examples, there's a 79-year old man working here now. He's doing the plaster work on the Onozaki's new storage building. Every morning he's up at 6, eats breakfast, packs a light lunch and takes off on his 10-speed for the bitter-cold 5-mile ride to work. He works out there by himself all day, every day. I could go on and on about the old folks-there's the 70 year-old barrel-maker who came to repair 3 of Mr. Onozaki's miso vats; the 69 year-old "traveling saleslady' who walks from house to house with a huge pack of wares on her back; the 85 year-old man who came bicycling up on his day off to buy some miso; the 78 year old grandmother we live with, etc., etc. They are such an inspiration to us.

We are the only foreigners living for miles around and the only Americans most of these people have ever talked to, so of course we attract a great deal of attention. Recently we have attracted the attention of the media. It all started when a local newspaper came to interview us and take our picture. This was followed by a magazine story, then Japan's leqding national newspaper, the *Asahi*, came. This resulted in one live radio interview, another magazine story and two fifteen minute TV stories on 2 national networks. All of this interest took us very much by surprise. They are mostly interested in our views on American foods as opposed to traditional foods, our ideas on Japanese tradition, and the relationship between food, health, and tradition. So, as you can see, this has been a most rewarding experience. . . ."

Miso may take a little getting used to in the beginning, but as you use it more and more you will come to love it. Through talking with many of my students and friends, and from observing the members of my family, I have found that men usually like the taste of miso more than women when first beginning macrobiotics. I think this is because women are generally more yin on the outside and more yang on the inside, and often prefer more yin or lighter types of food. Men are generally the opposite, and often desire more yang types of food. Of course, this varies from person to person.

Miso can be used in grain, vegetable, fish, and bean dishes, or in soups, pickles, condiments, spreads, sauces, breads, and candy, as medicine. Please experiment and discover some of the many uses of this wonderful food.

For further information on how to make and use miso, please refer to *How to Cook with Miso* by Aveline Kushi, published by Japan Publications, Inc.

Morning miso soup should generally not be too salty, but should be rather lightly seasoned. Because miso is so delicious, it is very easy to use too much. Since it is a more yang food item, try not to eat it in large quantities.

Basic Miso Soup

5–6 cups water
1 cup wakame, washed, soaked and sliced
1 cup onion, sliced in half moons
3 tsp. miso

Lightly wash wakame. Cover with water and soak for 3–5 minutes. Slice into small pieces.

Place onions, wakame and water in a pot. Bring to a boil, reduce flame to low, cover, and simmer until onions and wakame are soft. Reduce flame to very low so that the water does not bubble. When using miso for a medicinal purpose or in your morning soup, do not boil it as the beneficial bacteria will be destroyed by the intense heat. When using it as a seasoning in other dishes, however, you may boil the miso.

Place miso in a suribachi and add a small amount of soup broth. Purée until creamy. Add to the broth and vegetables and gently mix in. Simmer for 2 minutes and serve. Garnish with scallions, dulse, parsley, nori, etc. when appropriate.

Onion Miso Soup

5–6 cups water
one 2″ strip kombu
2 cups onion, halved and quartered
3–4 tsp. miso

Place kombu and water in a pot. Bring to a boil, reduce flame to low, cover and simmer 2–3 minutes. Remove kombu and save for future use. Add onions and simmer until onions are very soft. Reduce flame to very low and add puréed miso. Simmer 2 minutes, garnish, and serve.

Ozoni (White Miso Soup)

In Japan, *ozoni* is usually prepared on New Year's Eve and served just before midnight. It is usually prepared with white miso. Ozoni can be prepared with a variety of ingredients and misos.

- **6 cups water**
- **6 small rounds of daikon, about 1/4″ thick**
- **3 small taro potatoes, quartered**
- **12 pieces of brown rice mochi, about 2″ long**
- **3–4 Tbsp. white miso (*shiro* miso)**
- **6 sprigs watercress, boiled separately for less than a minute**

Place daikon and taro in a pot with water. Add a pinch of sea salt. Bring to a boil, reduce flame to low, cover and simmer until daikon and taro are soft. Purée miso in a suribachi with a small amount of soup broth. Reduce flame to very low so broth does not boil. Add puréed miso and mix very gently so as not to break the taro.

Place one or two pieces of pan-fried or baked mochi in each serving bowl. Add one piece of taro and daikon to each bowl and cover with broth. Place one sprig of watercress in each bowl and serve. You may also garnish with small strips of toasted nori.

Oyster Miso Soup

- **6 cups water**
- **2 cups daikon, cut into matchsticks**
- **1 cup fresh oysters, shelled and washed**
- **4 tsp. white or yellow miso**
- **6 tsp. finely grated carrot as garnish**

Place water in a pot and add oysters. Bring to a boil, reduce flame to low and simmer 5 minutes. Remove oysters and set aside. (You may chop the oysters and add them back to the soup during the final 2–3 minutes, or leave them out for use in another dish.) Add daikon. Simmer until daikon is soft. Reduce flame to very low. Purée miso and add to soup. Simmer 2–3 minutes. Place in serving bowls and garnish each with 1 teaspoon of grated carrot in the center of the bowl. Serve. This dish is very good for increasing strength and vitality.

Shiitake Miso Soup

- **6 cups water or kombu/bonito stock**
- **6 large shiitake mushrooms, soaked, destemmed and sliced**
- **1 dozen snow peas, with stems removed**
- **3–4 tsp. red miso**
- **toasted nori strips**
- **scallions**

Place kombu/bonito stock in a pot. Add shiitake, bring to a boil, reduce flame to low, cover and simmer 10 minutes. Reduce flame to very low, add snow peas and puréed miso. Simmer on a very low flame for 1–2 minutes. Place in serving bowls. Garnish each bowl with a few nori strips and scallions. Serve.

Taro Miso Soup

- **5–6 cups water**

3 taro potatoes, cut into bite-sized pieces
6 sprigs watercress, separately cooked less than one minute
1 onion, quartered
3–4 tsp. miso

Place taro, onions and water in a pot. Bring to a boil, reduce flame to low, cover and simmer until vegetables are soft. Reduce flame to very low and add puréed miso. Simmer 2 minutes. Place in serving bowls and add 1 sprig watercress to each bowl. This dish is also very good for strength and vitality.

Dulse Miso Soup

5–6 cups kombu/shiitake broth
1/3 cup dulse, soaked 2–3 minutes and sliced
1/2 cup onion, diced or sliced in half moons
3–4 tsp. miso

Place broth in a pot. Add onions and dulse. Bring to a boil, reduce flame to low, cover and simmer 10 minutes. Reduce flame to very low and add puréed miso. Simmer 2 minutes. Garnish and serve.

Natto Miso Soup

5–6 cups kombu/bonito stock
1 cup natto
scallions
3–4 tsp. miso

Prepare broth and heat up. Reduce flame to very low and add puréed miso. Simmer 2–3 minutes. Place in serving bowls and add 2 tablespoons of natto and a few sliced scallions to each bowl. Serve.

Okara Miso Soup

6 cups water or kombu stock
1–2 cups fresh okara
1/3 cup burdock, cut in matchsticks
1 onion, diced
1/2 cup carrot, cut in matchsticks
3–4 tsp. miso

Lightly sauté onions, carrots and burdock in a small amount of sesame oil. Place vegetables in a pot. Add water. Bring to a boil, reduce flame to low, cover and simmer until vegetables are soft. Add okara and simmer 2–3 minutes. Purée miso. Reduce flame to very low and add miso. Simmer 1–2 minutes. Serve.

Fu Miso Soup

5–6 cups water
2 cups fu, soaked and cut into bite-sized pieces
3 shiitake mushrooms, soaked, destemmed and sliced
1 onion, cut in half moons
1/2 cup Chinese cabbage, thinly sliced

    3–4 tsp. miso
    sesame oil

Lightly sauté onions, shiitake and cabbage. Squeeze fu to remove excess water. Add fu to vegetables and sauté lightly. Add fu and vegetables to water. Bring to a boil, reduce flame to low, cover and simmer until vegetables are soft. Purée miso. Reduce flame to very low and add miso. Simmer 2 minutes and serve.

Nori Miso Soup
    5–6 cups water
    1/2 cup sliced scallions
    1 cake tofu, cut into cubes
    2 sheets nori, toasted and cut into 1/4″ × 2″ long strips
    3–4 tsp. miso

Bring water to a boil. Add tofu and simmer 2–3 minutes. Reduce flame to very low and add puréed miso. Simmer 1–2 minutes. Turn off flame and add scallions. Place in serving bowls, garnish with nori and serve.

    This soup is very simple and quick to prepare when you are in a hurry.

Pumpkin or Squash Miso Soup
    5–6 cups water
    2 cups butternut or buttercup squash, or Hokkaido pumpkin, cubed
    1/2 cup onion, diced
    1/2 cup wakame, soaked and sliced
    3–4 tsp. miso

Place onions, squash and wakame in pot. Add water. Bring to a boil, reduce flame to low, cover and simmer until pumpkin or squash is soft. Reduce flame to very low and add puréed miso. Simmer 1–2 minutes, garnish and serve.

SOUP STOCKS

A variety of thoroughly nutritious and delicious soup stocks can be made from foods such as sea vegetables, roasted grains, vegetables, beans, noodle water, seitan water, shiitake mushrooms, fish (including boiled fish heads, bones and meat), bonito flakes, chuba, chirimen iriko (small dried fish), shellfish (including mussels, clams, and oysters), and dried vegetables, or from combinations of the above.

    Stocks such as these can really enhance the flavor of your soup and noodle dishes, and should be used whenever possible. They also provide a valuable use for various odds and ends left over from preparing other dishes.

    Always make sure that the stock you prepare is the most appropriate for the soup that you are making. If you choose the wrong stock, your soup may not taste as good as it could.

Kombu Stock (Kombu Dashi)
    5–6 cups water

one 3″ strip of kombu

If your kombu is dusty or covered with plenty of white powder (or if you wish to avoid too much salt), you may quickly wipe it off with a damp, clean sponge. Washing it under water will remove some of the valuable minerals that it contains. Add the kombu and water to a pot and bring to a boil. Simmer 2–3 minutes, remove kombu and place on a bamboo mat to dry. Save the kombu to use again in soup stock or for use in other dishes. The stock is now ready to use. If you do not have an immediate use for it, simply refrigerate it until needed.

Shiitake Mushroom Stock
5–6 cups water
4–5 shiitake

Place ingredients in pot and bring to a boil. Simmer uncovered about 5–6 minutes. Remove shiitake and dry on bamboo mat as above. Save for use in another stock or dish or as a garnish for noodles.

Kombu, Shiitake, and Bonito Flake Stock
5–6 cups water
4–5 shiitake
2 Tbsp. bonito flakes

Place kombu and shiitake in pot with water. Bring to a boil. Boil one or two minutes, remove kombu and dry as above. Save for later. Reduce flame to medium and simmer shiitake another 3–4 minutes. Remove shiitake, dry on mat as above, and save. Add bonito flakes and simmer 3–4 minutes. Turn flame off. When bonito flakes settle to the bottom of the pot, pour off the clear broth or strain through a strainer. Save bonito flakes and use again later. The stock is now ready.

Stock from Leftover Kombu, Shiitake, or Bonito Flakes
Simply prepare leftover dried out kombu, shiitake, or bonito in the same manner as above. However, boil them for a slightly longer time to get a stronger stock.

Combinations of the Above
Various stocks can be made by combining kombu, shiitake, or bonito flakes in different ways. For example, you can combine kombu and bonito, bonito and shiitake, shiitake and kombu, etc. Simply prepare as above.

Vegetable Soup Stock
Do not throw away the tops, ends, or roots of the vegetables that you cook, as you can prepare a very wonderful stock by simply boiling odds and ends such as these in 5–6 cups of water for about 5 minutes. When you have finished boiling, discard the vegetables or add them to your compost.

People often throw away things such as scallion roots and onion skins. This is not using food wisely. Scallion roots make a very delicious stock, or can be very finely chopped and added to fried rice or to soups. Onion skins can be washed before peeling the onion and used to make a stock for French onion or other soups. Vegetable stems or the cores of cabbages can also be used in this way. Be sure that these various parts are washed very thoroughly before preparing stock.

Other Seaweed Stocks

Sea vegetables such as dulse, wakame, or kelp can also be used to make soup stock. Simply prepare as above.

Dried Vegetable Stock

Root vegetables such as carrots, parsnips, turnips, rutabaga, daikon, radishes, burdock, etc., can be diced, shaved, sliced into rounds, or cut into very thin matchsticks and dried. Simply tie them on a string or string them on a piece of thread with a needle and hang them in a sunny place to dry. You may also spread them onto a bamboo mat and dry them in a warm but slightly shaded area. (They may take a little longer to dry this way.) Just make sure that they have fresh air circulating around and under them to prevent molding.

Vegetables become very sweet when dried in this manner, and make a delicious stock by boiling them as above.

While in Japan, I had the opportunity to observe daikon drying in the sun. The daikon were sliced very finely and spread evenly on a bamboo mat, so that the pieces received proper ventilation and were not too crowded. The bamboo mat was then placed outside with a bamboo curtain hanging over it. The curtain kept it out of direct sunlight but allowed just enough light to filter through.

Once the vegetables have dried completely, they may mold if place in a container.

Grain Stock

To prepare, simply roast rice, sweet rice, millet, buckwheat, barley, or any other grain until it becomes golden brown and releases a nutty fragrance. Boil for 4–5 minutes and remove grain from stock water. The grain can be used to make another stock by boiling it again for a slightly longer time.

Chirimen Iriko Stock

 5–6 cups water
 2 Tbsp. chirimen or chuba iriko

Place water and iriko in a pot and boil 3–4 minutes. Remove iriko and save for use again. The stock is ready

You may also add kombu to this stock to create a slightly different flavor. Boil the kombu 1–2 minutes, remove and save. Then boil the iriko as above and remove.

Fish Stock

If you have fresh or leftover fish heads, bones, or meat, you can prepare a soup stock by simply boiling them 3–5 minutes. Let the various pieces settle to the bottom and then drain off the clear stock.

Bean Stock
The water left over from cooking azuki beans, chickpeas, or any other bean can be saved and used as a soup stock.

Seitan Stock
The water left from cooking seitan can be diluted and used as a soup stock.

Noodle Stock
The water left over from cooking any type of noodles can also be saved and used as a soup stock.

Please refer to *Introducing Macrobiotic Cooking* for the following soup recipes: millet, rice and pumpkin, barley-lentil, split pea, kidney bean, black bean, chickpea, onion, squash, vegetable, tofu, watercress, basic miso, quick miso, watercress miso, daikon and sweet rice dumpling miso, Chinese cabbage and tofu miso, and daikon and wakame miso, along with a number of additional soup stocks.

4. Cooking with Vegetables, including Salad-Making

"Leaves of grass . . . green, simple,beautiful, natural . . . shapes endless in variety yet never strange, unfamiliar, artificial . . . . No one can duplicate this naturalness. We can analyze its parts, imitate its color or form but its vitality, its physiological and chemical activity, its power to grow—all this eludes us; human understanding cannot encompass it.

There is no factory in existence that can remove CO_2 from the air, produce its own oxygen and then change the whole thing into carbohydrate with the addition of a little sunshine. Yet this complex process simply and with little effort occurs in a blade of grass."
—George Ohsawa in *The Macrobiotic Guidebook for Living*

What is more magnificent, soothing, and refreshing than the vegetable kingdom? I never cease to marvel at this natural beauty which surrounds us. This wonderfully varied world endlessly produces fruits, nuts, berries and seeds; vegetables of all colors, sizes, shapes, tastes and textures; grasses, grains, herbs and flowers; wild vegetables like burdock, dandelion, milkweed, cattails, mugwort, Japanese knotweed and watercress; edible tubers like jinenjo, taro potato, and others. The list is almost endless.

If you observe children at play, they appear so free, happy, and comfortable when surrounded by nature. They seem very much at home when surrounded by trees, grass and forest. We all love to walk through fields and gardens or drive into the country to buy freshly picked fruits and vegetables from roadside stands or farmer's markets.

When I go shopping, the produce section almost always catches my attention before anything else in the store. From talking with our friends in the natural food business, we have heard that the success of any natural food store depends largely on the appearance and selection of produce. Vegetables and fruits add beauty and life to the store, and this naturally attracts customers.

The best fruits and vegetables for daily use are those which have been organically or naturally grown without chemical fertilizers, pesticides, herbicides, artificial additives, preservatives or processing of any kind other than natural methods such as sun drying, pickling, etc. Of course, it may not be possible to have organic produce daily, but you should try to buy it whenever you can. It will improve your health tremendously. As you continue to eat macrobiotically, you will begin to notice a tremendous difference in taste between organic and non-organic produce. I have found non-organic produce to be much less sweet, and the flavor of certain vegetables is often not as distinct. Also, you can often taste the chemicals in and on the skin of non-organic vegetables and fruits. One bonus that you receive from eating organic produce is that the skin is edible because it is not sprayed or waxed. Thus you receive added vitamins and minerals from your vegetables and fruits.

While in Japan, I had the opportunity to visit several very large, organic farms where no chemical or animal fertilizers of any kind were used in the soil. Instead, the farmers gathered leaves and grasses from the surrounding mountains and fields and spread them on the gardens for mulch. Gradually, this organic, natural mulch decayed and produced healthy soil with beneficial bacteria, enzymes, and nutrients in it. The soil was very much alive and healthy compared to the many plots of chemically fertilized land throughout Japan. At one farm about seventy miles west of Kyoto, I was shown a jar of organically grown rice which had been in storage for six years. It looked and smelled just like freshly harvested rice. I was then shown a jar of chemicalized rice which had been stored for the same amount of time. It was completely black in color, had a very bad odor, and was almost totally decomposed.

Several of the farmers also showed me how to distinguish whether a particular vegetable or piece of fruit was naturally grown (which means without animal-quality or chemicalized fertilizers), organically grown with animal fertilizers, or chemically grown. Naturally grown vegetables are generally very well balanced in size and shape, and are pleasant to look at. For example, naturally grown leafy greens have leaves that are generally all of the same height and size, and the core of the vegetable is located directly in the center. For example, when you cut a cabbage in half, you will find that it has a core at its base that extends up into the head. If the cabbage has been naturally grown, the core will be directly in the center, while the core of a chemically fertilized cabbage will sharply curve to one side. Cabbage grown with animal fertilizer will also have a slightly off-center core. The same is true for carrots and daikon. In these vegetables, the center ring or core is located directly in the center with natural mulch, extremely off-center with chemical fertilizer, and slightly off when grown with animal fertilizers. In the case of *mikan*, the small tangerines which grow throughout Japan, the sections of naturally grown mikan come together at the very center of the fruit, while the sections of chemically grown mikan come together far off-center. The sections of mikan grown organically but with animal fertilizers come together slightly off-center.

As with many neighborhoods throughout Japan, there were several organic "community gardens" not far from our house in Kyoto. An old farmer planted and cared for the vegetables, and rented several rows to each neighbor. The neighbors would only have to go and pick their vegetables whenever they needed them, which was often daily. It would be wonderful to have community gardens like this in America, as many people live in apartments or cities where there is little available space. Freshly-picked vegetables are so much more delicious than those which have been sitting on the shelf for several days.

Whenever possible, try to buy your greens daily. You can store them in a cool place, or refrigerate them when necessary. It is also best to buy locally grown produce. Of course, this is often not possible in the winter, so we in the North must often rely on produce from the Western or Southern states during this season. However, many ground and root vegetables, including onions, carrots, cabbage, squash, pumpkin, turnips, rutabaga, and others can be naturally stored in a cool place during the winter months. There are many books available on the subject of storing vegetables during the winter, and I suggest that you study these if you wish to learn more about this subject.

When selecting produce, try to buy the freshest items with the most brightly colored leaves and skin. Your vegetables should be crisp. Vegetables that have a dull color or that are limp and soft will spoil easily and must be used quickly. They are also less tasty. If you refrigerate your greens, it is best to keep them in paper bags. The paper will absorb moisture and thus reduce the chances of molding or softening. Plastic bags gather moisture and vegetables cannot breathe in them, thus causing early spoiling. No vegetable should be left in the refrigerator for too long, as it will eventually spoil.

The use of canned and frozen vegetables should be avoided. Once a vegetable has been picked and partially or totally cooked, it begins to lose its life energy. Many varieties of canned and frozen produce contain salt and preservatives which should also be avoided.

Naturally dried or pickled vegetables are fine for regular use. These include shiitake, daikon, lotus root, and dried fruit. These items are sun-dried, oven-dried or dried on racks in a natural manner.

Use a vegetable brush to clean your vegetables. They are sold in most natural food stores. Scrub your root vegetables gently, but firmly, so as not to remove the skin. Once the soil has been removed, rinse them under cold water. (They should not be washed under warm water.) Leafy greens can be simply washed under cold water without scrubbing. Organic vegetables usually have much soil left on them. Leave it on until you are ready to use the vegetable, as it will help to keep it fresher. Vegetables tend to become limp more quickly after they have been washed.

Always try to balance the sizes, shapes, colors and tastes of the vegetables and other ingredients that you use in cooking. For instance, suppose you prepare a soup with millet, a very small, yellow grain. Almost any vegetable will complement it in color, while it may be more appealing to the sight if the vegetables are cut into small pieces by dicing or quartering them. Since millet is a more yang grain, it often goes well with more yin vegetables such as celery, onions, cauliflower and scallions. You may use a small amount of yang vegetables with it, such as carrots or burdock, but the taste of these vegetables should not dominate the soup. Larger cuts can be used more often in stews or baked vegetable dishes. Try not to use too wide a variety of cutting methods in any one dish, and keep the size of the vegetables as uniform as possible. Otherwise, the smaller and thinner pieces will cook faster than the thicker and larger ones.[1]

There are a number of cooking methods that can be used to add variety to your meals, so try to use as many of them as possible. Don't stick with any one style or method of cooking. Occasionally vary the ingredients and methods of preparing your favorite dishes so that your meals reflect variety and change.

Garnishes are very important, as they stimulate the various tastes and add variety and color to meals. Some of the many garnishes which can be used occasionally include scallions, chives, raw onion, parsley, grated daikon and carrot, roasted or deep-fried bread cubes, watercress, various seaweeds, finely chopped green vegetables, roasted sesame or sunflower seeds, ginger, shiitake, fried tofu (on noodles), celery leaves, dill, slices of lemon, orange and grapefruit, roasted seeds, wasabi, horseradish, bonito flakes, dried fish, fresh mushrooms and others.

There are a number of cooking methods which can be used on a regular basis. Some should be used more often than others. For instance, we should generally avoid eating tempuraed or deep-fried foods on a daily basis. If eaten too frequently, these foods can cause skin, kidney or intestinal problems due to the amount of oil that they contain. The most frequently used cooking methods include sautéing, boiling, steaming, baking, pressure-cooking, broiling, Wok cooking and deep-frying (tempura). Some of these are more yang while others are more yin. Boiling and steaming are generally more yin, while the others are generally more yang. However, we can vary the degree of yin or yang within each method by adjusting our ingredients, cooking time, amount of salt, seasoning, pressure, oil, water and other factors. *Nabe* cooking and *sukiyaki* can also be used, and I will explain these in more detail later in this chapter.

SAUTÉING

There are two basic methods of sautéing that are used quite frequently in macrobiotic cooking. When sautéing, be careful not to use too much oil, salt or tamari.

---

[1] Please refer to *Introducing Macrobiotic Cooking* for a thorough explanation of various cutting techniques.

Generally, our food should be cooked with very small amounts of oil. We obtain enough fat and oil from grains, beans, desserts, pastries, etc., and therefore don't need to use too much in our vegetable cooking. One tablespoon of oil used in cooking is generally enough for ten people.

In the first method, slice the vegetables in the desired manner. Lightly brush a small amount of sesame oil in a skillet and heat. Place the vegetables in the skillet, and add a small pinch of sea salt to bring out their natural sweetness. Sauté the vegetables for a short time (about 4–6 minutes) on a medium flame, and occasionally move them gently from one side of the skillet to the other with chopsticks or a wooden utensil to avoid burning and insure even cooking. Do not stir the vegetables too quickly or in a chaotic manner, as this will affect the vibration of the food. Reduce the flame to low and cover when necessary. Not all foods need to be covered when sautéing. For instance, Chinese cabbage is more watery and yin. It cooks very quickly and does not always need to be covered. More yang vegetables such as carrots, turnips, regular cabbage, burdock, etc. which are harder, less watery and take more time to cook, often need to be covered. Sauté for another 10 minutes or until the vegetables are almost done. The necessary cooking time will differ slightly with each vegetable and will also depend on how thick, thin, large or small you slice them. Gently mix the vegetables from time to time to avoid burning and insure even cooking. Season to taste with sea salt, tamari or miso during the final 3–7 minutes and place in a serving bowl.

The second method requires the use of water as well as oil. Cut the vegetables into the desired size. Lightly oil the skillet as described above and heat. Place vegetables and a pinch of sea salt in the hot skillet. Sauté over a medium flame for 3–5 minutes, mixing occasionally. Then add enough cold water to lightly cover the bottom of the skillet. Cover the skillet, reduce the flame to low and cook until the vegetables are about 80% done. Add sea salt, tamari, puréed miso or other seasoning, cover and cook 3–4 minutes. Remove cover and cook away the excess liquid. Place in a serving bowl.

Carrot and Turnip Kinpira

    1 cup turnips, cut into matchsticks
    2 cups carrots, cut into matchsticks
    sesame oil
    pinch of sea salt
    1/8 cup roasted sesame seeds (black or white seeds are fine)
    tamari to taste

Lightly brush oil in a skillet and heat. Place carrots and turnips in skillet with a pinch of sea salt. Sauté 2–3 minutes. Add water to lightly cover bottom of skillet. Cover and cook until vegetables are about 80% done. Add tamari to taste, cover, and cook 2–3 minutes. Remove cover and cook off excess liquid. Mix in sesame seeds and place in serving bowl.

Sautéed Carrot Greens

    1 bunch fresh carrot greens (tops)

1/3 cup toasted sesame seeds
pinch of sea salt
sesame oil
tamari to taste

Wash carrot greens and chop very finely. Lightly brush skillet with sesame oil and heat. Place greens in skillet with a small pinch of sea salt. Sauté on medium flame for 2–3 minutes. Mix occasionally to avoid burning. Reduce flame to low, cover and sauté for 3–4 minutes. Stir occasionally. Remove greens and place in a bowl.

Wash sesame seeds and roast in a dry skillet as you would in making gomashio. Place seeds in a suribachi and grind as for gomashio. Add a small amount of tamari and mix.

Mix carrot greens together with ground seeds and place in a serving bowl.

This is a very delicious way to prepare carrot greens, as the sautéing and mixing with the seeds and tamari helps to cancel their somewhat bitter flavor. Miso can also be used instead of sesame seeds and tamari. Carrot tops are also very delicious when tempuraed.

Sautéed Mustard Greens and Daikon

1 bunch of mustard greens
1-1/2 cups of daikon, cut into thin rectangular shapes
pinch of sea salt
water
tamari to taste
sesame oil
roasted sesame seeds

Thoroughly wash mustard greens and daikon. Cut daikon into rounds and slice each round into thin rectangles. Lightly brush sesame oil in a skillet and heat. Add daikon and a pinch of sea salt. Sauté for 2–3 minutes on a medium flame, stirring occasionally. Add water as described, cover, reduce flame to low and sauté until daikon is almost done. Stir occasionally.

Slice mustard greens diagonally into 1-inch pieces, and place on top of the daikon. Add a few drops of tamari, cover and cook for 2–3 minutes. Remove cover and mix greens with daikon. Cook off excess liquid and place in a serving bowl.

Roasted whole sesame seeds may be added to this dish. Simply mix in before placing in a serving bowl.

Sautéed Lotus Root

1 lotus root section
sesame oil
tamari or sea salt to taste

Wash lotus root very thoroughly, as it often has heavy soil caked to it. Slice off both ends of the section and discard. Cut the remainder into thin rounds or dice. Sauté using method number one described previously. You do not need to add water, as lotus root is already quite watery. When the root is almost done, season with tamari or sea salt and cook until finished. Place in serving bowl.

Sautéed Jinenjo and Onions
2 cups jinenjo, diced
1 onion, diced
pinch of sea salt
sesame oil
tamari to taste or sea salt

Lightly brush skillet with sesame oil. Heat and add onions. Sauté on a medium flame, stirring occasionally until onions become translucent. Add jinenjo and a pinch of sea salt. Cover and reduce flame to low. Sauté until jinenjo is almost done. Add tamari or sea salt to taste and cover. Continue to cook until jinenjo is soft. Stir occasionally. Place in a serving bowl.

Shiitake and Snow Peas
1 lb. snow peas (remove hard stem that runs along the spine of each pod)
5–6 medium shiitake, soaked, destemmed and thinly sliced
sesame oil
tamari to taste

Lightly oil a skillet and heat. Add shiitake, cover and reduce flame to low. Stir occasionally. Sauté 3–4 minutes. Add snow peas and seasoning. Cover and cook for 2–3 minutes until peas are done. The peas should be bright green and slightly crisp so do not overcook. Mix together with mushrooms and serve.

Escarole and Fresh Mushrooms
1 cup fresh mushrooms, washed and thinly sliced
1 bunch escarole
tamari to taste (very little)
sesame oil

Wash escarole and slice into 1-inch pieces. Lightly oil a skillet and heat. Add mushrooms, cover and sauté for 3–4 minutes. Add escarole and tamari to taste. Cover, reduce flame to low and sauté until escarole is done. Do not overcook. The escarole should have a bright green color.

Green Beans and Almonds
3 cups green beans
1/3 cup slivered almonds
tamari to taste
sesame oil

Wash green beans and remove stems. Slice diagonally into thin pieces. Lightly oil a skillet and heat. Add beans and sauté over a medium flame for 2–3 minutes. Add a pinch of sea salt. Add enough water to lightly cover the bottom of the skillet, cover and reduce flame to low. Sauté until beans are about 80% done. Season lightly with tamari to taste and cook until done. (Beans should be bright green.) Mix in almond slices and sauté 1 or 2 minutes more. Place in a serving bowl.

Sautéed Cucumbers and Miso
> **3 cucumbers, quartered and sliced diagonally into half-inch pieces**
> **sesame oil**
> **1 Tbsp. puréed miso**

Lightly oil skillet and heat. Add cucumbers, cover and sauté 2–3 minutes. Add puréed miso, reduce flame to low, cover and sauté until cucumbers are done. Place in serving bowl.

Sautéed Cabbage and Black Sesame Seeds
> **1/2 cabbage, cut into one-inch pieces**
> **1/8 cup black sesame seeds**
> **sea salt to taste (very little is needed)**
> **sesame oil**

Sauté using either method. Add sesame seeds during the last 2 minutes. Place in a serving bowl.

Chinese Style Vegetables
> **1-1/2 cups Chinese cabbage, sliced diagonally**
> **1 stalk celery, sliced diagonally (thin)**
> **1 cup mung bean sprouts**
> **1/4 cup sliced shiitake mushrooms**
> **1/2 cup diced lotus root**
> **1 small onion, diced**
> **sesame oil**
> **pinch of sea salt**
> **tamari to taste**
> **3 cups water**
> **1/4 cup kuzu, dissolved in 1 Tbsp. water**

Lightly oil skillet and heat. Add onions, lotus root, and shiitake. Cover and sauté until onions are translucent. Add celery and sauté 3–4 minutes. Add sprouts, cabbage and water. Bring to a boil, reduce flame to low and stir in diluted kuzu and tamari. Cover and cook 2–3 minutes. Place in serving bowl. This dish is delicious when served with deep-fried or freshly cooked udon or somen, or by itself.

BOILING

Boiling your vegetables on a daily basis is very important. Try to include at least one dish every day that is prepared with this method. Because it uses water, and since most greens require a very short cooking time, it supplies us with a very good quality of yin (including vitamin C) in our diet. If a person has an overly yang condition, boiled vegetables are very helpful in restoring balance. Boiled vegetables are also excellent for children. Too many heavily cooked vegetables may cause children to become too yang, while excessive oil may cause intestinal or leg problems.

Generally, your vegetables should be slightly crisp after being boiled or steamed. Greens should not be soft and overcooked, while root vegetables can be cooked a little longer until soft. For young children, you may cook greens until they are a little softer than usual so that they can be properly chewed.

Also, you should not cover a hot dish of greens even with a bamboo mat, as this causes the heat to remain in the vegetables and they will continue to cook for a short time. This will result in dull colored greens or greens that are too soft. Root vegetables can be covered, as they do not lose their color as quickly as green vegetables.

There are many ways to prepare boiled vegetables so that they are both delicious and beautiful. The standard way is to place a small amount of water in a saucepan or pot. Bring to water to a boil, and add the vegetables with a small amount of sea salt. Reduce the flame to low and simmer until the vegetables are done. I will discuss several of the other ways in the following recipes.

Broccoli and Cauliflower

> **1 medium-sized bunch of broccoli**
> **1 small head of cauliflower**
> **1/8 tsp. sea salt**
> **water**

Wash the broccoli and cauliflower. Remove the base of the cauliflower and separate flowerettes from stem. If flowerettes are large, cut in half. Remove the large, thick stem from the broccoli and separate the flowerettes from the stem. Slice in half if necessary. If the califlower and broccoli leaves are fresh and green, slice them into thin slices. If not, save for use in soup stock. Slice the broccoli stem diagonally into thin rounds or half-moon shapes. If the remaing stems are too hard, they can be used in making soup stocks.

Place a small amount of water in a pan (enough to cover bottom with half an inch). Add the cauliflower and half of the above sea salt. Cover and bring to a boil. Reduce flame to low and simmer until cauliflower is done. Remove and place in the center of a serving bowl. Place broccoli in the same water used for cooking the cauliflower. Add remaining salt, cover and bring to a boil. Reduce flame to low and simmer until broccoli is done. (It should be slightly crisp and bright green in color.) Remove broccoli and arrange along with cauliflower.

This dish is especially attractive when the cauliflower is placed in the center of the bowl and the broccoli is arranged in a ring around the outside.

You may occasionally serve with a miso-lemon or miso-*tahini* sauce.

Boiled Cabbage, Sweet Corn, and Tofu

> **1 onion, diced**
> **2 ears fresh sweet corn, with kernels removed**
> **1 cake fresh tofu, cut into small cubes**

2 cups Chinese cabbage (or regular cabbage), cut into squares
pinch of sea salt
2–3 drops of tamari

Layer onions and corn in a pot with the onions on the bottom and corn on top. Add enough water to cover the bottom of the pot. Add a pinch of sea salt and bring to a boil. Cover and reduce flame to low. Simmer 4–5 minutes. Add tofu and Chinese cabbage. (If you use regular cabbage, you may add it on top of the corn at the beginning.) Add a couple of drops of tamari, cover and cook until cabbage is done. (This takes only a couple of minutes or so.) Mix vegetables and place in a serving bowl.

Mixed Vegetables

1 medium onion, diced
2 carrots, diced
1 cup fresh green peas
1/2 cup deep-fried tofu strips, diced
pinch of sea salt
2–3 drops tamari

Layer the vegetables in a pot as follows: onions on the bottom, then tofu, green peas, and carrots. Add enough water to cover the bottom of the pot and a pinch of sea salt. Bring to a boil, cover and reduce flame to low. Simmer until peas and carrots are tender. Add a very small amount of tamari and cook 2–3 minutes more. Place in a serving dish.

You may omit the fried tofu if you wish to reduce your intake of oil.

Stuffed Chinese Cabbage Rolls

15 Chinese cabbage leaves
1/2 onion, diced
1/2 stalk celery, diced or minced
1 carrot, finely diced
1/2 cup cooked rice
1 cup cooked millet
one 6″ strip of kombu
tamari
water

Boil cabbage leaves for 2–3 minutes in water with a pinch of sea salt. Remove leaves and rinse under cold water. (Save boiling water for use as soup stock.) Slice off part of the hard base of the cabbage leaves.

Place rice, millet, onion, carrot, and celery in a bowl and mix well. Add a small amount of water to hold together. Add a little tamari. Shape the grain and vegetable mixture into oblong rounds. Roll the stuffing up inside the cabbage leaves and fasten with a toothpick or dried gourd strip.

Place a 6″ strip of kombu in a skillet or pot and place cabbage rolls on top. Add enough water to cover the bottom of the skillet. Add a few drops of tamari, bring to a boil, cover and reduce flame to low. Simmer 15–20 minutes. Arrange rolls on a plate or platter and serve.

You may add pieces of diced seitan to the stuffing or serve with a very light kuzu sauce over each roll, using the kombu cooking water as a base for the sauce.

Creamed Carrots and Onions

> **2 cups diced carrot**
> **1 cup diced onion**
> **1/2 cup fresh peas (optional)**
> **corn oil**
> **sea salt to taste**
> **2 cups water or kombu stock**
> **1/3–1/2 cup rice flour**

Lightly brush oil in a skillet and heat. Add onions and a pinch of sea salt. Sauté, stirring occasionally until onions are translucent. Add carrots and peas. Sauté 2–3 minutes over medium flame. Reduce flame to low, cover and sauté until carrots and peas are about 80% done. Add rice flour, stirring constantly to mix evenly with vegetables. Sauté 2 minutes. Gradually add water and stir constantly to prevent lumping. Bring to a boil. Place a flame-deflector under pot to prevent burning. Reduce flame to low, cover and simmer 15–20 minutes. Stir occasionally. Season to taste with sea salt and cook 5–10 minutes more. Place in serving bowl. Garnish with chopped parsley.

This method can be used to make creamed onions, celery, broccoli, cauliflower, etc. You can also use different soup stocks to create a variety of flavors.

Boiled Daikon

> **1 medium-sized daikon**
> **one 3″ strip of kombu**
> **water**
> **pinch of sea salt**
> **tamari to taste**

Wash daikon and slice into 1/4-inch thick rounds. Place kombu in bottom of a pot and add daikon. Add a pinch of sea salt and enough water to cover half the daikon. Bring to a boil, cover and reduce flame to low. Simmer 20–25 minutes. Add a small amount of tamari, cover and simmer another 15–20 minutes. The daikon should be very sweet and soft, and should not taste salty. Slice kombu into half-inch squares and mix in with daikon. Place in a serving bowl.

This dish is very delicious if you add sake lees to it. Simply purée a small amount of lees with water and add during the final 30 minutes.

Boiled Watercress

> **2 bunches of watercress**
> **pinch of sea salt**
> **1 cup water**

Wash the watercress thoroughly under cold water. Since watercress grows on the banks of pond and streams, there are often baby eels and snails attached to it.

Place water in a saucepan with a pinch of sea salt and bring to a boil. Place about one-fourth of the watercress in the pot and cover. Boil less than one minute on a medium flame. Remove immediately from water, place in a colander and rinse under cold water to stop the cooking process. This rinsing will keep the watercress bright green. Then place another fourth of the watercress in the same water. Cover, cook as above and rinse. Repeat until all watercress has been cooked. Arrange on a plate as is or first slice into 1-inch pieces.

This rinsing process can also be used with Chinese cabbage, Swiss chard, bok choy and other greens to stop the cooking process and keep their color very bright.

Swiss Chard Rolls
    10–12 medium to large Swiss chard leaves
    2 carrots, quartered lengthwise
    pinch of sea salt
    water

Place about an inch of water in a cooking pot with a pinch of sea salt and bring to a boil. Add the carrot strips, cover, reduce flame to low and simmer until done. (They should be slightly crisp; not soft.) Remove, rinse under cold water and set aside. Place Swiss chard leaves in same water, cover and simmer 2–3 minutes. Remove and rinse under cold water. Squeeze excess water out of leaves. Cut off the white stem and save. Spread a leaf flat on a cutting board. Then place another leaf on top so that the bases point in opposite directions. Now you will have a double thickness of leaves. Place carrot strips (one or two per roll) lengthwise along the long edge of the leaves. Roll the carrot inside the leaves, similar to nori-maki, pressing firmly to produce a compact log or roll shape. Slice each roll in half and slice each half into equal sized rounds of approximately 1–1-1/2 inches in length. Arrange on a platter standing on end so that the carrot shows on top. The rounds look very attractive with the orange carrot center surrounded by the green chard.

Repeat above until all leaves and carrots are used up.

Chinese cabbage, bok choy or other large, leafy green vegetables can also be used instead of Swiss chard.

The white stems from the Swiss chard leaves can be sliced diagonally into thin pieces and placed in a serving bowl or saved for soup or soup stock.

NABE

While in Japan I learned of the wonderful art of *nabe* cooking. A nabe is a ceramic casserole dish, usually very attractively painted, that is used to heat vegetables. Usually the ingredients which go into nabe are pre-cooked and attractively arranged on a platter and placed on the dining table. Meanwhile, a light tamari, miso or kuzu broth is placed in the nabe, and everyone sits around the table and chooses something that he or she wishes to place in the broth. Once the ingredients are in the nabe, it is heated up.[2] The ingredients are then served on plates along with a bowl of broth as a dip.

This is a wonderful way to bring family and friends together for dinner, or for small, informal get-togethers or parties. It can be a lot of fun.

You may be able to purchase a nabe in an Oriental food or department store. If not, an attractive enameled, overn-proof or cast iron casserole dish can be used on the hot plate.

Nabe is a one-dish meal with many ingredients usually served along with rice, a sautéed vegetable, and pickles.

Udon-Vegetable Nabe
    1 package udon or somen
    1 bunch watercress
    1 cake of tofu
    10–12 slices of deep-fried tofu
    6–8 diagonally sliced carrots
    6–8 rounds of daikon
    6 scallions, sliced daigonally into 2″ strips
    10–12 pieces of pre-cooked seitan
    4–5 Chinese cabbage leaves, sliced diagonally into 1/2″ strips
    one 3″ strip of kombu
    tamari to taste

Cook udon or somen, rinse and set aside. Place 5–6 cups of water in a cooking pot with a small amount of sea salt and bring to a boil. (This water should be used to boil all of the ingredients and will serve as the nabe broth.) Place the Chinese cabbage leaves in the water and cook until done. Rinse under cold water and drain. Next, boil the tofu. Then boil the carrots and rinse. Boil the daikon next, and rinse and drain when done. Then boil the watercress for 1 minute and rinse and drain. Then deep-fry the tofu and drain. Arrange all of the above ingredients very attractively on a large platter so that the colors are balanced. The seitan does not have to be cooked again, while the scallions take only a minute or so and can be cooked at the table.

Place the kombu in the cooking water and boil 2–3 minutes. Remove and save for later use. Season the broth lightly to taste with tamari and simmer for about 5 minutes.

Next plug in the hot plate and transfer the broth into an attractive cooking pot or casserole dish and place on top of the hot plate to heat up.

Each person should have a plate, bowl, and chopsticks in front of them. Dip the individual vegetables and udon into the broth and heat. Then, each person transfers their portion to their plate and dipping bowl. You can ladle a small amount of the broth into each bowl for dipping the vegetables and noodles. The

---

[2] In Japan, many dining tables have heating or cooking units built into them. In this country, you may have to use a hot plate to heat the broth and vegetables.

remaining broth can be eaten as a soup with a few sliced scallions served in it.

You may use any ingredients you wish in preparing nabe. Seafood and shellfish can be used, as well as various noodles and vegetables. The broth can also be seasoned with miso, sea salt, or sake.

SUKIYAKI

Sukiyaki is another wonderful Japanese dish that is usually prepared in a cast iron skillet. It may be prepared at the table or in the kitchen prior to serving. Sukiyaki usually contains many different ingredients which are attractively arranged and seasoned with a broth made from kombu stock, tamari, *mirin* (sweet cooking sake), or a small amount of regular sake. The ingredients are then cooked in the broth and served with a dip sauce. You can prepare an all-vegetable sukiyaki or a seafood and vegetable, noodle and vegetable, or noodle, seafood, and vegetable sukiyaki.

Vegetables which require a longer time to cook should be placed in the skillet first and cooked until they are almost done, while those which require shorter time should be added toward the end. Sukiyaki can be served hot from the kitchen stove or placed on a hot plate at the table to keep the ingredients warm. Each person can then eat from the skillet as they would for nabe.

Udon and Seafood Sukiyaki
>   1 package of udon, cooked, rinsed and drained
>   6–7 cups kombu or kombu-shiitake broth, seasoned with tamari to taste or
>   with 1 Tbsp. sake or mirin if desired
>   1/4 lb. scallops
>   1 dozen clams, left in shells (scrubbed to remove sand)
>   10–12 medium or large shrimp, shelled and deveined
>   1 bunch of watercress, washed
>   8–10 large shittake, soaked 10–15 minutes, destemmed and sliced thick
>   6 scallions, sliced diagonally into 1-1/2″–2″ lengths
>   1 Chinese cabbage with base removed, sliced into 1-1/2″ pieces

Place broth in a large, cast iron skillet. Arrange all ingredients very attractively in the skillet and simmer on the kitchen stove for about 5–7 minutes. Transfer to the dining table and serve.

If you wish to cook at the table, place the hot broth in the skillet and set on a hot plate. Arrange udon on one platter, the seafood on another, and the vegetables on a third, along with a few lemon wedges for use with the fish. Place a portion of the ingredients in the skillet and cook 5–7 minutes. Everyone can then help themselves to the portion that they wish to eat. Gradually add the remaining ingredients and cook as above until they are used up.

The broth can be ladled into individual bowls (only a small amount, as you will need the rest for cooking) for use as a dip sauce.

Tofu and tofu products can also be used in this dish.

STEAMING

Steamed vegetables are also an important part of the macrobiotic way of eating, and should be included regularly in the diet.

There are several types of steamers available which can be used to prepare vegetables. One type is made of stainless steel and is expandable, and can be folded or contracted to fit just about any size pot or saucepan. It is available at most stores with a kitchen or household section, as well as in natural food stores. The second type is from Japan or China and is made of bamboo which is tied together to form a round steamer. It usually comes with two or three separate steaming sections and a cover. The sections can be stacked or used individually. Place the steamer on top of a pot to use. Another type which I have used is made of glazed clay. It is round and has a hollow cone in the center to allow steam to enter. It should also be placed on top of a pot to use. If you do not have a steamer, a small colander will do. Simply set it down inside the pot and place vegetables inside.

To steam vegetables, place about 1/4–1/2 inch of water in a pot and bring to a boil. Place the vegetables in the steamer, add a pinch of sea salt, cover and steam until done.

Steamed vegetables should not be overcooked, but should be slightly crispy. Save the vegetable water for use in soup stocks, sauces, etc.

Steamed Kale and Tofu
 1 small bunch of kale
 1 cake of tofu, cubed
 pinch of sea salt

Wash kale and slice diagonally into small pieces. If leaves are very wide, first slice them lengthwise down the center and then diagonally.

Place 1/4–1/2 inch of water in pot. Place steamer in or on top of the pot. Place kale in steamer and set cubes of tofu on top. Sprinkle with a pinch of sea salt. Bring to a boil, cover and reduce flame to low. Simmer until kale is done. It should be slightly crisp and bright green. If you steam it for too long, it becomes a dull green color. Place in a serving bowl and mix tofu in with kale.

Steamed Hokkaido Pumpkin
 1 medium Hokkaido pumpkin
 pinch of sea salt

Wash pumpkin and cut in half. Remove seeds and hard stem. Then cut into wedges about 1 inch thick. Cut each wedge in half. Place in a steamer with a pinch of sea salt. Cook as above.

The pumpkin will take about 10–12 minutes to steam. Poke with a chopstick to test whether it is done.

Place attractively in a serving bowl.

BAKING

Baked vegetables are more appropriate during the fall and winter months. Baking is a more yang cooking method, and usually involves the use of root and ground vegetables instead of greens.

Vegetables can be baked with or without oil. You can also add kombu to them for a different flavor. Sea salt, tamari or occasionally miso can be used as seasonings. Root vegetables such as carrots and burdock can also be rolled in pastry dough and baked.

Baked Squash

Fall or winter squashes such as Hokkaido pumpkin, buttercup, acorn, butternut, blue, green or red Hubbard and Turbin squash are all delicious when baked. First wash and then cut them in half. Clean out the seeds and save. (They can be roasted as I will explain later.) Oil a baking dish or cookie sheet with a little sesame oil and rub a very small amount of the oil on the skin of the squash to keep it from splitting. (One or two drops should be enough.) Then, rub a pinch of salt on the inside of the squash or add a little tamari about 75% of the way through cooking. Place the squash upside down on the baking dish with the skin up and hollow part facing down. This will help to retain moisture, thus shortening the cooking time and preventing the squash from drying out too soon. Bake at 375°–400° F. for about 45–60 minutes, depending on the type and thickness of the squash used. When the squash is just about done, turn it over, allowing the inside moisture to evaporate and the squash to turn slightly brown. Remove and slice. Place in a serving dish.

If the squash is not organic and the skin is waxed, bake as above, however, when the squash is done, scrape the pulp out of the shell and place it in a serving bowl. Discard the skin.

Halved squash can be stuffed with seitan, bread cubes or different grains and vegetables and then baked. Whole squash can be similarly baked, as I will describe later.

Summer squash can also be halved and baked, but requires only about 25–35 minutes cooking time.

Stuffed Acorn Squash

    1 acorn squash, washed, halved and seeds removed
    1 cup cooked millet
    1 small onion, diced
    4–5 fresh mushrooms, diced
    1/2 stalk celery, diced
    1/4 carrot, chopped fine or minced
    water
    tamari or sea salt

Mix millet and vegetables thoroughly. (Add just enough water to moisten along with a little tamari or sea salt.) Place the millet and vegetable mixture into each hollow of the squash. Fill to the top.

Place squash in a baking dish and cover, or cover the top of the dish with aluminum foil. (Place squash on an oiled cookie sheet if using foil. This will keep the moisture in while baking.)

Bake at 375°–400° F. for 35–40 minutes. Remove cover or foil and bake another 10 minutes or so to brown and allow moisture to evaporate.

Place in serving dish or platter. Slice at table while serving.

Any of the other varieties of squash can be prepared in this way, while different grains such as wild rice, brown rice, cous-cous, barley and others can be used in the stuffing.

Baked Sweet Corn
6–8 ears of freshly picked sweet corn

Remove corn silk and any outer leaves that are very long. Leave all other leaves on the corn. Wash under cold water to moisten the corn husks.

Bake in 350° F. oven for about 35 minutes. Remove husks either just before serving or individually at the table.

Serve with a little umeboshi paste or plum to rub on the corn. This gives it a very delicious flavor.

The natural corn flavor and juices are held in by the husks. When boiling or steaming corn, however, some of the flavor and nutrients go into the cooking water.

Baked Pumpkin or Squash Seeds
any kind or amount of pumpkin or squash seeds
tamari

Wash the seeds and separate from pulp. Discard the pulp. Spread seeds on dry cookie sheet and put in 350° F. oven for 10 minutes or so, mixing occasionally so that they roast evenly. Bake another 5 minutes or until all moisture has evaporated from the seeds. Add a little tamari and mix well. Spread seeds out again. Bake another 3–4 minutes until tamari is dry on the seeds. Place in a bowl.

These are great for an anytime snack or at parties. Do not make them too salty, however as they will make you very thirsty. Seeds such as these contain a good balance of more yang minerals such as calcium, iron, zinc, etc. and more yin protein and fat.

Vegetable Pastry Rolls
2 carrots (preferably long and not too thick)
1 piece of burdock
2 cups whole wheat pastry flour
1/8 tsp. sea salt
1/16–1/8 cup corn oil
1/2 cup cold water

Wash carrots and burdock and cut away tops and ends. The burdock should be boiled or steamed for 3–5 minutes and allowed to cool before wrapping it in the pastry, as it takes longer to cook than carrots. (If you overbake, the crust becomes too hard.)

Mix flour and salt, add corn oil and mix in well. Gradually add water and form dough into a ball. Knead 1–2 minutes and roll out as for pie crust. Cut dough in lengthwise strips wide enough to wrap a whole vegetable. Wrap dough around whole carrots and burdock and seal ends and seams.

Place on a lightly oiled cookie sheet and bake at 350° F. until crust is golden brown. Remove and allow to cool. Slice each roll in half. Then slice each half into equal size rounds about 1–1-1/2 inches long and arrange on a platter.

Baked Root Vegetables
> **2 carrots, cut into irregular shapes**
> **1 burdock root, cut diagonally or in irregular shapes**
> **2 medium onions, halved and quartered**
> **4–5 taro potatoes, halved (or quartered if large)**
> **one 3″ strip kombu**
> **1/2–3/4 cup water**
> **pinch of sea salt**
> **sesame oil (optional)**

Wash vegetables and cut as directed. Lightly oil a casserole dish and place kombu in bottom. (You may omit the oil if you wish.) Place vegetables on top of kombu, keeping each type separate or in its own space in the dish. Add water and a pinch of sea salt. Cover and bake at 350°–375° F. for 35–45 minutes or until done. Remove cover during the last 5 minutes or so to brown slightly.

The juice can be saved for soup stock.

Vegetables such as turnips, squash, rutabaga, cabbage, daikon, Brussels sprouts, jinenjo, lotus root, mushrooms, corn and others can be used in this recipe. Tiny carrots, taro or small onions can be baked whole rather than sliced.

PRESSURE-COOKING

Pressure-cooking is used mostly for grains and beans and is not often used for vegetables, as most of them require a relatively short cooking time. But if you are in a hurry to prepare a meal, pressure-cooking may be practical, especially for squash, root vegetables, sweet corn, broccoli, Brussels sprouts and other ground vegetables.

Pressure-cooked vegetables are very sweet and delicious, as none of their juices and nutrients can escape during cooking. The leftover cooking water also makes a very good soup stock. Pressure-cooking requires very little water, a lower flame and less time for cooking, while boiling and steaming require a little more water and time.[3]

---

[3] A table with the specific cooking times and water content for a variety of vegetables is included in *Introducing Macrobiotic Cooking*.

Pressure-Cooked Root Vegetables

    1 stalk burdock, sliced diagonally into 1/4" pieces
    1/2 daikon, cut into 1/4" rounds or halved
    1 lotus root section, cut into 1/4" rounds or halved
    5 shiitake, soaked, destemmed and halved or quartered
    1 12" strip kombu, soaked and sliced into 1" squares
    1 onion, quartered
    1 Tbsp. tamari
    1-1/2 cups water

Place kombu in pressure-cooker and add shiitake and onions. Place daikon on top. Then place lotus root on top of daikon and add burdock on top of that. Add water and tamari and bring to pressure. Reduce flame to low and cook 15–20 minutes. Allow pressure to come down slowly. Remove top, mix vegetables and place in a serving bowl.

This dish is very good to eat if you have a cold or are feeling weak.

Deep-fried tofu or *yuba* can also be added to this recipe.

Pressure-Cooked Hokkaido Pumpkin

    1 Hokkaido pumpkin, washed, halved, seeds removed and cut into 1"–1-1/2" slices
    water
    pinch of sea salt

Place pumpkin in pressure-cooker with a pinch of sea salt. Add enogh water to cover the bottom of pressure-cooker. Place top on and bring to pressure. Reduce flame to low and pressure-cook 3–4 minutes. Allow pressure to come down. Remove top and place squash in a serving bowl.

BROILING

Broiling is used mainly when preparing fish or tofu dishes, but can be used occasionally for vegetables or when making shish-kebab. When you broil vegetables, you will usually need to prepare a sauce to baste them with. This keeps the vegetables moist and prevents them from burning or drying out too quickly. When making shish-kebab, we usually broil with quicker cooking vegetables, such as onions, shiitake, scallions, fresh mushrooms, broccoli, Brussels sprouts, etc., while tofu, seitan, shrimp and other types of fish can be included with the vegetables.

Shish-Kebabs

    5–6 medium to large shrimp or scallops
    5–6 shiitake or fresh mushrooms (if using shiitake, first soak and destem)
    5–6 cubes tofu (about 1"–1-1/2" square)
    5–6 slices of scallion (about 1-1/2" long) or small, white onions
    5–6 broccoli flowerettes
    5–6 slices carrot, cut diagonally or in irregular shapes (boil for one minute
      before skewering)
    basting sauce

If using shrimp, remove shells, devein and leave tails attached. Place one piece of each of the above items attractively on a metal or bamboo skewer.

Basting Sauce No. 1
    1/2 cup tamari
    1/4 cup yinnie syrup
    1 tsp. arrowroot
    1/4 tsp. grated ginger
    a little water if necessary

Bring all ingredients to a boil, reduce flame to low and simmer 3–4 minutes.

Basting Sauce No. 2
    1/4 cup tamari
    1/4 cup water or sake
    1 Tbsp. yinnie syrup
    1 tsp. grated onion
    1/2 tsp. chopped or minced parsley
    1/2 tsp. lemon juice

Mix ingredients and let sit for 15–20 minutes.

Baste each shish-kebab with either of the above sauces. Place under broiler for 1–2 minutes, baste again and turn over. Broil until done, basting when necessary. Serve one shish-kebab to each person.

WOK COOKING

A *wok* is a deep, rounded frying pan from China. It is used mostly for frying or sautéing vegetables, and often requires a higher flame, more constant stirring and a shorter cooking time than regular sautéing.

To use, simply place a small amount of oil in the wok and heat. Add greens, fish, tofu or other vegetables with a pinch of sea salt or a little tamari. Stir ingredients constantly from side to side to ensure even cooking and avoid burning. Cook until all ingredients are done. They should be somewhat crispy.

A wok can also be used for deep-frying and making tempura, as it heats up quickly and holds heat well.

TEMPURA

Tempura originated in Portugal (where some of the world's most delicious seafood can be eaten) and was introduced in Japan by merchants and sailors who went there to trade. Tempura is made from vegetables, fish, shellfish or tofu which have been dipped in a batter and deep-fried until they are golden brown and crisp. Tempura is very delicious and can be fun to prepare. Because it is quite oily, it is often served with a dipping sauce made from ingredients such as tamari, water, sake, grated ginger, grated daikon, etc. It is also usually eaten along with a small serving of freshly grated daikon to which several drops of tamari are added. This helps to "cut through" the oil, thus making it somewhat easier to digest.

Among oils, light sesame is the best for making tempura. Dark sesame oil is too heavy, while corn oil is very yin and will expand too quickly and spill over the sides of your tempura pot. Other oils such as safflower or sunflower are inexpensive, but are not so good for your health. Because they are more yin, they are harder to digest. Since tempura is quite oily, it is not advisable to eat it regularly or in large quantities. This is especially important for those with any type of intestinal, gall bladder, liver or skin problems. Some people may have to avoid it entirely until their condition improves.

Any kind of pot, such as a saucepan, Chinese wok, deep, cast iron skillet or Dutch oven, will do for making tempura. For best results, always make sure you have about 2–3 inches of oil in the pot. When making tempura, the oil should be heated to about 345°–355° F. A lower temperature will cause soggy tempura, while a higher temperature will cause it to burn.

Heat the oil. Do not allow it to smoke. To test for correct temperature, drop a small morsel of batter into the pot. If it sinks to the bottom and remains there for a minute or so before rising to the top, the temperature is too low. If it does not sink to the bottom, but stays on top of the oil, it is too high. The batter should sink to the bottom and rise quickly to the top. This indicates that your oil is of the correct temperature.

Make sure that you wash, cut and drain all of your vegetables before heating the oil. Some green leafy vegetables may need to be patted dry with a towel before deep-frying to avoid splashing the oil. Prepare your batter while the oil is heating. If the batter sits for too long, it will become too thick. Do not mix the batter too much. If you are making a large amount of tempura for many people, make small amounts of batter at a time. Make additional batter as needed.

Vegetables can be cut into various shapes such as diagonal slices, thin rounds, half-moons, rectangles, flowerettes or matchsticks. If you cut your vegetables into matchsticks, you can place them all into the batter at once. Then pick a chopstickful or spoonful out at a time and deep-fry. When using fish, it should be in the form of fillets cut into 1-1/2"–2" pieces, while shrimp should be cleaned, shelled and deveined prior to use. To keep shrimp from curling up, make two small, diagonal slices in the underside about an inch apart. Leave the tails on the shrimp. Just about any type of vegetable, fish or shellfish can be used for tempura, and nori strips, tofu, cooked seitan and even apple slices or rounds are also good.

After you have cut your vegetables or other ingredients, dip them in the batter one piece at a time. The ingredients should be lightly coated with batter for the best results. If they are coated too thickly, the end result will be oily, soft tempura. Then drop the batter-coated ingredients one at a time into the hot oil. (This will prevent the oil from splashing or the pieces from sticking together.) Continue to add the ingredients until you have 4–5 pieces in the oil. Do not add too many pieces at once, as this will lower the temperature of the oil considerably, resulting in soggy, oily tempura. If, while cooking, the batter separates from the vegetables and spreads throughout the oil, you may have used too much water in it. If this happens, add a little more flour to the batter. (If the batter is too thick, add a little more water.) Deep-fry until golden brown, turning each piece with chopsticks to evenly brown on both sides. When done, place each piece on a wire draining rack or on paper towels to drain. Arrange on a platter or bamboo serving basket with a napkin placed under the tempura to soak up remaining oil that will drain as the tempura sits.

If you prepare a tempura dish which includes fish and vegetables, deep-fry the vegetables first. If you cook the fish before or together with the vegetables, the flavor of the fish will penetrate the oil and dominate the taste of the vegetables. If you are using a variety of vegetables, do them one kind at a time. This will help each variety to retain its own unique flavor.

To rid your oil of the taste or smell of fish or other impurities, deep-fry an umeboshi plum in it until it turns black. Also, clean the oil with a wire oil skimmer after each use to remove bits of deep-fried or burned batter. Always keep your oil clean for best results. It will also store longer if kept clean.

To store used tempura oil, allow it to cool and place it in an airtight container (glass jar) and store in a cupboard or pantry (away from the heat of the stove) until you use it again. You can occasionally add new oil as needed. New oil will sometimes bubble up, so in order to avoid spilling, do not heat the oil too quickly. If it does boil or bubble up, quickly remove the pot from the flame, lower the flame and place it back on the stove. You can also place two cooking chopsticks on top of the rim of the pot, forming a V-shape. This will help to prevent spilling.

To keep tempura warm while you are frying the remaining ingredients, place it on a cookie sheet in a warm oven (about 200° F.).

Pastry and Corn Flour Batter
>3/4 cup whole wheat pastry flour
>1/4 cup corn flour
>1–1-1/4 cups water
>1/4 tsp. sea salt

Whole Wheat and Rice Flour Batter
>1/4 cup whole wheat flour
>1/4 cup brown rice flour
>1–1-1/4 cups water
>1/4 tsp. sea salt

Pastry and Arrowroot Flour Batter
>1 cup whole wheat pastry flour
>1 Tbsp. arrowroot
>1–1-1/4 cups water
>1/4 tsp. sea salt

Mix all dry ingredients. Then gradually add water and mix. Do not mix too thoroughly or make too thin. If batter sits for too long in a warm kitchen it will become too thick.

Below are some of the dip sauces that can be served with tempura:

Daikon Sauce
    1/2 tsp. grated daikon
    2 Tbsp. tamari
    2 Tbsp. water

Ginger Sauce
    1/4 tsp. grated ginger
    2 Tbsp. tamari
    2 Tbsp. water

Tentsuyu Sauce
    1 cup kombu stock (warm)
    1/4 cup tamari
    1/4 cup sake
    1/2 tsp. grated ginger
    1/4 tsp. lemon juice

Tamari Sauce
    1 cup warm shiitake soup stock
    1/4 cup tamari
    1 Tbsp. grated onion

Serve a small dish of one of the above to each person as explained previously. The dip sauce should be slightly warm when served. Serve a small dish of grated daikon or turnip with a drop or two of tamari added along with the dip sauce.

Burdock Eel
    2 pieces of burdock root, sliced diagonally about 1/4 inch thick
    2 carrots, sliced diagonally about 1/4 inch thick
    2 medium-sized onions, halved and then quartered
    10–12 fresh mushrooms or shiitake which have been soaked
      (leave whole or halve them)
    tempura batter
    water
    tamari

Wash and slice vegetables. Prepare tempura batter while the oil is heating. Dip vegetables in batter and deep-fry until golden brown. Drain on paper towels. Pat each piece with paper towels to remove most of the oil. Layer the vegetables in a baking or casserole dish. Add water to just cover the vegetables and sprinkle with a little tamari. Cover baking dish. Bake at 375° F. until batter separates from the vegetables and creates a thick, creamy sauce. This may take about 1–1-1/2 hours. If necessary, season with more tamari toward the end and remove cover. Bake 10 more minutes or so. Serve in the casserole dish.

    Burdock eel is considered to be more yang than other vegetable dishes; however, it is also quite oily. It is very delicious but should not be eaten too often.

DEEP-FRYING

Practically everyone is familiar with deep-frying. Prepare just as you would tempura, only omit dipping the ingredients in batter. Fry until golden brown on both sides. Seitan, tofu and some vegetables can be prepared in this way, as can rice-balls, seaweed (kombu), sushi that has dried out, bread cubes, etc.

Lotus Root Chips
> **2 lotus root sections**
> **oil**
> **dip sauce**
> **grated daikon**

Wash and cut away ends of lotus root. Slice into very thin rounds. Deep-fry until golden brown and crisp. Drain on paper towels and arrange on a platter or bamboo serving plate. Serve with dip sauce and grated daikon.

Kombu Chips
> **two 12″ strips of kombu**
> **oil**

Brush kombu with a wet sponge. Slice into 2″ pieces and deep-fry until crisp.

These are somewhat salty and make good party snacks to accompany various beverages.

Deep-Fried Rice Balls
> **2 cups leftover cooked rice**
> **oil**
> **tamari**
> **grated daikon**

Wet hands and form rice into small balls, triangles or rolls. Make sure to pack it firmly so that it does not fall apart. You may wrap a strip of toasted nori around each rice ball for variety. Deep-fry until crisp and golden brown on both sides. The inside will be soft and warm. Serve with a drop of tamari on each, or with a dip sauce. You can also serve with grated daikon to help digest the oil.

Deep-Fried Bottom Rice
Occasionally your rice may burn on the bottom or scorch. Never discard this. Place it on a bamboo mat to dry for 2–3 days or until it becomes very hard. Then break it into bite-sized pieces and deep-fry until golden brown and very crispy. Children especially enjoy this as a snack or as part of a meal. Serve with a little tamari or a dip sauce.

SALADS

There are numerous ingredients to choose from when making a salad. These include rice, cous-cous, bulghur, noodles, beans, seitan, tofu, shrimp, crab, lobster, tuna and other fish, sprouts, seaweeds, fruits, agar agar, and of course vegetables. Bread crumbs and seeds can also be used as garnishes.

With a little imagination, you can prepare wonderful raw, boiled, pressed, noodle, sea vegetable, fruit, seafood, fruit and vegetable combination salads and others.

Salads can be very helpful in aiding the body in discharging stored animal fats and salts.[4] They are also very good for pregnant and breastfeeding women, as they help to balance their more yang condition. On the other hand, if you eat too many salads, your condition will start to become too yin.

Raw salad should be eaten mainly in the late spring and summer in order to balance the warmer weather and to aid in the discharge of excessive yang accumulated during the colder months. If you eat a large quantity of raw vegetable or fruit salad during the colder months, however, you may feel weak or chilly. Also, many fruits and vegetables are not in season during the colder months. The other salads mentioned above can be eaten in moderate quantities during all four seasons.

There are a variety of natural and healthful dressings which can be used on your salads. I will discuss these in a later chapter.

Boiled Salads

To prepare a boiled salad, place about an inch of water and a pinch of sea salt in a pot or saucepan and bring to a boil. Boil each vegetable separately for 1–2 minutes. (More yin vegetables such as Chinese cabbage, onions, watercress, etc. require only a minute or less, while carrots, daikon, kale, cabbage, etc. may require one and a half to two minutes boiling time.) All vegetables should be slightly crisp but not raw. You may use the same water to cook all of the vegetables, but boil those with the mildest flavors first (Chinese cabbage, onions, carrots, etc.) and those with the strongest flavor (daikon, celery, turnips, etc.) last. Watercress leaves a bitter taste in the water and should be the very last vegetable to be boiled. In this way, each vegetable retains its own distinct flavor. Incidentally, watercress should be boiled for only 20–30 seconds.

After you boil each vegetable, remove it and place in a colander and rinse under cold water until cool. Allow each vegetable to drain and place in a bowl. When all of the ingredients have been added to the bowl, mix them together with chopsticks or wooden utensils. Rinsing your vegetables will stop the cooking process and keep their color very bright, thus making your salad more attractive and aesthetically pleasing.

Add the dressing of your choice and serve. A tofu or umeboshi dressing is especially delicious with boiled salads. You can also serve the salad without mixing in the dressing while allowing each person to add it at the table.

Boiled Salad No. 1

1 cup Chinese cabbage, sliced into thin, diagonal strips
1/2 cup carrot, cut into matchsticks
1/2 cup daikon, cut into matchsticks
1/2 cup onion, cut into thin half-moons
1/2 cup celery, cut diagonally very thin

---

[4] This is one reason why vegetarian and fruitarian diets are becoming increasingly popular in America, Europe and other parts of the world where animal products are consumed in large quantities.

1 bunch watercress or Swiss chard (cut watercress sprigs into thirds, and
  slice chard diagonally into thin strips)
water
pinch of sea salt

Boil vegetables as described, in the following order: cabbage, 1 minute; onions,
1 minute; carrots, 1–1-1/2 minutes; daikon, 1-1/2 minutes; celery, 1 minute; and
watercress, 20–30 seconds. Rinse, drain and place in bowl as described. Mix and
serve with dressing.

If you wish to omit the dressing, simply roast a few sesame or sunflower seeds
in a dry skillet, grind in a suribachi until about 40%–50% crushed and mix with
salad or sprinkle on top. Whole, roasted seeds can also be mixed in with or
sprinkled on your salad.

Boiled Salad No. 2

1 bunch mustard greens, cut diagonally into strips
1 cup daikon, cut into matchsticks or thin rectangles
1/2 cup carrot, cut into matchsticks or thin rectangles
water
pinch of sea salt

Boil as above in the following order: carrots, 1–1-1/2 minutes; daikon, 1 minute; lotus root, 1-1/2–2 minutes; and mustard greens, about 1 minute. Rinse,
drain and place in a bowl. Mix and serve with a dressing.

Boiled Salad No. 3

1 cup shredded cabbage
1 cup kale, cut diagonally into thin strips
1/4 cup celery, cut diagonally very thin
1/2 cup carrot, cut into matchsticks or thin rectangles
1/2 cup onion, cut into half-moons
2–3 red radishes, halved and thinly sliced
1 sprig Italian parsley, finely chopped (leave raw)
water
pinch of sea salt

Boil as above, in the following order: onions, 1 minute; carrots, 1–1-1/2 minutes; cabbage, 1–1-1/2 minutes; kale, 1–1-1/2 minutes; radish, 1 minute; and
celery, 1 minute. Leave the parsley raw. Rinse, drain and place vegetables in a
bowl. Mix and serve with a dressing. Add raw parsley.

Macaroni Salad

2 cups elbow, shell or alphabet macaroni
1 cup cooked chickpeas, drained
1/2 cucumber, quartered and sliced diagonally
1 stalk celery, cut into thin diagonals
1 onion, cut into thin half-moons (boil 1 minute before mixing in)
1/2 cup grated carrot

**1 cup shredded iceberg lettuce or tiny flowerettes of broccoli
(parboil broccoli before mixing with other ingredients)
dressing**

Cook, rinse and drain macaroni. Mix all ingredients together except onions.
Boil onions about 30 seconds to 1 minute with a pinch of sea salt. Add onions
to other ingredients and mix. Serve with umeboshi-sesame dressing. Garnish with
a small sprig of parsley, watercress or very tiny daikon leaves.

Bean Salad
**1 cup cooked kidney beans
1/2 cup cooked chickpeas
2 cups steamed green beans, cut into 1-1/2″ pieces
1 cup steamed yellow wax beans, cut into 1-1/2″ pieces
1/2 cup minced onion**

Cook kidney beans and chickpeas as outlined in bean chapter (season with sea
salt). Steam greens and wax beans until done. Mix all ingredients together and
serve with umeboshi-parsley dressing. Let beans sit in dressing for 15–20 minutes
before serving.

Hijiki Salad
**1/2 head iceberg lettuce
1/2 cucumber, sliced diagonally
1/2 cup alfalfa sprouts
2 red radishes, sliced into thin rounds
1/4 bunch of watercress
1/2 onion, sliced into thin rings or rounds
1 cup cooked hijiki**

Wash hijiki and soak 4–5 minutes. Place in saucepan and boil 15–20 minutes without seasoning. Remove, drain and allow to cool. Slice hijiki into 2″ pieces. Arrange ingredients very attractively in a salad bowl, so that the various colors
are well balanced. Top the bowl with hijiki. Allow everyone to choose from the
salad bowl and place their portion in individual plates. Serve with tofu, sesame,
plum or sesame oil and rice vinegar dressing.

Wakame Salad
**1 cup wakame (wash, soak 10 minutes, boil 2–3 minutes, rinse under cold water,
drain and slice into 1″ pieces)
1 head Romaine lettuce, separated into small, bite-sized pieces
1 cucumber, sliced into thin rounds**

Prepare wakame as directed. Cut both ends off the cucumber and rub a little sea
salt on the ends of the main sections. Rub one of the smaller pieces in a spirallic
or circular motion on both salted ends of the main piece for about 30 seconds.
This will help to remove any bitter flavor in the cucumber. Wash salt off and slice
cucumber into thin rounds. Place all ingredients in a bowl, except for a few slices

of cucumber, and toss together. Arrange remaining cucumber slices attractively on top of the salad. Serve with an umeboshi-tahini dressing.

This salad is also good with a miso-tahini-scallion dressing.

Wakame-Cucumber Salad

2 cups wakame, prepared as above
1/2 cucumber (not too big around), sliced into very thin rounds, soaked in salt water, pressed about 30 minutes, rinsed and drained
1/2 cup medium-sized or small chuba (dried sardines), dry-roasted for several minutes on a low flame until crisp
brown rice vinegar or umeboshi, lemon or fresh orange juice

Arrange portions of wakame and cucumber in individual serving dishes. Place several chuba on top. Pour 2–3 drops of brown rice vinegar or other above mentioned juices on each dish of salad and serve. This is very nice in the summer.

Dulse Salad

1 cup Chinese cabbage, finely sliced and boiled less than 1 minute
1/2 cup daikon, cut into matchsticks and boiled 1-1/2 minutes
1/2 cup carrot, cut into matchsticks and boiled 1-1/2 minutes
1/4 cup onion, sliced in half-moons and boiled one minute
1/4 cup dulse, washed, soaked and sliced into 1/2″ pieces

Mix ingredients together in a salad bowl and serve with an umeboshi dressing.

Waldorf Salad

3-1/2 cups shredded cabbage
1/4 cup grated carrot
1/2 cup roasted, chopped walnuts
1/4 cup celery, finely sliced diagonally
1 apple, cut into 1/4″ slices or chunks
1/4 cup raisins

Mix ingredients together in a salad bowl. Add a tofu-sesame dressing and mix. Cool before serving.

Cous-Cous Salad

2 cups steamed cous-cous (toss while cooling to make fluffy)
1 cup cooked chickpeas
1/2 minced onion
1/4 cup finely chopped carrot
1/4 cup fresh green peas, boiled with a pinch of salt until done

Mix ingredients together in a bowl. Mix in a dressing made with umeboshi juice, lemon juice and parsley. Serve.

Bulghur Salad

2 cups cooked bulghur (toss while cooling to make fluffy)
1/4 cup minced parsley

    1/4 cup minced onion

    1/2 cup minced carrot, lightly boiled 1 minute

    1/2 tsp. sesame oil

    1/2 tsp. tamari

    1 tsp. lemon juice

Toss bulghur with chopsticks or fork to cool and make fluffy. Mix in vegetables. Blend sesame oil (heated first), tamari and lemon juice in a suribachi. Mix in with bulghur and let sit 30 minutes before serving.

Rice Salad No. 1

    4 cups cooked brown rice

    1/4 cup shiitake, soaked in lemon juice or brown rice vinegar

    1/4 cup lotus root, quartered, sliced and steamed 1–2 minutes

    1/2 cup broccoli stems, quartered, sliced and steamed 1 minute

    1/2 cup carrot, cut into matchsticks and steamed 1-1/2 minutes

    1/4 cup burdock, cut into matchsticks and steamed 2 minutes

    1/2 cup boiled or sautéed shrimp, diced

    1/4 cup daikon, sliced into matchsticks and boiled 1-1/2 minutes

    lemon juice

    parsley

Cook rice, allow to cool and mix to make fluffy. Mix in other ingredients. Squeeze lemon juice or brown rice vinegar over salad and mix. Let sit for several minutes before serving. Garnish with parsley.

    Umeboshi juice with finely chopped shiso leaves can be used in place of lemon juice or vinegar. You can also add parsley, scallions or chives. A little tamari or sea salt mixed in with the rice also helps to create a different flavor.

Rice Salad No. 2

    3–4 cups cooked brown rice, prepared as above

    1/4 lb. shrimp, shelled, deveined and cut into 1/4″–1/2″ pieces

    1/2 cup diced carrot

    1/2 cup green peas, boiled until done

    1/4 cup shiitake, soaked, destemmed and thinly sliced

    1/2 cup deep-fried tofu strips (dice after frying)

    1/2 head Romaine lettuce

    1 scallion, sliced diagonally

    1/4 cup onion, diced

    1/2 cup cooked seitan (squeeze out liquid and cut into small chunks)

Cook rice as in the above recipe. Mix to fluff. Sauté all vegetables except for the scallions and lettuce. Season with a little sea salt or tamari while sautéing. Add shrimp and seitan during the final 3–4 minutes. Mix all ingredients with the rice with the exception of the lettuce. Sprinkle with sea salt, tamari or lemon juice and mix.

    Place lettuce leaves on individual salad plates or in a large platter. Scoop rice salad onto lettuce leaves and serve.

Pressed Salad No. 1

1/2 head lettuce (separate into bite-sized pieces or shred)
1 cucumber, sliced diagonally into thin pieces
1 stalk celery, sliced diagonally into very thin pieces
2 red radishes, sliced into thin rounds
1 onion, sliced into thin rounds
sea salt

Place vegetables in a pickle press or large bowl and sprinkle with a little sea salt. Mix. Apply pressure to the press. If you use a bowl, place a small plate on top of the vegetables and place a stone or weight on top of the plate. Leave it for at least 30–45 minutes. Pour off water as it rises. You may leave up to 3 or 4 days, but the longer you press the vegetables, the more they resemble light pickles.

Pressed Salad No. 2

1/2 cucumber, sliced into thin rounds
4–6 Chinese cabbage leaves, cut diagonally into thin strips
1 small onion, sliced into thin rounds
1/2 stalk celery, sliced diagonally into very thin pieces
2 scallions, cut into 1-1/2″ pieces
1/2 cup daikon, sliced into very thin rectangles
2 cups umeboshi juice

Place vegetables in pickle press or bowl and prepare as above. Leave about 45 minutes to an hour. Drain and serve. Save umeboshi juice, as it can be used several times.

Crab Salad

1/2 head Romaine lettuce, separated into bite-sized pieces
1/2 head iceberg lettuce, separated into bite-sized pieces
1 cucumber, halved and sliced diagonally
3 red radishes, sliced into thin rounds
1/2 carrot, cut into very thin flower shapes
1/2 cup celery, sliced into very thin diagonals
2 cups cooked crabmeat, cut into 1/2″ pieces

Mix ingredients together or arrange each in a separate section of a large salad bowl. Serve with umeboshi, tamari-lemon, sesame oil and rice vinegar dressing or any other suitable dressing. This is also delicious with a white miso dressing.

Seafood such as cooked shrimp, lobster and other varieties can be added or used in this recipe. You may also garnish with dry, roasted bread cubes or seeds.

Fruit Salad No. 1

1-1/2 cups small broccoli flowerettes, boiled
1/2 cup daikon, cut into rectangles and boiled
1 cucumber, sliced diagonally
2 apples, cut into 1/2″ pieces (wash in salt water)
1/2 cup carrot, halved, thinly sliced and boiled

1 cup halved strawberries, washed in salt water
pinch of sea salt

Cook vegetables as directed, rinse under cold water and drain. Wash fruit slices as directed and drain. Mix all ingredients together and serve.

Fruit Salad No. 2

1 bar agar agar or prepackaged flakes or powder (follow directions on label)
2 cups water
1/2 cup raisins
1 tangerine (peel and separate sections)
2 peaches, sliced
1 cup halved strawberries
1 apple, sliced

Break agar agar into pieces and soak in 2 cups water. Bring to a boil, reduce flame and stir constantly until dissolved. Pour liquid into a shallow bowl, cake pan, etc. Allow to cool and become hard. Cut hardened agar agar into 1/4–1/2 inch pieces or cubes.

Mix all ingredients together with a pinch of sea salt. Chill and serve.

SPROUTING

Sprouts can be made very easily at home by using a quart canning jar, top and a round piece of wire screen or cheesecloth. They require very little time to make and are much more delicious when freshly made for salads or vegetable dishes. The most common types of sprouts are made from either mung beans, soybeans, chickpeas or alfalfa seeds.

How to Make Sprouts

Place any *one* of the above mentioned beans or seeds in a one-quart canning jar which has a removable center disc top. Cover the seeds or beans with water, and let sit for 3–4 hours. Drain off water.

Cut a piece of wire screen to the same circumference as the outer rim of the jar top and place it inside the jar top. The screen will allow air to circulate in the jar. Screw the cover on the jar. If you do not have the correct jar top or wire screen, you can either use cheesecloth or punch several holes in the top of a regular jar to allow air in.

Place the jar in a dark cupboard or pantry with a temperature of about 70°–72° F.

Rinse and drain the beans or seeds with cold water two or three times per day. It will take about 3–5 days for the beans or seeds to produce 2–3-1/2 inch long sprouts.

After the sprouts are long enough, rinse with cold water, drain off the hulls or shells and place in an airtight container. Place container in the refrigerator or other cool place until ready to use.

Alfalfa seeds take the least amount of time to sprout, while chickpeas take the longest. If you do not rinse and drain your sprouts as directed, they may mold and decay.

For additional vegetable recipes, including burdock-carrot *kinpira*, baked summer squash, sukiyaki, tempura, and stuffed lotus root, along with a more detailed discussion of the method of pressure-cooking vegetables, please refer to *Introducing Macrobiotic Cooking*. Recipes for bean, chickpea, noodle, fruit, and fruit salads are also included.

5. Bean Dishes, including Tofu and Natto

As well as being very delicious, beans are a valuable source of protein, calcium, iron, minerals and vitamins. Beans can be combined with vegetables, seaweeds, grains and noodles, or, when combined with fruit, can provide a nice dessert.

They can be seasoned with sea salt, tamari or miso to create different flavors. They can be cooked with kombu, which helps them to cook faster and makes them easier to digest.

People sometimes say that beans are difficult to digest and create intestinal problems. The factors which may influence the digestibility of beans include the proper cooking and combinations of ingredients, thorough chewing, proper seasoning, cooking them long enough and eating them in a moderate volume and not too late in the evening. Beans generally require more time to be digested than a food such as noodles. In China and Japan there is a proverb, "A man who eats too many beans becomes a fool." Perhaps this is based on the tendency of beans to produce intestinal problems when eaten in large quantities, which often leads to irritability and unclear thinking.

It is very important to watch the intake of beans among small children. If they eat too many beans, or begin eating them before they develop the gastric enzymes necessary to digest them properly, they may develop gas pains, bulging stomachs or very weak legs.

Some varieties of beans are quite yin and may cause more intestinal disorders than the more yang varieties. The more yang beans are azuki, lentils and chick-peas, and these are generally smaller and more compact and have a lower fat content. Beans such as kidney, pinto, black beans, navy beans and red lentils are generally more yin, since they are either larger or have a higher fat content. Lima beans and soybeans are both very yin, and require thorough chewing. They should be eaten only on occasion and in small quantities.

There are several methods for cooking beans which will aid in their proper digestion and also make them more delicous. The first method is to simply boil them for a long time. First, soak the beans for several hours or more. This will soften their skins and reduce their cooking time. Lentils, split peas and red lentils do not require soaking, as they cook very quickly. Chickpeas are very hard and require a longer soaking, from a minimimum of four hours to overnight. Kombu can be placed on the bottom of the pot when cooking chickpeas, soybeans, lima beans or kidney, pinto and navy beans. I have found that kombu definitely improves their flavor and, because of its high mineral content, creates a very balanced dish. Place the soaked beans in a pot. For each cup of beans add 3-1/2 to 4 cups of cold water. Bring to a boil, reduce flame to low, cover and simmer until about 80% done. Then add approximately 1/4 teaspoon sea salt for each cup of beans. The volume of salt may be less if you are preparing a large quantity. Continue cooking until beans are soft. Remove cover, turn flame to medium, boil off excess liquid and serve. The total cooking time may vary from one hour for lentils to two hours for other beans and up to four or more hours for chickpeas. The longer you cook your beans, the softer and more easily digestible they become. For practical purposes, however, most beans are generally finished after cooking for an hour and 45 minutes to two hours.

The second method is pressure-cooking. This requires less cooking time, less water, and soaking is often not necessary. Wash beans, place in pressure cooker and add water. Cover and bring to pressure. When pressure is up, reduce flame to low and cook for 45 minutes. (Chickpeas require soaking before pressure-cooking, and need to be cooked for between an hour and 15 minutes to an hour and a half.) Allow pressure to come down and remove the cover. Season with the same amount of salt as for boiled beans and continue to simmer until excess liquid is cooked away.

Do not add salt at the beginning or the beans will not cook properly and their skins will remain tough.

I have found that azuki beans taste better if they are boiled. Lentils, split peas, Japanese black beans, red lentils and soybeans will often clog the pressure gauge of your pressure-cooker, so it is best to boil them. Soybeans can be boiled for half an hour. Skim the foam off the top as it rises, and when no more foam rises to the surface you may then place them in a pressure-cooker and continue cooking until done. You may also roast soybeans before pressure-cooking to avoid clogging. If Japanese black beans are first roasted and combined with rice, they will not clog the gauge when pressure-cooked.

The third method was introduced to me by Aveline Kushi. She calls it the *shocking method,* and it is simply a variation on the boiling method. Place beans in a pot and add only enough water to cover the surface of the beans. Bring to a boil and reduce flame to low. Place a cover which is slightly smaller than the top of the pot you are using down inside the pot so that it rests on the beans. This will keep the beans from jumping up and down, and will reduce their cooking time. Since they are more yang, azuki beans do not require a cover. They have a tendency to go downward and not jump around while cooking. (You may also place a small strip of kombu under the beans before cooking.) As the beans absorb water and expand, add just enough water to barely cover them and place the cover back on top. Pour the water slowly down the side of the pot so as not to upset or drastically shock the beans. In this way, the beans will peacefully adapt to the change in temperature caused by the addition of cold water. Repeat this process until they are about 80% done. Add the same quantity of sea salt as for the other methods. Remove the cover and simmer until the beans are soft, adding water when necessary. When beans are soft, turn up flame slightly to boil off excess liquid and serve.

The fourth method is to bake them. First, place the beans in a pot and add 4–5 cups of water for each cup of beans. Place pot on stove and bring to a boil. Boil 15–20 minutes to loosen bean skins. (Add kombu, if desired, to baking dish.) Pour beans and water into a baking or bean baking crock, cover and place in the oven at 350° F. Bake until beans are 80% done. Depending on type of bean used, the cooking time may be from 3–4 hours. Add more water as the beans need it. Cook until beans are soft and creamy. Remove cover to brown. You may also add diced onions, carrots or other root vegetables to the beans when they are about 50%–60% done, and can also season with miso instead of sea salt. If you want a sweet dish, you may add raisins, dried apples, etc. at the beginning.

Azuki Beans with Squash

2 cups azuki beans, washed
2 cups buttercup squash or Hokkaido pumpkin, cubed with skin left on
1/4–1/2 tsp. sea salt per cup of beans
water

Use method No. 1 or No. 3 described above. Add squash or pumpkin at the beginning.

Azuki Beans with Apples and Raisins

2 cups azuki beans, washed
1 cup dried apples, soaked and quartered
1 cup raisins, soaked
raisin and apple soaking water
additional water if needed
1/4–1/2 tsp. sea salt per cup of beans

Add apples and raisins at the beginning. Use method No. 1 or No. 3 described previously. Season with sea salt when 80% done. Continue cooking as directed.

Chestnut Azukis

    2 cups azuki beans, washed
    1 cup dried chestnuts, roasted until golden or soaked
    1/4–1/2 tsp. sea salt per cup of beans

Roast chestnuts in a dry skillet until golden, or soak in water for one hour. Add to beans at beginning. Use method No. 1 or No. 3 and cook as directed. Season with sea salt when 80% done and continue cooking as directed.

Lentils

    2 cups lentils, washed
    water
    1/4–1/2 tsp. sea salt per cup of beans

Use method No. 1. Cook lentils for about 45 minutes. Season with sea salt and continue cooking another 15–20 minutes.

Red Lentils

    2 cups red lentils, washed
    1 onion, diced
    water to just cover (4–5 cups)
    1/4–1/2 tsp. sea salt per cup of beans

Place onions on bottom of pot. Before you wash the lentils, place them a handful at a time on a plate and sort out small stones. Wash the beans and add to pot with onions. Use method No. 1. Do not cover as they will boil over the pot. Cook as directed for 35–40 minutes. Add sea salt and continue cooking another 10 minutes. These beans will harden as they cool, so if there is a little excess liquid in them it is allright.

Chickpeas (Garbanzo Beans)

    2 cups chickpeas, soaked overnight
    one 2″ strip of kombu, soaked and cut into strips
    1 onion, diced
    1/2 cup carrot, diced
    1/4 cup lotus root, diced
    5–6 cups water
    1/4–1/2 tsp. sea salt per cup of beans

Layer kombu, onion, carrot and lotus root in that order in a pressure cooker. Add water, cover and bring to pressure. Pressure-cook as directed for 1-1/4–1-1/2 hours. Allow pressure to come down and remove cover. Add sea salt or miso. Continue cooking until most of the liquid is boiled away.

Pinto Beans

    2 cups pinto beans, washed
    1 onion, diced
    1/2 cup carrot, diced or quartered
    water
    1/4–1/2 tsp. sea salt per cup of beans

Use whichever method you prefer. With methods No. 1 and N o. 3, add vegetables when beans are 80% done, season and continue to cook as directed. With methods No. 2 and No. 4, add vegetables at the beginning. Continue to cook until done.

Kidney Beans
> 2 cups kidney beans, washed
> water
> one 2″ strip of kombu
> water
> 3–4 tsp. puréed brown rice miso

Place kombu on bottom of pot. Add beans. Use the *shocking method* described previously. When the beans are 80% done, add puréed miso. Continue to cook as directed.

You may use any of the other methods described, and may season with sea salt instead of miso. You may also add vegetables for variety.

Japanese Black Beans (Black Soybeans)
> 2 cups Japanese black beans
> sea salt
> tamari water

Wash beans quickly under cold water. Soak overnight with 1/4–1/2 teaspoon of sea salt per cup of beans added to the water. This will prevent the skins from peeling. Place beans and soaking water in a pot. You do not need to add additional salt, but may need to add enough water to keep the surface of the beans covered. Bring to a boil, reduce flame to low and simmer. (Don't cover.) A black foam will rise to the surface of the beans. Skim and discard. When foam no longer floats to the surface, cover the beans and cook for 2-1/2–3 hours, adding water when and if needed just to cover. Toward the end, remove cover and add a small amount of tamari to keep the skins a shiny, black color. Cook excess liquid away. When beans are finished, shake the pot up and down to coat the beans with liquid. There should be just enough liquid left to coat them. Serve.

These beans are traditionally served on New Year's Day. They are beneficial in treating problems with the sexual organs, and are good for overly yang conditions which result from an excessive intake of animal food.

Soybeans
The soybean is often referred to as the meat of the East because it is much higher in protein than most varieties of animal food. It also has a very high fat content. It is widely eaten in the Far East in the forms of tofu, okara, and fermented as natto, *tempeh*, miso and tamari. Soybeans are one of the more yin of the beans, and are best when cooked together with more yang ingredients such as burdock, lotus root, seaweed and miso. However, since they are fermented and aged with sea salt and grains, miso and tamari have a more yang nature.

Soybeans are somewhat difficult to digest, so they must be cooked and chewed very thoroughly. Soybeans and the various products made from them are very delicious, and should be included in your diet. Miso and tamari can be used daily, while soybeans and their various products can be occasionally eaten as side dishes.

Soybeans with Kombu and Burdock

> **2 cups soybeans, washed and roasted in a dry skillet**
> **one 6″ strip of kombu, soaked and sliced into small squares**
> **1/2–1 cup burdock, washed and quartered**
> **water**
> **1/4–1/2 tsp. sea salt per cup of beans**

After washing, roast soybeans in a dry skillet until golden brown. Do not roast too long or over too high a flame, or they will burn. Soak kombu and slice into small squares. Wash burdock thoroughly with a vegetable brush, but gently enough so as not to remove the skin. Slice burdock as directed.

Place kombu on bottom of pot and add soybeans. Add burdock and just enough water to cover. Use method No. 3 and cook as directed. Add sea salt when beans are 80% done, and continue to cook as directed. There should not be too much liquid left over after they are finished.

Soybeans with Lotus Root and Salmon

> **2 cups soybeans, washed**
> **one 2″ strip kombu, soaked and cut into squares**
> **1 cup lotus root, diced**
> **1/2 cup diced carrot**
> **1/2 cup diced daikon**
> **1 small salmon head, sliced thin**
> **sesame oil**
> **sea salt to taste**
> **water**

Cook the salmon head until the bones become soft. Sauté the vegetables in a small amount of sesame oil for several minutes. Roast the soybeans as above or soak overnight before cooking. Place soybeans in a pot and add vegetables and fish. Add enough water to cover the surface of the vegetables and fish. Use method No. 3 and cook as above.

This dish is very good to give a person strength.

(For other soybean recipes, see the Tofu, Natto, Sea Vegetable or Condiment sections of this book.)

TOFU

Tofu is a soybean product that is believed to have originated in China and later taken to Japan. It is now becoming a very popular protein source in the United States and Europe, especially among vegetarian and macrobiotic people.

Tofu can be made by soaking soybeans (preferably slightly green soybeans), blending them, cooking the pulp, and mixing the soymilk with a natural solidifier called *nigari*, which is high in magnesium. There are now many small and large tofu shops in America which produce fairly high quality tofu, making it available in almost all natural food stores, and even in some supermarkets. Tofu is also sold in Oriental food stores, but the quality is often inferior as a result of using lemon juice, vinegar, alum and chemicals as solidifying agents rather than natural nigari. Some varieties are made with chemical nigari, so make sure you read the label and ask how the tofu was made before you purchase it. If you cannot find tofu that is made with natural nigari, the next best choice is one made with lemon juice.

While in Japan, we had the opportunity to visit one of the most famous tofu shops in the country, located in the Arashiyama section of Kyoto. They are so careful about the quality of their products that they told us to eat them on the same day that we purchased them. If not, they told us to throw them away! This is because tofu tastes the best when eaten immediately before being over-exposed to warm temperatures. Of course it is still good to eat if refrigerated and stored in water for up to 3–5 days.

In most cities in Japan, there are trucks which travel throughout each neighborhood delivering fresh tofu twice per day. It's a wonderful treat to have freshly made tofu delivered right to your door. Tofu is a staple in the Japanese diet, and there are many varieties available, such as deep-fried tofu (*aburage*) cubes, pouches, strips, and deep-fried tofu cakes with vegetables and seaweed inside. I hope that some day all of these delicious products will be available for all of us to enjoy in America. In the meantime, however, you can prepare many of them at home.

Making tofu is quite an involved process that requires much attention and time. Sometimes it is more practical to buy it at a natural food store, but everyone should make it at home at least once, and preferably more often, just for the experience. Besides, homemade tofu is usually very delicious.

Tofu is a versatile food that can be prepared in many different ways. It can be pan-fried, deep-fried, boiled, steamed, baked or broiled. It can be occasionally eaten raw, especially in summer, or if your condition is overly yang. However, since it is very yin, raw tofu should not be eaten on a daily basis.

Another by-product of the tofu-making process is called *okara*, which is the soy pulp that is separated from the soymilk. It is sometimes referred to as *uno-hana*. I remember very clearly the first time I purcahsed okara in Kyoto. Several of the ladies in the neighborhood were also buying tofu. When they heard me ask for okara, they all started to chatter at once, with looks of astonishment on their faces. They could not believe that an American knew about okara and how to prepare it. I must have spent about half an hour trying to explain to them, in my childish Japanese, how I had learned about it. After that, they started to bring dishes of cooked okara for me to taste. They knew that we were macrobiotic and prepared these dishes especially with all natural ingredients.

Homemade Tofu

 3 cups soybeans, washed and soaked overnight
 4–4-1/2 tsp. nigari (crushed to a fine powder in a blender or suribachi)
 6 quarts cold water
 tofu box
 white cotton sack or cloth
 cheesecloth

Drain soaking water from beans and discard. Grind beans in an electric blender. If you have the time and patience, you can grind them in a Foley food mill. Place water in a large pot. Add soybeans. Bring slowly to a boil. As soon as the water begins to boil, reduce flame to low and simmer about 5 minutes. Make sure to stir constantly to avoid burning. Do not cover the pot, as the beans will foam up and spill over the sides. As soon as the water starts to boil, sprinkle cold water on top to stop the bubbling. Bring gently to a boil again. Again add a little cold water to stop bubbling. Repeat this once again, then turn off the flame.

You can now do one of the following: Make a cotton muslin sack with three sides sewn shut. Make it long enough so that all the beans fit inside and there is still room at the open top to hold onto; or —place a large cotton cloth in a strainer. Place the strainer or sack in a bowl to catch the soymilk. You can use either method when making tofu.

Pour the hot liquid, called soymilk, and the soybean pulp into either the cotton sack or the strainer. (If you use the strainer method, pull the four corners of the cloth together and hold tightly so as to form a sack.) Squeeze the remaining liquid from the sack into the bowl. Save the okara (pulp) which remains in the sack.

After you have placed the soymilk in a bowl, sprinkle the powdered nigari over it. Using a wooden spoon, gently make two deep strokes in the soymilk, forming an X. Allow soymilk to sit about 10–15 minutes undisturbed in the bowl, after which the tofu liquid should start to curdle.

A special tofu box is needed to complete the process, and this can be purchased at most natural food stores. It is basically a wooden or stainless steel box with holes in the sides. If you do not have one, a bamboo steamer basket will do. Line the box or steamer with cotton cheesecloth and gently spoon the tofu liquid (soymilk) into the box. Place a layer of cheesecloth on top of the tofu, and place the wooden lid (which comes with the box) gently on top. Do not push it down. Place a small weight, not too heavy, on top of the lid. Allow tofu to sit, undisturbed, for approximately an hour or until it forms a cake. Then carefully place tofu in a flat bowl or baking dish filled with cold water, and let it sit for half an hour. Your tofu is now ready to eat or refrigerate for later use. When you store tofu in the refrigerator, always make sure that it is covered with water to keep it fresh. Tofu will spoil very quickly if exposed to warmth, so it should always be regrigerated until it is used. Your tofu should keep for several days if it is stored in this way.

Tofu with Scallions (Summer Tofu)

 2 cakes raw tofu

1/2 cup finely sliced scallions
1/4 cup grated fresh ginger
1/4 cup finely shaved bonito flakes (not the same kind used for soups)
tamari

Cut raw tofu into slices or squares. Place one or two slices in each serving dish (small dishes or saucers will do). Place a small amount of scallion, ginger and bonito flakes on top of each serving and add several drops of tamari. Serve.

This dish is very good during the hot summer months when you may desire a cool, refreshing snack.

Tofu with Bonito Flake Broth

6–8 cups water
1–1-1/2 cakes fresh tofu, cut into 2″ cubes
1–1-1/2 Tbsp. bonito flakes (same kind as above)
1/2 cup thinly sliced scallions
tamari

Place water and bonito flakes in a pot. Bring to a boil, reduce flame to low, cover and simmer 5–6 minutes. Uncover and place tofu in the pot. Lightly season with tamari. Bring to a boil. Simmer one or two minutes. Turn off flame and add scallions. Serve hot.

Baked Tofu with Miso/Lemon Sauce

2 cakes tofu, cut into slices
1 Tbsp. miso
2–3 tsp. lemon juice
water
roasted sesame seeds
scallions

Stack slices of tofu in a shallow baking dish so they are slightly tilted (/////) and lean on one another as illustrated.

Blend miso and lemon juice together in a suribachi. Add enough cold water to make a creamy sauce. It should not be overly thick or too thin. Spoon sauce over tofu.

Bake at 350° F. for about 15–20 minutes. Garnish with scallions and freshly roasted sesame seeds. Serve.

As a variation, add 1 teaspoon sesame tahini to the sauce, or use orange or tangerine juice instead of lemon juice.

Broiled Tofu

2 cakes tofu
tamari
scallions

Slice tofu into pieces about 2″ wide, 3″ long, and 1/2″ thick. Sprinkle a little tamari on each side of the tofu or dip in tamari and grated ginger. Place in broiler and broil until slightly brown on both sides. This does not take very long, so be careful not to burn the tofu. Attractively arrange on a platter, garnish and serve. You may also broil tofu with a miso sauce rather than tamari.

Tofu Loaf

2 cakes soft tofu (32. oz.)
5 shiitake mushrooms, soaked for 15 minutes and destemmed
2 Tbsp. bonito flakes
one 6″ strip kombu
1-1/2 cups water
watercress
3 scallions, sliced
tamari to taste

Grind tofu in a suribachi until creamy. Slice shiitake very thin.

Place water, kombu, shiitake and bonito flakes in pot and bring to a boil. Remove kombu after 3–4 minutes. Slice kombu very finely and add back to broth. Add tamari to taste and simmer 5–6 minutes. Pour the broth slowly into the suribachi a little at a time and mix. It should not be soupy. Place tofu mixture into a bread or loaf pan.

Place in oven and bake about 30–35 minutes at 375° F. Boil several sprigs of watercress for less than a minute and garnish each bowl with one piece. Serve with a little tamari.

Steamed Tofu Rolls

2 cakes tofu
3 mushrooms (shiitake), soaked, destemmed and sliced
1/4 cup finely chopped carrot
1/2 cup sliced scallions
pinch of sea salt
tamari
3–4 sheets toasted nori
sesame oil
6–8 *kanpyo* (dried gourd strips) about 5″–6″ long, soaked about 5 minutes

Brush a skillet lightly with sesame oil and heat. Sauté carrots and mushrooms 9–10 minutes. Season with a little tamari.

Place tofu in suribachi and grind until creamy. Add carrots, mushrooms, scallions and a pinch of sea salt. Mix well.

Place nori on a bamboo mat. Spread tofu mixture about 1/4″ thick on nori leaving 1″–1-1/2″ at the top and half an inch at the bottom uncovered. Roll in the same way as nori-maki (directions are in the chapter on grains). Tie each roll at both ends with a piece of gourd strip. Place rolls in a steamer and steam for about 10–12 minutes. Gently remove and allow to cool. (If you slice while hot, the nori will fall apart.) Untie gourd strips and slice into eight equal pieces (rounds) as you would for nori-maki. Arrange on a platter and serve.

Deep-Fried Tofu Cakes

> 2 cakes tofu, drained
> 1/2 cup carrot, very finely diced
> 1/2 cup scallion, sliced into small pieces
> 1/4 cup burdock, very finely diced
> sesame oil
> tamari
> toasted nori

Sauté carrots and burdock in a small amount of sesame oil for 5 minutes. Add a little water, cover and cook until vegetables are soft. Season with a little tamari and cook 3 minutes. Remove cover and cook water away.

Grind tofu in a suribachi. Add vegetables and scallions to tofu. Mix well. Shape into patties or rolls. Wrap a strip of toasted nori around the patties. Deep-fry in hot sesame oil until golden brown and drain. Serve with a tamari-ginger dip sauce.

Aburage (Age or Deep-Fried Tofu)

Aburage is the Japanese name for tofu that has been drained of excess liquid, sliced, and deep-fried until golden brown. It can be cut into a variety of shapes before frying. In Japan it is often cut into cubes, triangles, large strips, pouches and cakes.

To prepare, place a cake of fresh tofu on a wooden cutting board. Place a weight or plate on top to squeeze excess liquid from the tofu. Place a small dish under one end of the board and prop it up so that it is slightly tilted. This will allow the liquid from the tofu to drain off properly. Let the tofu sit for about an hour to drain properly, and slice it into pieces about 1/3–1/2 inch thick.

Lightly coat each piece with arrowroot flour and place in hot sesame oil. Do not put too many in at once, as this will lower the temperature of the oil and the tofu will not cook properly. Deep-fry until golden brown. Drain on paper towels to remove excess oil. You may also boil the deep-fried slices in water to remove any remaining oil.

These strips can be cut into pieces and added to soups, sauces, on top of noodles, etc. Or you may leave them whole and use them to make stuffed tofu pouches, which are explained below.

Stuffed Age Pouches

> 5–6 age pouches
> 1/2 cake fresh tofu
> 1/2 cup diced onions
> 1/4 cup very finely diced carrot
> 1/4 cup green beans, very finely diced
> kuzu
> water

tamari to taste
kanpyo (6 strips 6″ long, soaked for 10 minutes)

Boil age pouches in water to remove excess oil and rinse under cold water. Slice one end off of each rectangularly shaped pouch. Using a vegetable knife, gently separate the top and bottom from the inside portion of each pouch. Be careful not to push the knife all the way through the opposite side of the pouch. Open pouch and gently spoon out inside portion.

Lightly sauté vegetables for 5–7 minutes in a small amount of sesame oil. If necessary, add a little water to soften, and lightly season with tamari.

Grind tofu in a suribachi. Add sautéed vegetables and mix thoroughly. Fill each pouch with tofu/vegetable mixture. Do not stuff to capacity. Tie the open end of each pouch with a piece of gourd strip.

Place a piece of kombu in a pot and add stuffed pouches. Add just enough water to cover the pouches and a pinch of sea salt. Bring to a boil, reduce flame to low, cover and simmer 5–7 minutes. Add a little diluted kuzu to the water to make a sauce. Season with tamari to taste, and cook for 10 minutes. You may also season the sauce with a few bonito flakes and some diced onion.

These pouches may be stuffed with other ingredients such as cooked rice, tofu, and vegetables; okara and vegetables; tofu and hijiki; mochi; and others. Please experiment.

Okara

2 cups fresh okara
1/2 cup onion, diced
1/2 cup carrot, cut into matchsticks
1/4 cup burdock, cut into matchsticks
2 shiitake mushrooms, soaked, destemmed and sliced thin
1/2 cup kombu soup stock
1/2 cup sliced scallions
tamari to taste

Lightly sauté all vegetables (except scallions) for 2–3 minutes in a skillet with a small amount of sesame oil. Add kombu broth, cover and simmer over a low flame for 3–4 minutes. Add okara, cover and simmer on low for 5–6 minutes. Add a small amount of tamari to taste and simmer for an additional 3–4 minutes or until all liquid has been absorbed. Mix in scallions. Place in serving bowl. To make okara lighter, dry roast in a skillet for 3–4 minutes before adding vegetables.

Okara Croquettes

Croquettes can be made by mixing okara with pastry or rice flour. Enough flour and water should be added to make the mixture hold together. Add diced vegetables and mix with a small amount of tamari. Spoon or form into cakes and deep-fry in hot sesame oil until golden brown. Drain oil on paper towels. Serve with tamari-ginger or tamari-daikon dip sauce to help digest oil.

NATTO

Natto is a fermented soybean product which you can easily make at home. All you need is a pilot light in your oven. For directions on how to make natto, please see *Introducing Macrobiotic Cooking*.

Sautéed Natto
2 cups fresh natto
1/2 cup diced onion or sliced scallions
sesame oil
tamari to taste

Lightly brush a skillet with a small amount of sesame oil and heat. Sauté onions until translucent. Add natto and a small amount of tamari to taste. Sauté 2–3 minutes. Serve. If you use scallions, you may add at the same time as the natto.

Natto Rice or Noodles
Mix natto with a few scallions or diced raw onion and add a small amount of tamari. Garnish each bowl of freshly cooked brown rice or noodles with one or two tablespoons of natto and a few small strips of toasted nori. Serve.

Natto Tempura
2 cups fresh natto
1/2 cup diced onion
1/4 cup diced carrot
1/4 cup sliced scallions
arrowroot flour
tamari

Mix natto, onions and scallions with a small amount of tamari and enough arrowroot flour to hold together.

Place tablespoons of natto into hot sesame oil and deep-fry until golden brown. Drain on paper towels. Serve with tamari-ginger sauce or grated daikon.

Dried Natto
2 cups fresh natto
cookie sheet

Place natto on a cookie sheet and bake at a low temperature until each bean is completely dry and hard.

Please refer to *Introducing Macrobiotic Cooking* for additional information on the preparation of azuki and other beans, as well as recipes for tofu; okara; corn and tofu; tofu, onions and watercress; dried tofu; yuba; vegetables and yuba; *gan-modoki*; and natto.

6. Cooking with Sea Vegetables

For centuries, people around the world who lived near the salty oceans and seas have harvested kelp and other sea vegetables to use in their cooking. For instance, in America a number of the Indian tribes who lived near the coasts harvested and used a variety of seaweeds. Of course, the Japanese and other Oriental peoples have traditionally relied upon sea vegetables for thousands of years as a source of iodine and minerals, and still use them widely in their cooking. The Scottish and Irish people harvested dulse and Irish moss, while sea vegetables are a part of the native cuisine in places like the Hawaiian Islands, Philippines, the South Pacific islands, Australia, South America, Iceland, the U.S.S.R., and many other countries.

Today, most of our sea vegetables come from Japan. Recently, however, some kombu, kelp and hijiki have been harvested off the coast of Maine and Nova Scotia, while dulse has been harvested off the Maine coast for quite some time now. America is very fortunate to have thousands of miles of coastline on the Atlantic and Pacific oceans where a wealth of edible sea vegetables are just waiting to be harvested. All of these edible seaweeds are rich in calcium, iron, Vitamin A, niacin, Vitamin C, protein, iodine and other minerals. Since the sea salt that we use in macrobiotic cooking has no iodine added to it, sea vegetables are a valuable and necessary item in our diet.

Because Americans are generally not accustomed to eating sea vegetables, their taste and texture may seem strange at first. But when properly prepared, you should come to love the various seaweeds that are available in natural food stores and they will, hopefully, become a regular item in your diet. Also, the more you eat these sea vegetables, the sooner you will come to notice the beneficial effect that they have on your health. For example, sea vegetables help strengthen the intestines, liver, pancreas, sexual organs and bloodstream. In some cases, you may notice that your hair has become stronger and darker in color, with fewer split ends after beginning to eat sea vegetables. Since they are so rich in calcium, they are excellent for producing and strengthening bones and teeth.

Some of the seaweeds that you may encounter in a natural food store are kombu, wakame, nori, green nori flakes, hijiki, arame, dulse, kelp, *mekabu*, Irish moss, agar agar and Corsican seaweed.

Kombu can be used in many ways. It can be roasted and ground into a powder for use as a condiment, or can be used in a variety of soups, salads, soup stocks, vegetable and bean dishes, pickles, etc. In many cases, wakame can be substituted for kombu. Wakame is one of my favorite seaweeds, and is delicious when added to miso soup and salads. Nori is very high in protein, and I find it especially satisfying during pregnancy. It has often helped me to satisfy cravings for other protein foods, such as fish.

Nori is very easy to prepare and is great as a snack, as a garnish for soups and other dishes, in riceballs, nori-maki, etc. Nori is also very high in iron, which makes it especially good food for pregnant women who may be concerned about iron levels. Green nori flakes are sold prepackaged and are mostly used as a condiment over rice and other foods. This type of nori is the highest in protein and iron.

Arame is dark brown in color and has a very mild flavor. I am sure that you will find it to be one of the easiest of the sea vegetables to acquire a taste for. It does not have as strong an ocean flavor as its cousin, hijiki. Hijiki is thicker and coarser in texture, and has a much stronger flavor. It is black in color, and when soaked unwinds into very long strands. Both of these seaweeds can be cooked with lotus root, carrots, onions, daikon and other vegetables, or with tofu, deep-fried tofu, soybeans and many other foods. They can also be combined and cooked with rice, millet or barley, and can be used in making vegetable or vegetable-grain pies and sea vegetable pastries. Salads made with hijiki are very nutritious and are especially good along with a tofu or umeboshi dressing.

Dulse is highest of all the seaweeds in iron, and has a very salty flavor. If you wish to reduce your intake of salt, simply wash or soak dulse before using. However, do not wash or soak your seaweeds for too long, as this will cause many of their valuable vitamins and minerals to be lost. Dulse makes a delicious condiment when combined with sesame seeds, soups, salads, aspics, etc.

Mekabu has a somewhat strong flavor, but is delicious when used in soups and vegetable dishes. Irish moss can be used in soups and stews, as a gelatin dessert and in jellies, aspics and puddings. Kelp can be used as a seasoning or condiment, or in soups and vegetable dishes. Agar agar is a translucent seaweed used as a gelatinous base for desserts which are called *kanten*, and in various types of aspics. Corsican seaweed is usually sold in the form of a tea which is helpful in discharging various types of worms from the body.

The following are only a few of the many ways to prepare sea vegetables. Additional recipes can be found in the other chapters of this book.

Hijiki with Soybeans
Hijiki is one of the more yang seaweeds, and is often prepared with sesame oil, vegetables, and soybean products. Those who wish to restrict their intake of oil

can also omit it if they choose. The following recipe is especially good if you wish to restrict your oil intake.

> **2 cups soaked hijiki (or arame)**
> **1/2 cup soybeans**
> **water (soaking water from hijiki to cover seaweed)**
> **tamari to taste**

Wash hijiki or arame very quickly under cold water. Place in a bowl, cover with water and soak 5–10 minutes. Remove and drain. Slice hijiki strands into 1″–2″ pieces.

Wash soybeans and roast on a low flame until golden brown. Do not roast too long or on too high a flame, as these beans burn very easily. (You may also wash the beans and soak them overnight instead of roasting.) Do not use oil in the skillet when roasting. Stir constantly to evenly roast and avoid burning.

Place soybeans in a pot. Place hijiki on top and do not mix. Add enough of the soaking water to cover the top of the seaweed. Bring to a boil, cover, and reduce flame to low. Simmer until beans are about 80% done. Season with tamari to taste and simmer until beans are done. Remove cover, raise the flame slightly and cook until almost all liquid evaporates. Serve.

Hijiki and Deep-Fried Tofu

> **2 cups soaked hijiki (or arame)**
> **1/2 cake tofu**
> **water to cover**
> **tamari to taste**

Wash, soak and slice hijiki or arame as above. Drain tofu and slice into rectangular pieces. Deep-fry until golden brown on both sides. Remove and place on paper towels to drain oil. Cut tofu slices into thin strips and place in a pot. Place hijiki on top of tofu. Add hijiki soaking water to cover. Bring to a boil, cover and reduce flame to low. Simmer about 5 minutes. Season with tamari to taste and simmer another 20 minutes. Remove cover and cook away excess water. Serve.

Hijiki Rolls

> **2 cups cooked hijiki (or arame) and vegetables or tofu**
> **1 large pie crust (see dessert section)**

Roll crust out as you would in making a pie. Drain excess liquid from hijiki or arame and place seaweed evenly on the crust. Leave about one inch around the outer edge of the crust uncovered by hijiki. Roll up the crust, seal the edges with water and press with a fork as you would for strudel. Bake at 350° F. for about 30–35 minutes. Allow to cool. Slice into one-inch rounds as you would nori-maki and serve on a platter with rounds placed on their sides. Each piece should have a spiral appearance, with the hijiki and pastry spiraling into the center of the roll. Serve.

Hijiki or Arame with Sautéed Vegetables

Any of the recipes which call for hijiki can also be made with arame. In general, arame requires slightly less cooking time than hijiki.

When preparing these sea vegetables with sautéed vegetables, first lightly brush the skillet or pot with sesame oil. Add desired vegetables and sauté for several minutes. Add seaweed and cook as for the hijiki and deep-fried tofu recipe presented above.

Arame with Lotus Root

> **2 cups soaked arame**
> **1 cup lotus root, sliced into quarters, matchsticks, or diced**
> **sesame oil**
> **water**
> **tamari to taste**

Wash, soak and slice arame as you would hijiki. Lightly brush sesame oil in a skillet and heat. Place lotus root in skillet and sauté 5–7 minutes. Add arame with soaking water to cover. Bring to a boil, cover, reduce flame to low and simmer 30–35 minutes. Season with tamari to taste and continue to cook another 20 minutes. Remove cover, turn flame up slightly and cook away excess water. Serve.

Arame or Hijiki with Dried Daikon

Dried daikon is very sweet and high in calcium, vitamins and minerals. It is available prepackaged in many natural food stores and Oriental markets.

> **2 cups soaked and sliced arame or hijiki**
> **1 cup dried daikon, soaked and sliced**
> **seaweed and daikon soaking water**
> **tamari to taste**

Cook as above until the dried daikon becomes soft.

Wakame, Carrots and Onions

> **2 cups soaked and sliced wakame**
> **1 onion, cut into half-moons**
> **1 carrot, cut in small, irregular shapes**
> **water**
> **tamari to taste**

Wash wakame very quickly. Soak 5–7 minutes and slice. Place onions and carrots in a pot and place wakame on top. Add enough wakame soaking water to cover the top of wakame. Bring to a boil, cover and reduce flame to low. Simmer about 15–20 minutes. Add tamari to taste. This dish should be very lightly seasoned. The carrots and onions will become very sweet. Simmer another 10–15 minutes. Remove cover, turn up flame and cook off excess liquid. Serve.

Wakame and Ginger
  2 cups soaked and sliced wakame
  2 Tbsp. fresh grated ginger
  water
  tamari

Wash, soak and slice wakame. Place in a pot and almost cover with soaking water. Bring to a boil, reduce flame to low and simmer about 10–15 minutes. Remove wakame and drain. Save cooking water for use as soup stock. Place wakame in individual serving dishes and add a couple of drops of tamari to each. Peel skin off fresh ginger and grate. Place about 1/4 teaspoon of grated ginger on top of each dish and serve.

I first heard about this very delicious dish from one of my neighbors in Kyoto. The ginger makes it a little spicy, but I feel that it is a good dish to help balance an over-yang condition cuased by eating too much fish and salt. It also helps to dissolve deposits of animal fat and oil, as well as providing beneficial vitamins and minerals.

Wakame and Fresh Tuna
  2 cups wakame, washed, soaked and sliced
  one small fillet of fresh tuna (about 3″ × 2″)
  water
  tamari to taste

Place wakame in a pot and cover with water. Bring to a boil, cover and reduce flame to low. Simmer 25–30 minutes.

Place tuna in a very small saucepan with a little water and a pinch of sea salt. Bring to a boil. Reduce flame and simmer 2–3 minutes. Cut tuna into small chunks and add to wakame. Season lightly with tamari and simmer for 10 minutes. Boil off excess liquid. Serve.

Baked Wakame
  2 cups wakame, soaked and sliced
  1 cup onion, cut in half-moons
  1-1/2–2 Tbsp. sesame tahini
  1/4 cup roasted sesame seeds
  water
  tamari

Place onions in a saucepan and add a very small amount of wakame soaking water. Bring to a boil, cover, reduce flame to low and simmer about 5 minutes. Remove onions and place in a small casserole dish.

Mix onions with wakame. Dilute tahini with about 1/2 cup wakame soaking water and mix with wakame and onions. Mix in a small amount of tamari. Smooth out wakame and onions in casserole dish and sprinkle lightly toasted sesame seeds on top. Cover dish and bake in 350° F. oven for 25–30 minutes. Remove cover and bake another 10–15 minutes to evaporate excess liquid and slightly brown top. Serve.

Kombu, Burdock, and Lotus Root

1 cup burdock, sliced diagonally about 1/4″ thick
1 cup lotus root, quartered and sliced 1/4″ thick
one 12″ strip kombu
water
tamari to taste

Wash vegetables and slice as directed. Quickly wash kombu, soak for 5–7 minutes, and slice into one-inch squares. Place kombu in the bottom of pot, place vegetables on top and add enough kombu soaking water to almost cover. Add a pinch of sea salt. Bring to a boil, cover and reduce flame to low. Simmer until vegetables are done. Season with tamari to taste and simmer another 15–20 minutes. Remove cover and cook away almost all excess liquid. Serve.

This dish is also very good with a few soybeans added to it. Simply dry-roast beans until golden brown or soak overnight. Place beans on top of kombu, vegetables on top of beans, and cook as directed until beans are just about done. Season with tamari and cook until done.

Kombu-Vegetable Rolls

one 12″ strip kombu, about 2-1/2″–3″ wide
1 large carrot, quartered lengthwise
kanpyo (dried gourd)
water
tamari to taste (about 1 Tbsp.)

Lightly brush kombu with clean sponge and soak until soft and easy to handle.

Soak kanpyo until easy to use. You will probably need about ten 6″ long strips.

Place kombu strip flat on a cutting board. Place carrot strips lengthwise along the strip of kombu. Roll up kombu very tightly around carrots and tie in the middle and at both ends. Tie leftover strips around kombu roll so that they are evenly spaced.

Place roll in a pot and half cover with kombu soaking water. Bring to a boil, cover and reduce flame to low. Simmer about 45 minutes. Season with tamari and allow to simmer another 20 minutes or so. Remove kombu roll and slice into even rounds between each gourd strip. Arrange on a plate with roll slices standing on end so that carrot shows.

Burdock can also be used in this recipe. Simply quarter it if it is very thick, or halve it if it is thinner and place it lengthwise on the roll together with the carrots.

Shio Kombu

(please see condiment section)

Nori

Nori is used most frequently as a garnish, for riceballs, nori-maki or simply as a snack.

198

It is easily prepared by holding a sheet with the shiny side facing you about 10 inches from the flame of your stove. Do not roast both sides as this destroys some of the valuable vitamins and minerals. Rotate the sheet above the flame so that it is evenly toasted. The color will change from black or puple to green when done.

To use as a garnish, simply cut roasted sheets into squares or strips with a pair of scissors. For rice balls, nori-maki, etc., please see the Chapter on "Cooking with Whole Grains."

Tempura Nori

> 2–3 sheets nori, cut into strips 1/2″ wide by 2″ long
> 1 cup tempura batter (see vegetable section for recipe)
> sesame oil
> tamari-ginger dip sauce

Slice nori as directed. Heat sesame oil. Dip strips of nori into batter with chopsticks or use fingers to evenly coat with batter. Drop into hot oil and deep-fry until golden brown on both sides. Do not place too many strips in the oil at once or they will stick together and lower the temperature of the oil. Drain on paper towels. Serve with a tamari-ginger dip sauce.

Shio Nori

> (please see condiment section)

Tempuraed Nori-Tofu Rolls

> 2 sheets toasted nori
> 1/2 cake tofu, drained and ground in a suribachi with a little tamari
> tempura batter
> sesame oil
> tamari-ginger or tamari-daikon dip sauce

Prepare nori-tofu rolls as you would nori-maki (see grain section). Slice into even rounds and dip into tempura batter. Place in hot sesame oil and deep-fry until golden brown. Serve with dip sauce to help digest oil.

Sautéed Dulse and Vegetables

> 1 cup dulse, washed, soaked and sliced
> 1/2 cup carrot, cut into thin rectangles
> 1/2 cup daikon, cut into thin rectangles
> sesame oil
> small amount of tamari

Lightly brush skillet with sesame oil. Add daikon and carrots and sauté 5–7 minutes on a medium flame, stirring constantly to avoid burning. Add chopped dulse and several drops of tamari. Cover and reduce flame to low. Simmer 10 minutes or so. Remove cover and cook off any excess liquid. Serve.

Agar Agar
(please see vegetable section for vegetable aspic recipes and dessert section for kanten recipes)

For additional sea vegetable recipes, please refer to other sections of this book, or see *Introducing Macrobiotic Cooking* for more information on the preparation of arame, wakame, boiled kombu and vegetables, baked kombu and vegetables, shio kombu and riceballs.

7. Natural Baking including Whole-Grain Bread, Waffles, Pancakes and Doughnuts

Recently, while walking through a local supermarket, I started reading the labels of various breads and bread products. I was quite surprised at the long lists of additives. I remember that only a few years ago the lists of additives and ingredients seemed to be much shorter. You could still find a decent loaf of rye or Italian bread made only from flour, water, salt and yeast. Now it is more difficult to find even a loaf of bread such as this. Even the whole wheat or dark rye breads sold today in most supermarkets contain many additives, preservatives and coloring agents. I have often heard people from Europe comment on how much better the bread is there.

Fortunately, however, amidst this trend of mass produced, chemicalized, over-yeasted and lifeless bread, there is a growing interest in making homemade, good quality, nutritious breads once again, both on a small scale in many houses and on a somewhat larger scale in small bakeries throughout the country.[1] Now you you can find many delicious varieties of whole wheat, rye, pumpernickel and other types of bread, muffins, rolls, etc.

When making your own bread, it is best to use freshly ground, organic flour. This may not always be possible, but try to use it whenever you can, as fresh flour makes a big difference in the flavor of your bread. Also, once flour has been milled, it begins to oxidize and lose many of its valuable nutrients and its natu-

---

[1] One of the most outstanding naturally baked breads in this country is made by the Baldwin Hill Company in Massachusetts. Made only from whole wheat, sea salt, well water and a special sourdough starter, Baldwin Hill bread is baked in an authentic brick oven according to traditional European methods. Thousands of people throughout New England enjoy this bread on a regular basis. For a brochure about the bread and how it is made, write to: Box B, Baldwin Hill Bakery, Baldwin Hill Road, Phillipston, Mass. 01331.

rally sweet flavor. You will also notice a tremendous difference between bread made from organic flour and that made with non-organic flour. Your bread will also rise better if it is made with freshly ground flour.

The best kind of whole wheat to use in making bread is hard, red winter wheat. It is very high in protein and gluten, which causes the bread to rise. Pastry or other types of spring wheat are generally low in gluten and protein and do not produce good bread. These wheats are used mainly in making cookies, cakes, pies and other pastries.

Flours which are made from corn, millet, barley, oats, rye, sweet rice, and brown rice help to make delicious breads when combined with whole wheat flour. When used by themselves these flours do not make very good bread, because they do not contain enough gluten. When preparing flour, first wash your grains and then roast them in a dry skillet until a slightly nutty fragrance is released. Use a low flame and stir to avoid burning. Then mill the roasted grain in either a stone or steel-toothed mill. Stone ground flour generally produces the best quality bread.

Cooked whole grains can also be used along with whole wheat flour to produce good bread. I have found that breads made with flour and cooked grains are much easier to digest than those made with flour alone. Whole oats, oatmeal, millet, sweet rice, amazake, rice, soft rice, rye and barley all make delicious bread. The grain can either be cooked as it would in a regular grain dish, or until it is very soft. Cooked grain that is three or more days old and which has become slightly sour acts as a very good leavening agent, helping the bread dough to rise naturally. It also produces a very moist, sweet-flavored bread.

Oil is not necessary in making good bread. In fact, many breads taste much better without it. Also, breads made with oil have a tendency to spoil easily, as oil becomes rancid if not used quickly. Oil can be used now and then to make your bread lighter and more moist, but the bread should be eaten more quickly.

It is not at all necessary to add sweeteners to your bread. If you do use sweeteners, however, the best quality ones are barley malt, yinnie syrup, rice honey (*ame*), or amazake.

Natural sea salt should be used in making your bread, while well water is the best type of water to use in bread baking. Fresh spring water is the next most preferable, while if neither of these are available, tap water will do. Distilled water is not suitable for drinking or making bread. It is a lifeless form of water, totally lacking in minerals, energy, etc. It is better to use tap water than to use distilled water.

Yeast is unnecessary in making good bread. For thousands of years, people have been making delicious bread without the use of yeast. In many countries throughout the world, yeast is still not used as leavening agent. Bread will rise naturally if it is kneaded properly (about 350 times) and allowed to proof (sit or rise) for 8–12 hours or more in a warm place. There are many natural leavening agents which you can use to promote fermentation. These include sourdough starters, sour noodle cooking water, and others. If eaten excessively, yeast bloats the stomach, causes indigestion and often hiccups, thins the blood, and weakens the intestines. However, you may occasionally eat yeasted breads at parties, during special meals, or when dining at a restaurant, but they should not be eaten in your home on a regular basis. Your health may decline considerably if they are overused. If and when you use yeast in baking bread at home, you need only add a small amount to cause the bread to rise. If you use too much, it may tend to override the natural sweetness and flavor of the bread.

Yeasted bread tends to mold and decay much more quickly than unyeasted bread. Unyeasted breads usually dry out before they mold. If this happens, simply slice it and steam it for several minutes. You may also steam it whole. Bread becomes very moist and soft when steamed, as if freshly baked. If you store your bread in plastic bags, it may tend to mold more quickly because of the moisture that is held in. Paper bags are better to wrap the bread in. If the crust does mold, simply remove the moldy portion and slice, steam or toast the remainder. Hard or dry bread can also be used for croutons or stuffings, so don't throw it away.

Other factors which may affect the quality of your bread include the time of day you make it, the phase of the moon, and, most importantly, your own physical and mental condition. I have found that if I make bread early in the morning (corresponding to the more expansive time referred to as *tree nature*) and bake it around dinner time, it rises or ferments (yinnizes) much more smoothly than if I make the bread at night (during the more contractive time known as *metal nature*) and bake it in the morning. Also, my bread seems to rise better on warm, sunny (more yang) days than on cold, rainy (more yin) days. Fermentation, which is a more yin process, naturally becomes more active under more yang conditions. Also, if your physical condition is not good, you may discharge this feeling or vibration through your hands into the dough, and your bread will not turn out as well. At the same time, if you are feeling unhappy, worried, depressed, etc., these vibrations are often discharged into the dough and the bread will not rise as well. I have found that if I maintain a more happy and positive attitude while kneading my bread, it rises more smoothly and tastes better.

As with other things, practice and patience are important. The more you grow accustomed to working with flour and baking at home, the better your bread will become.

Corn Bread

    3 cups corn meal
    1 cup pastry flour
    1/4 tsp. sea salt
    2–3 Tbsp. sesame oil
    1/2 cup barley malt (optional)
    2-1/2–3 cups water

Mix flour and salt well. Add oil and sift in with hands. Add barley malt and mix a little. Gradually add in water until dough becomes like a thick cookie batter.

Oil a bread or oblong cake pan with sesame oil. Heat oiled pan in 325° F. oven until hot but not smoking. Place batter in pan and spread out evenly. Bake at 325° F. for half an hour and at 350° F. for about 50–60 minutes, or until light brown and top starts to crack open a little.

Corn-Rice Bread

>   3 cups corn meal
>   1 cup pastry flour
>   1 cup cooked brown rice
>   1/4 tsp. sea salt
>   2–3 Tbsp. sesame oil
>   3 cups water

Mix and bake as above.

   Apple-corn bread can be made by adding about a cup of diced apples to the batter. Other grains can also be used instead of rice. Also, fresh sweet corn removed from the cob and mixed in with the batter makes a very sweet, delicious bread.

Sourdough Waffles

>   1-1/2 cups pastry flour
>   1 cup whole wheat flour
>   2 Tbsp. sesame oil
>   1/4 tsp. sea salt
>   1 cup soft rice
>   1 cup soured seitan starch water
>   1 cup cold water

Combine all ingredients and allow to sit overnight in a warm place. Use a large bowl to let the batter sit in, as it will ferment from the sour seitan water and rise. It may spill over if the bowl is too small.

   Oil waffle iron and heat. Add batter and cook until golden brown.

Pancakes

Use same recipe as above and cook as for pancakes. As a variation, you may omit the grain or use other grains or flours, such as buckwheat, corn, rice or whole wheat. Buckwheat, corn and rice flours should always be used in combination with whole wheat or pastry flour. The whole wheat or pastry flour should comprise a larger portion of the batter than the other flours.

Rye Bread

>   5 cups whole wheat flour
>   3 cups rye flour
>   1/2 tsp. sea salt
>   2 Tbsp. oil (optional)
>   water (about 4 cups)

Combine flour and salt. Mix well. Add oil, if desired, and mix well with hands. Gradually add water to form a ball of dough. Knead about 350 times, adding flour as needed as dough becomes sticky. Oil 2 bread pans with light sesame oil.

Divide dough in half and shape into loaves. Place in pans and press down around the edges to round the loaves. Make a shallow slit in the top center of each loaf. Lightly brush loaves with sesame oil and cover with a warm, damp cloth or dish towel. Allow to sit 8–12 hours in a warm place. Bake at 300° F. for about 30 minutes and 350° F. for about 1-1/4 hours. Allow to cool, and slice.

You may add a few caraway seeds to this recipe for a different flavor, or add a cup of sourdough starter or sour seitan-starch water for a sourdough rye bread. If you do use a sourdough starter, reduce the amount of water used accordingly.

Barley-Millet Bread

    5 cups whole wheat flour
    2 cups barley flour
    1 cup millet flour
    2 Tbsp. sesame oil (optional)
    1/2 tsp. sea salt
    water

Roast barley and millet separately in a dry skillet. Grind each separately into flour. Combine flours and salt. Add oil and mix well. Add in water to form a ball of dough. Knead 350 times. Place in oiled bread pans, shape into loaves, and oil the top of the loaves lightly with sesame oil. Allow to sit, covered with a damp towel, in a warm place for 8–12 hours. Bake as in the above recipe.

Rice Kayu Bread

    2 cups rice
    8 cups water

Place rice in a pressure-cooker and add water. Cook for 1 hour or more. Allow pressure to come down. Remove cover and place rice in a large bowl to cool. Add the following ingredients while rice is still slightly warm:

    2 tsp. sesame oil (optional)
    1/2 tsp. sea salt
    enough whole wheat flour to form into a ball of dough

Add oil and salt to rice and mix well. Add enough flour to form into a soft ball of dough. Knead about 350 times, adding flour to the ball as needed to keep it from getting too sticky. Place the dough in two oiled bread pans, shape into loaves and allow to rise 8–12 hours. Be sure to cover the loaves with a damp towel and set in a warm place while rising. Bake at 300° F. for 30 minutes and 350° F. for one hour or until golden brown. Cool and slice.

You may also add a few raisins to this recipe for raisin-rice kayu bread. Boil the raisins for a very short time to soften before adding to the dough.

Raisin-Rice Bread

    4 cups cooked rice
    4 cups whole wheat flour
    1/2 tsp. sea salt
    2 Tbsp. sesame oil (optional)

> **1-1/4 cups water**
> **2 cups raisins**

Boil raisins for about 10 minutes in 1-1/4 cups water. Allow to cool.

Mix flour and salt. Add oil and sift with hands. Add rice and sift well to evenly mix. Add cooled water and raisins. Form into a ball and knead 350 times, adding a little flour occasionally while kneading to prevent sticking.

Oil two pans, divide dough equally in half and place in pans. Oil the surface of the loaves and shape dough so that it is rounded. Cover the pans with a damp cloth or towel and place in a warm area. Allow to rise for 8–12 hours. Bake at 300° F. for 30 minutes and 350° F. for 45 minutes to an hour.

Crêpe Batter

> **2 cups pastry flour**
> **2 cups water**
> **1/4 tsp. sea salt**

Mix ingredients well and whip in a blender or with an egg beater. This makes the batter lighter.

Pour onto a hot, oiled pancake griddle or pan and smooth out with a spoon until very thin and round. This can be done by making a circular motion, very lightly, on the batter with a spoon.

Cook until done. Do not burn.

Prepare a vegetable or fruit filling and fill. Roll crêpes up and serve. (Fasten with a toothpick if necessary.)

Yeasted Doughnuts

> **1-1/2 cups pastry flour**
> **1-1/2 cups whole wheat flour**
> **1/4 cup chestnut flour**
> **1/4 cup warm water**
> **1/2 Tbsp. dry yeast**
> **1 Tbsp. whole wheat flour**
> **1/3 tsp. cinnamon**
> **1 cup raisins**
> **1-1/2 Tbsp. sesame oil**
> **1 tsp. sea salt**
> **1 cup warm water**

Dissolve yeast in 1/4 cup warm water and let sit for 5 minutes. Add a tablespoon of whole wheat flour and let sit for an additional 5–10 minutes. Combine flours, salt, cinnamon and oil. Mix well with hands. Add raisins.

Gradually combine yeast and water with flour mixture. Knead for 5–7 minutes. Place dough in an oiled bowl and cover with a damp towel. Let rise in a warm place for about 4 hours. Dough should double in size by then. Push dough down and let rise for one hour more. Push down again and roll out on a floured board as you would for a pie crust. Dough should be about 1/4–1/3 inch thick. Cut out and deep-fry in hot oil until golden brown on both sides. Drain on paper towels to remove oil. Cool before serving.

Yeasted Whole Wheat Bagels
    1/2 Tbsp. dry yeast
    1/4 cup warm water
    1 Tbsp. pastry flour
    1-1/2 cups whole wheat flour
    1-1/2 cups pastry flour
    1/4 cup yinnie syrup
    1 diced onion (optional)
    1/2 cup sesame oil
    2–2-1/2 cups whole wheat flour
    1 tsp. sea salt

Dissolve yeast in 1/4 cup warm water and 1 tablespoon of pastry flour. Let sit for about 10 minutes.

Mix 1-1/2 cups whole wheat flour, 1-1/2 cups pastry flour, water, yinnie syrup, onion and yeast. Cover with a damp towel and let rise until double in size.

Add oil, sea salt and remaining 2–2-1/2 cups whole wheat flour. Knead for 5–7 minutes. Cover with a damp towel and let rise for one hour.

Press down and let rise another 20 minutes. Roll into log shape and connect ends, or cut out center as you would a doughnut.

Dip into boiling water for 10 minutes. Place on an oiled cookie sheet and let rise for 20 minutes.

Bake at 375° F. for about 25 minutes or until golden brown.

Cool before serving.

Yeasted Rolls
    (see Holiday Menu—Thanksgiving section)

For recipes for rice, raisin-rice, amazake, whole wheat, corn and steamed breads, please refer to *Introducing Macrobiotic Cooking*.

8. Natural Desserts

The dessert recipes presented in this chapter do not call for the use of eggs, dairy or soy products, honey, maple syrup, or tropical spices.

The best quality sweeteners to use in dessert cooking are those made from whole grains. Barley malt, yinnie syrup, amazake, or rice honey (*ame*) are the four sweeteners which I recommend most highly. They are available in most natural food stores throughout this country. (Amazake may not be readily available, but it can be made very easily at home.) Fruits such as apples, strawberries, pears, peaches, cherries, raisins, currants, apricots and others can also be used to sweeten your desserts. (Tropical fruits and juices are not recommended for this climate.)

As much as possible, try to use locally grown, seasonal fruits (such as those recommended in the Standard Diet) in your desserts, or, during the winter, fruits such as apples and pears which keep fairly well during the colder months. Raisins, currants, and other dried fruits can also be used in preparing winter desserts, as they are harvested in late autumn and store very well during the cold months. Walnuts, chestnuts, almonds, pecans and peanuts can be used in desserts, along with sesame and sunflower seeds. Other varieties of nuts should be used only occasionally.

Pastry, rice, whole wheat, sweet rice, oat and millet flours can be used in making various cakes, cookies, crusts for pies, strudels, etc., as can rolled oats. For the best tasting desserts, try to use only freshly milled flour.

Various nut and grain milks can also be used in custards, puddings and fillings. To make oat milk, for example, cook one cup of whole oats with 5 cups of water until very creamy and done. Purée the oats, place them in a cheesecloth sack and squeeze out the milk. The leftover grain or bran part can be used in breads, etc. Rice milk can be made in the same way. Almond milk can be made by boiling almonds and puréeing them in a blender until the liquid is creamy.

The only spices that I use in dessert cooking are fresh ginger root and cinnamon. Cinnamon is more yang than most other tropical spices, but should be used only occasionally and in small quantities. I don't recommend that you use it in all of your desserts.

Use only the best quality oils in your desserts, such as light sesame and corn oil. Do not overuse them though, as the combination of oil, fruit and flour can result in health problems if eaten too frequently or in excessive volume. Corn oil makes lighter, crispier crusts and cookies, while sesame oil leaves a slightly stronger flavor in pastries.

Apple cider jelly, apple butter, cooked and puréed dried fruits, squash butters, currants and raisin purée can be used as dessert fillings. Sesame butter, tahini, and occasionally peanut and almond butters, may be used in cookies, custards, etc.

Desserts made without milk, butter, soy butter, soy milk, eggs or leavening agents may not be as light as those which you are used to eating, but they are very delicious and are best for your health.

Soy products such as soy butter, soy milk, and tofu are very yin, and should generally not be used in desserts, regardless of the popularity of items like tofu custard and tofu cheesecake. Tofu is already very high in yin factors, such as protein and fat, and should not be used in combination with sweeteners, spices, fruit and other more yin items. Tofu should be prepared and served along with more yang items such as tamari, miso, bonito, kuzu, root vegetables, etc. In Japan, people intuitively avoid combining tofu with various yin items. They intuitively know that it would be unhealthy. I know from experience that tofu desserts can produce an upset stomach and headaches. Therefore, I never prepare them in my kitchen and don't buy them in natural food restaurants or stores.

Through experience, I have also discovered that the best desserts for overall · health are those which are simply made and do not contain a long list of ingredients. Rich, heavy desserts will eventually cause stagnation in the intestines, stomach, liver, spleen, pancreas and gall bladder, and can result in an overall decline in vitality if eaten regularly.

Sweet Rice Cookies (1 dozen)
> **1 cup sweet rice flour**
> **1-1/2 cups pastry flour**
> **1/2 cup roasted sesame seeds**
> **1/2 cup roasted sunflower seeds**
> **1-1/2 cups apple juice**
> **2 Tbsp. corn or sesame oil**
> **1 cup raisins or currants**
> **1/4 tsp. sea salt**

Mix dry ingredients together. Add oil and mix with your hands. Add raisins and apple juice and mix well. Place a tablespoonful at a time onto an oiled cookie sheet. Spread out very thin. Bake for 25 minutes at 350° F.

Raisin Cookies (about 1-1/2 dozen)
> **3-1/2 cups pastry flour**
> **2 Tbsp. corn or sesame oil**
> **1/4 tsp. sea salt**

1 cup barley malt
1/4 tsp. cinnamon
3/4 cup chopped walnuts
1 cup raisins
1-1/4 cups water

Combine flour, salt and cinnamon. Mix in oil. Add barley malt, raisins and nuts and mix well. Add water. Spoon onto oiled cookie sheets and press flat. Bake at 325° F. for approximately 20 minutes.

Peanut Butter Cookies (1-1/2 dozen)

1-1/2 cups peanut butter
1-1/2 cups pastry flour
1 cup barley malt
1/4 tsp. sea salt
1 cup water

Combine flour and sea salt. Add peanut butter and barley malt. Mix in well. Add water and mix until all ingredients are thoroughly blended. Place by tablespoonfuls onto an oiled cookie sheet. Press each cookie until flat with a wet fork. (The cookies should be rather thin.) Bake at 350° F. for 15–20 minutes.

You can place half a piece of walnut in the center of each cookie before baking if desired. Do not overbake, as these cookies burn easily and become very hard.

Apple Butter Cookies (about 1-1/2 dozen)

3 cups pastry flour
1/4 tsp. sea salt
1/2 tsp. cinnamon
1 cup barley malt
3 Tbsp. corn oil
1/2 cup water
apple butter or apple cider jelly

Combine dry ingredients. Add barley malt, oil and water. Mix well. Drop by tablespoonfuls onto oiled cookie sheets. Press down so each cookie is about 1/4-inch thick. Make a small indentation in the center of each cookie with your thumb or a spoon. Place about 1/2–1 teaspoon of apple butter, apple cider jelly, or other fruit filling into indentations. Bake at 350° F. for about 10 minutes or until light brown on the bottom.

Oatmeal Cookies (2 dozen)

3 cups rolled oats
1-1/2 cups whole wheat pastry flour
3 Tbsp. corn oil
1 cup chopped walnuts
1/4 tsp. sea salt
1 cup yinnie syrup
1 cup water

Combine dry ingredients. Add oil and mix in well. Add walnuts, yinnie syrup and water. Mix. Spoon batter onto an oiled cookie sheet and press down flat. Bake at 350° F. for about 20–25 minutes or until golden brown.

You may leave out the sweetener and add 1 cup raisins and a little more water. You can also use 2 cups of apple juice or amazake to sweeten instead of water and yinnie syrup.

Fruit-Nut Cake

   3 cups pastry flour
   1 cup whole wheat flour
   1/3 cups barley malt
   1/2 tsp. sea salt
   1 tsp. cinnamon
   1 cup chopped walnuts
   1/2 cup raisins
   2 cups water
   1/4 cup corn or sesame oil

Mix dry ingredients together. Add oil and mix well. Add barley malt and water and mix until smooth. To make the cake lighter, you may place the mixture in a blender or blend with an egg beater. Then mix in raisins and walnuts and place in an oiled cake pan. Fill almost to the top, as the cake will rise only slightly.

Bake at 325° F. for 1/2 hour and at 375° F. for 1/2 hour or so. Serve plain or topped with apple sauce.

Rice Pudding

   3-1/2 cups cooked brown rice
   1-1/2 cups apple juice (or half water and half juice)
   1/4 tsp. sea salt
   1/3–1/2 cup water
   1/4 tsp. cinnamon
   1/2 cup almonds
   3/4 cup water
   3–4 Tbsp. tahini

Boil almonds in 3/4 cup water and 3–4 tablespoons of tahini. Purée in blender. Place all ingredients in a pressure-cooker and cook for 40–45 minutes. Allow pressure to come down. Place ingredients in a baking dish or covered casserole and bake at 350° F. for 45 minutes to an hour. Remove cover and brown top.

Strawberry Shortcake

Cake

   2 cups corn meal
   1 cup pastry flour
   1/2 tsp. sea salt
   1/2 cup barley malt
   1/2 cup yinnie syrup

Topping

   2 qts. fresh strawberries
   1/2 cup yinnie syrup
   1/2 cup arrowroot flour
   pinch of sea salt
   1/4–1/2 cup water

3 Tbsp. sesame oil
1 cup water

Cake: Mix dry ingredients. Add oil and mix well. Add barley malt and yinnie syrup. Add water and mix. Place in an oiled cake pan or in muffin tins. Fill to the top. Bake at 250°–275° F. for 15 minutes and 375° F. for another 15–20 minutes.

Sauce: Wash strawberries, remove stems and cut berries in half. Place strawberries, water, salt and yinnie syrup in a pot. Add arrowroot and mix in well. Bring to a boil. Reduce flame to low and simmer until arrowroot thickens and strawberries are done. Stir to prevent lumping and sticking.

Cut the cake into squares and spoon topping over it. Serve. You can also use blueberries, applesauce, peaches, etc. instead of strawberries in the topping.

Apple Muffins (12 pieces)
    2 cups pastry flour
    1 cup whole wheat flour
    3 Tbsp. corn oil
    1/4 tsp. sea salt
    3 apples, diced
    1-3/4 cups apple juice (or half water/half juice)
    1/4 tsp. cinnamon (optional)

Combine dry ingredients. Add oil and blend well. Add water or juice and mix. Place apples in batter and mix evenly.

Oil muffin tins and heat oil in 350° F. oven until warm. Fill each muffin cup to the top with batter. Bake at 350° F. until golden brown.

Peaches or blueberries can be substituted for apples.

Rice Muffins (12 pieces)
    2 cups whole wheat flour
    1 cup rice flour
    1 cup corn meal
    1 cup cooked rice
    1/2 tsp. sea salt
    3 Tbsp. corn oil
    3-1/4 cups water
    1 cup raisins

Combine dry ingredients. Add rice and sift with your hands. Add oil and mix well again. Add water and raisins and mix well.

Place batter in oiled muffin tins, filling each section to the top. Bake at 325° F. for about 2 hours.

Corn Muffins (2 dozen)
    3 cups corn meal
    1-1/2 cups pastry flour

1/4 tsp. sea salt
1 cup barley malt (or half barley malt/half yinnie syrup)
2–3 Tbsp. sesame oil
1-1/2–2 cups water

Combine dry ingredients, then other ingredients. Mix well. Fill oiled muffin tins to the top with batter. Bake at 325° F. for 10 minutes and 375° F. for 15 minutes or until golden brown.

Peach Crisp

10–12 peaches, washed and sliced
pinch of sea salt
2 Tbsp. arrowroot flour
1/4 cup water
1 cup rolled oats
2 Tbsp. yinnie syrup or barley malt

Combine peaches, sea salt, arrowroot and water. Place in a baking dish and spread out evenly.

Roast oats and walnuts separately until golden brown. Chop nuts. Mix oats, walnuts, and yinnie syrup together. Spread topping evenly on peach mixture. Cover dish and bake at 375° F. for about 20 minutes or until peaches are cooked. Remove cover and brown topping (about 5–10 minutes).

For blueberry crisp, use 1 quart of blueberries and bake for a shorter time. For apple crisp, bake 20–30 minutes and brown topping for 5–10 minutes. Apples and pears are also good when combined in this crisp.

Apple-Pear Crunch

5–6 apples, sliced (leave skins on)
5–6 pears, sliced (leave skins on)
pinch of sea salt
1/2 cup water
2 Tbsp. arrowroot flour
1-1/2 cups granola
1/2 cup roasted, chopped walnuts
2 Tbsp. barley malt

Combine apples, pears, sea salt, water and arrowroot flour in a pot. Cover and cook on a low flame until fruit is soft and liquid has thickened. This should take only a few minutes. Place apple-pear mixture in a baking dish.

Combine granola, walnuts and barley malt. Place topping evenly on fruit. Bake uncovered at 350° F. until topping is golden brown.

Cherry Strudel

3 cups cherries, washed and pitted
3 tsp. arrowroot flour
2 tsp. water
1 cup walnuts, chopped
pinch of sea salt

Place cherries, water, sea salt and arrowroot in a saucepan. Mix well to dilute arrowroot. Bring to a boil, reduce flame to low and simmer for 3–5 minutes. Stir to prevent lumping and sticking. Remove from flame and allow to cool. Add walnuts. Spread cooled cherry filling evenly on rolled-out pastry dough. Roll up in a log shape. Wet ends of dough and seal to hold liquid in. Place on an oiled cookie sheet. Using a fork, poke several small holes in the top of the dough to keep it from splitting and to allow steam to escape. Bake at 375° F. for about 30 minutes or until crust is golden brown. Remove and allow to cool. Slice into 1–1-1/2 inch rounds and serve.

Apple Strudel

2-1/2 cups apples, washed and sliced
1 cup raisins
1/2 cup walnuts, chopped
3–4 tsp. arrowroot flour
1/4 cup water
pinch of sea salt

Prepare as above. (Bake at same temperature and for the same amount of time.) Cool, slice into rounds, and serve.

Apple Cous-Cous Cake

2 cups cous-cous, washed and steamed
1 cup raisins
1 cup diced apples
3/4 cup water or apple juice
pinch of sea salt

Wash, drain, and steam cous-cous for 5–7 minutes. Remove and fluff with chopsticks or a fork while cooling.

Place apples, raisins, water (or juice), and sea salt in a saucepan. Bring to a boil. Reduce flame to low, cover and cook until apples are done. This should take only 2–3 minutes. Remove and mix with cous-cous. Place mixture in a cake pan and spread out evenly. Cover the pan with a top or foil to hold in moisture. Allow to cool. Cut into squares and serve.

Cherry Cous-Cous Kanten

1 pint cherries, washed and pitted
2 cups water
2 cups apple juice
pinch of sea salt
5 Tbsp. agar agar flakes (read directions first)
1 cup steamed and fluffed cous-cous

Spread steamed cous-cous evenly in a casserole dish or shallow bowl.

Place cherries, water, juice, sea salt and flakes in a saucepan and stir. Bring to a boil, reduce flame and simmer for 2–3 minutes. Pour cherries and liquid gently over the cous-cous. Allow to cool and harden. Serve.

Cranberry Sauce
 (see Holiday Menu—Thanksgiving section)

Blueberry Kanten
 1 pint blueberries, washed
 2 cups water
 2 cups apple juice
 pinch of sea salt
 5 Tbsp. agar agar flakes (read directions first)
Wash blueberries and place in a pot with water, juice, sea salt and flakes. Mix well. Bring to a boil, reduce flame to low and simmer 2–3 minutes. Place in a shallow dish or mold. Chill until hardened. Serve.

Tahini Custard
 3 medium apples, peeled and sliced
 1/2 cup raisins
 2 cups water
 2 cups apple juice
 pinch of sea salt
 2–3 Tbsp. tahini
 5 Tbsp. agar agar flakes (read directions first)
Cook as above. Remove from flame. Place in a shallow bowl and chill until almost hardened. Place in a blender and blend until smooth and creamy. Place back in bowl and chill again. Serve.

Popcorn Balls
Prepare popcorn as usual and add a little sea salt. Heat barley malt or yinnie syrup in a saucepan until it boils. Reduce flame and simmer 2–3 minutes. Remove from flame and pour over popcorn. Use enough sweetener to evenly coat the popcorn. Mix well. Mix in chopped walnuts, pecans or peanuts if desired. Wet your hands and form popcorn mixture into round balls, packing firmly to hold them together. (You may spread the sweetened popcorn on a cookie sheet instead of forming it into balls.) Place in oven and bake at 350° F. for several minutes or until the sweetener starts to bubble and become darker in color. Remove and allow to cool. The baking will cause the sweetener to harden during cooling.

 These make wonderful snacks and are great to take to the movies or offer to trick-or-treaters on Halloween.

Sweet Rice Crunch
Soak sweet rice for about an hour. Drain well. Place in a dry skillet and roast on a low flame until the rice pops open like popcorn. Stir constantly with a wooden spoon or rice paddle to prevent burning and to insure even popping. Pour hot yinnie syrup over the popped rice and mix well. You may add roasted sesame or sunflower seeds if desired. Spread on a dry cookie sheet or form into small balls and bake at 350° F. for several minutes. Remove and allow to cool.

Blueberry Pie (1 large or two small pies)

> 2 qts blueberries, washed
> pinch of sea salt
> 1/8 cup water
> 1/4 cup arrowroot flour
> 1/4 cup yinnie syrup

Place blueberries, sea salt and water in a pot. Bring to a boil. Reduce flame to low, cover and simmer 2–3 minutes. Add yinnie syrup. Dilute arrowroot in a very small amount of water. Mix in well with the berries, stirring constantly to prevent lumping. Cook until thick. Allow to cool.

Prepare pastry dough and roll out. Place rolled-out shells in pie plates and press edges down with a wet fork or with your thumbs. Poke several holes in the shells with a fork. Bake empty shells at 375° F. for about 10 minutes or so.

Add filling to shells. Bake again at 375° F. for 25–30 minutes, or until crust is golden brown. Cool and slice.

Apples, peaches, other berries, pears, etc. can be substituted for blueberries.

Apple Pie

> 10–12 baking or cooking apples, sliced (remove skin if desired)
> pinch of sea salt
> 1/4 cup yinnie syrup or barley malt
> 2 Tbsp. arrowroot flour
> 1/4 cup water
> 1/4–1/2 tsp. cinnamon (optional)

Place all ingredients in a pot and bring to a boil. Mix well to prevent lumping and burning. Reduce flame to low, cover and cook until apples are soft. Cool slightly.

Prepare pie dough, roll out and partially bake the bottom crust for about 10 minutes as in the above recipe. Add filling, cover with top crust and seal edges together. Poke several holes in the top crust with a fork to let steam escape. Bake at 350°–375° F. for about 45 minutes or until crust is golden brown.

Squash Pie

> (see Holiday Menu—Thanksgiving section)

Basic Pie Dough (2 crusts)

> 4 cups whole wheat pastry flour
> 1/4 tsp. sea salt
> 1/8–1/4 cup corn oil
> 3/4–1 cup cold water

Combine dry ingredients. Add oil and sift with hands to mix in well with flour. Add water gradually and form into a ball. Knead 2–3 minutes. Let sit for a few minutes before rolling out. Divide in half and roll out.

Oatmeal Crust
>**3 cups rolled oats**
>**1-1/2 cups whole wheat pastry flour**
>**2–3 Tbsp. corn oil**
>**1/4 tsp. sea salt**
>**2 cups water**

Mix dry ingredients together. Blend in oil with your hands. Add water to form a thick batter. Spread evenly and very thinly on oiled cookie sheets, cake pans, or round pie plates. If using cookie sheets or cake pans, make sure to leave a ridge or lip around the edge to hold the filling in the crust. Pre-bake at 375° F. for 10–15 minutes before filling with fruit or squash. After filling, bake again at 375° F. for another 25–30 minutes or so.

Please refer to *Introducing Macrobiotic Cooking* for additional dessert recipes, including those for apple, apple-squash and squash pie; oatmeal-raisin cookies, kanten, apple crisp, applesauce, baked apples, raisin strudel, sweet azuki beans, apple tarts, and amasake.

9. Seafood

Whenever you buy fish or shellfish, make sure that it is as fresh as possible. Frozen, pre-breaded or pre-stuffed seafood is not recommended. Breaded or stuffed seafood often has eggs, monosodium glutamate (MSG), spices and preservatives added to it. Once you have purchased seafood, make sure to keep it refrigerated or in a very cool place until you use it. It is preferable to prepare it on the same day that you purchase it.

There are many kinds of ocean and freshwater fish and shellfish to choose from. Generally, white meat, slower-moving fish are more yin. A few of these are flounder, sole, haddock, scrod, codfish, whitefish, carp, etc. Dark meat, faster-moving fish such as tuna, salmon, bluefish, herring, eel, sardines, trout, mackerel, etc. are generally more yang. Among shellfish, there are also more yin and yang types. The slow-moving, more yin types are clams, oysters, scallops, mussels, octopus and abalone; while faster-moving squid, shrimp, prawns, lobster, crab, etc. are more yang. As a general rule, it is preferable to eat mostly the more yin varieties. This is especially true for women. Men can occasionally select more yang varieties, but should not eat them in large quantities.

Whenever you prepare seafood at home or eat it in a restaurant, make sure that you have plenty of vegetables or salad to help balance its more yang quality. Of course, when you prepare fish at home, brown rice or other grains should also be eaten along with plenty of other vegetable quality foods so as to balance the seafood.

Seafood should not comprise more than 5%–10% of your diet or of any one meal. A good way to eat seafood is in the form of *sashimi*; raw fish that is sliced and served along with a dip sauce. This sauce is often made with tamari and water or kombu broth as a base, to which either grated ginger, daikon, wasabi, sliced scallions, parsley, etc. are added. Since it is not cooked, sashimi is a more yin form of animal food. After eating it, you usually do not feel the strong yang effects that you would after eating cooked seafood.

There are many other ways to prepare seafood, such as baking, broiling, boiling, steaming, stuffing and pan-frying. Seafood can also be used in tempura, chowders, soups, stews, sukiyaki, fish cakes and in many other ways. I will discuss some of these in the recipes presented in this chapter.

Baked Haddock
2 lbs. fresh haddock
1/4 cup tamari
1/4 cup water
1 Tbsp. grated ginger
1 onion, sliced into very thin rounds
chopped parsley

Wash and slice fish into 2-1/2″–3″ chunks. Combine water, tamari and ginger in a bowl. Place the fish in the mixture and marinate for 30–60 minutes. Oil a baking dish lightly with sesame oil and place sliced onions on the bottom. Set fish on top of the onions, cover and bake at 375° F. for about 15 minutes or until fish is tender. Remove the cover, sprinkle with a little chopped parsley or sliced scallions and continue to bake, uncovered, just long enough to brown the fish. Serve.

Baked Stuffed Cod
1-1/2–2 lbs. fresh cod
1/2 tsp. sea salt
water to cover fish
1/2 cup cous-cous, washed and steamed 5–7 minutes
1/2 onion, diced
1 stalk celery, diced
2 mushrooms, diced
sesame oil
pinch of sea salt
1/2 cup fresh green peas, parboiled until almost done
chopped parsley

Place water and 1/2 teaspoon of sea salt in a bowl. Marinate fish in salt water for 30–60 minutes.

Steam cous-cous, fluff with a fork and set aside. Lightly oil a skillet with sesame or corn oil and sauté onions, celery, mushrooms and green peas. Mix cous cous and vegetables. Add a pinch of sea salt or a little tamari to the stuffing. Place stuffing in an oiled baking dish and place fish on top. Cover with lid or foil and bake at 375° F. for about 20 minutes or so. Remove cover and brown for another 10 minutes. Sprinkle with chopped parsley while browning the fish. You may squeeze a little lemon juice on the fish after serving.

Broiled Fillet of Sole
2 lb. fillet of sole

1/4 cup water
1/4 cup tamari
1 Tbsp. grated ginger

Wash sole and marinate in water, tamari and ginger for 10–15 minutes. Remove and place on an oiled baking sheet. Broil for 4–5 minutes on one side only. Remove, place on a serving platter and garnish with sprigs of parsley and lemon wedges. Serve a small dish of grated daikon to each person to help balance the fish.

Broiled Flounder

2 lbs. flounder fillets
tamari
sesame oil
lemon juice
slivered almonds
chopped parsley

Wash fillets, place on an oiled baking sheet and lightly brush with sesame oil and tamari. Squeeze a little lemon juice on the fillets, and then sprinkle them with slivered almonds and a little chopped parsley. Broil about 5 minutes or so, or until fish is tender. Do not overcook, or fish will become tough. Place on a serving platter and serve.

Pan-Fried Trout

brook or rainbow trout, scaled and cleaned (leave entire fish intact)
2 cups whole wheat flour
2 Tbsp. seaweed or kelp powder
pinch of sea salt
slices of lemon
parsley sprigs
sesame oil

Mix flour, salt and seaweed powder together. Roll the cleaned fish in it. Place about 1/4-inch of sesame oil in a skillet and heat up. Fry the trout in hot oil until golden brown. Turn over and fry until the other side is golden brown. You may sprinkle a little tamari on it for added flavor while cooking. Place on a serving platter. Garnish with lemon wedges or rounds and sprigs of parsley or watercress.

Pan-Fried Perch

6–8 perch fillets
1 cup corn meal
1/4 tsp. sea salt
tamari
lemon wedges
sprigs of parsley
sesame oil

Wash fish. Mix corn meal and salt and use to coat fish. Pan-fry as above. Sprinkle a little tamari on fish as you are frying it. Fry until golden brown on both sides. Garnish with lemon wedges and sprigs of parsley after placing on a serving platter.

Tempura Fillet of Sole and Daikon

> **5–6 sole fillets**
> **2 cups tempura batter**
> **1 cup kombu or kombu-shiitake soup stock, seasoned to taste with tamari**
> **1-1/2 cups grated daikon**
> **thinly sliced scallions**

Wash fish, pat dry, and dip into tempura batter. Deep-fry until golden brown on both sides. Remove and drain on paper towels.

Season soup stock with tamari and place in skillet. Bring to a boil. Place fried fish in the skillet along with grated daikon. Reduce flame to low and simmer 3–4 minutes. Place fish on a serving dish and spoon the broth and daikon over it. Garnish with scallions and serve.

Deep-Fried Smelt

> **several smelt, cleaned (leave entire fish intact)**
> **1 cup whole wheat pastry flour**
> **1/2 cup corn meal**
> **1/4 tsp. sea salt**
> **sesame oil**

Heat oil for deep-frying. Combine salt, flour, and corn meal and use to coat smelt. Deep-fry until golden brown on both sides and drain on paper towels. Serve with tamari, water, and grated ginger dip sauce and a small serving of grated daikon.

Koi-Koku (Carp Miso Soup)

This soup is especially good for increasing strength and vitality. That is one reason why it is traditionally served to women who have just given birth and are breastfeeding. It also helps to produce good quality milk. However, not all mothers may need this special dish after giving birth, especially those who are still strong. If a mother is generally yang after giving birth and eats *koi-koku* everyday for one week, she may become too yang. I had this experience after the birth of my first child. Generally, if a new mother feels tired and weak after birth, then one small bowl of koi-koku a day over a period of a week will help her become strong.

Since this soup is very delicious, it is easy to eat too much of it. If you include it as a special side dish, it is better to use it during the cold, winter months. Try to use it occasionally and only in small amounts.

> **1 small carp (about 2 lbs.)**
> **burdock, shaved or cut into matchsticks (volume should equal that of carp)**
> **sesame oil**
> **used bancha tea leaves and twigs (1/2–1 cup)**
> **cheesecloth**

    grated ginger

    mugi miso to taste (puréed)

Buy a live carp and ask to have the gall bladder removed at the fish market, being careful not to break it. Leave scales, bones, head, fins, etc. on the carp. Slice the carp, bones included, into 1/2-inch square chunks.

Shave or slice the burdock into matchsticks and sauté for several minutes in sesame oil. Place the carp in a pot and add water to cover. Tie up some used bancha leaves and twigs in a piece of cheesecloth to form a sack. Drop into the pot with the carp and add the burdock. Bring to a boil, reduce flame to low, cover and simmer until bones, scales, etc. are very soft. This may take 4–6 hours. (You may pressure-cook the soup for 2 hours instead if you do not have time to boil.) As the water evaporates, add more when necessary.

When bones are soft, remove the tea sack and discard. Purée miso in a small amount of the soup broth. Reduce flame to very low, add miso and simmer for several minutes. Serve with a little grated ginger in a bowl.

Refrigerate to store. Koi-koku will keep for about a week in the refrigerator.

Stuffed Cucumbers

    2–3 cucumbers

    1 lb. sole, lobster or crab meat (boiled until tender with a little sea salt and

      very finely chopped)

    tamari

    lemon juice

Mix cooked seafood with a small amount of lemon juice and tamari. Slice cucumbers into one-inch rounds, remove the seeds and hollow out the center with a spoon. Fill each cucumber with fish mixture. Arrange attractively on a platter and serve.

Seafood Pancakes

I discovered this very delicious recipe in Japan, and I hope that you will also enjoy it.

    cleaned seafood, cut into small pieces (use a wide variety such as oysters,

      clams, shrimp, octopus, squid, etc.)

    shredded cabbage

    shredded carrot

    diced onion

    sea salt

    pastry flour

    unbleached white flour

    water

Mix half pastry and half unbleached white flour along with a little sea salt into a thin batter. Add shredded vegetables and seafood. The batter should be fairly thick with seafood and vegetables.

Lightly oil a skillet or pancake griddle with sesame oil and heat it up. When hot, place spoonfuls of the batter mixture on the griddle to form a regular sized pancake. Cook until golden brown, turn over and fry the other side. Continue until all batter is used up.

Serve with a dip sauce made of tamari, water and ginger. Sprinkle the pancakes with a small amount of bonito flakes and green nori flakes after serving. Each person should then pour a little dip sauce over their pancake.

10. Condiments

Condiments play an important role in the macrobiotic way of eating, as they aid digestion and are an excellent source of vitamins and minerals.

When making condiments for small children, however, please use much less salt than for an adult, and the quantity given to them should be very small. Condiments should not be used on an infant's food. Gomashio and various seaweed powders are the most suitable condiments for small children.*

Condiments play a very important part in the diet of women during pregnancy, as they often need more minerals at this time. If a woman's iron level is low during pregnancy, condiments will usually help to supply her needs. However, a pregnant woman should not eat more yang condiments or large quantities of condiments if her condition is already overly yang. Prepare your condiments with less salt at this time.

Shio (Salt) Kombu No. 1
2–3 strips kombu, about 12″ long
water
tamari

Soak kombu in water until soft enough to cut. Cut each strip into 1/2-inch squares or 1/4-inch strips which are about 1-1/2 inches long. Place kombu in a saucepan. Cover with mixture of half water and half tamari (use kombu soaking water). Bring to a boil, reduce flame to low and simmer until the kombu is very soft and the tamari and water are almost all cooked away.

For a saltier condiment, cover the kombu with straight tamari only and cook as above.

Shio Kombu No. 2
2–3 strips kombu, about 12″ long
1/4 cup chirimen iriko (small dried fish)
water
tamari

Soak and slice kombu as above. Place kombu in a pot and add chirimen iriko. Cover with a half tamari/half water mixture and cook as above.

For a saltier condiment, use only tamari to cover.

You may add a little grated ginger after cooking for a different flavor.

---

* For a discussion of the salt needs of both children and adults and information about salt in general, refer to the section called "Preparation for Cooking" in *Introudcing Macrobiotic Cooking*.

Shio Nori

5–6 sheets toasted nori, cut into 1/2″ squares
water
tamari

Cook as above; however, this dish may take less time for all the liquid to cook away.

Daikon and Tamari

1 cup grated daikon
tamari

Grate daikon and place 1–2 tablespoons on each person's dish. Sprinkle several drops of tamari onto each serving.

You may also substitute grated carrot or turnip, or combine them with daikon.

Chirimen Iriko or Chuba

1 cup dried fish
tamari water
grated ginger

Roast fish in a dry skillet or oven until crisp. Pour a mixture of 1/3 water and 2/3 tamari (or use full-strength tamari) over the fish. Mix with a little grated ginger. Allow to sit and marinate for about 1/2 hour. Serve.

Furikake

1 cup shiso leaves

Mince shiso leaves very finely. Roast in a dry skillet or oven, or place in the sun until completely dry. *Furikake* can be sprinkled on grains or on salads.

Scallion Miso

1 cup sliced scallions (chives can be used instead)
1 Tbsp. mugi miso
1 Tbsp. water
1 tsp. sesame oil

Sauté scallions or chives over a low flame for 1–2 minutes in a little sesame oil. Purée miso with a little water and gently mix in. Cover and simmer over a low flame for 5–7 minutes. Stir occasionally to prevent sticking.

Green Peppers and Miso

4 diced or sliced green peppers (leave seeds in or remove if desired)
4 Tbsp. mugi or genmai miso
1/2 cup water
sesame oil

Slice peppers lengthwise or dice. Sauté in a small amount of sesame oil for 2–3 minutes. Purée miso with water, add to peppers, and cook for several minutes on a low flame until water evaporates.

Kombu-Chuba Powder
    1 oz. dry kombu
    1/4 cup chuba (or chirimen iriko)

Roast kombu and fish in 350° F. oven until fish becomes very crisp and kombu becomes brittle. Break kombu into small pieces and grind for several minutes in a suribachi. Add fish and grind into a very fine powder.
    Sprinkle on grains, vegetables, salads, etc.

Wakame-Sesame Powder
    1 oz. dry wakame
    1/4 cup sesame seeds

Roast wakame in 350° F. oven until crisp and dark. Remove and grind to a fine powder in suribachi. Place washed sesame seeds in a dry skillet and roast on a low flame until they release a nutty fragrance. Stir constantly so roasting will be even. Add sesame seeds to wakame powder and grind until seeds are about 50% crushed. Use as above.

Wakame-Fish Powder
    1 oz. wakame, roasted as above
    1 Tbsp. shiso leaves
    1 Tbsp. bonito flakes or dried shrimp
    1 Tbsp. roasted sesame seeds

Roast wakame as above. Roast the shiso leaves, bonito or shrimp, and sesame seeds separately in a dry skillet. Grind wakame in suribachi until it is a fine powder. Finally, add the sesame seeds and grind until they are about 50% crushed.
    Use as you would other powders.

Dulse-Sesame Powder
    1 oz. dry dulse, roasted in oven as above
    1/2 cup roasted sesame seeds

Prepare as in above recipe. Add the sesame seeds last and grind until 50% crushed.
    Use as you would other powders. This condiment is very high in iron.

Other Seaweed Powders
Various powders can be made by combining the different seaweeds, dried fish, shiso leaves and sesame seeds. You may also make condiments out of seaweed alone. Please experiment and invent your own condiments.

Roasted Seeds
Sesame, sunflower, pumpkin and squash seeds can be dry-roasted and sprinkled on grains, vegetables, salads, and noodles. You may lightly season the seeds with tamari while roasting.

Gomashio
>1 cup sesame seeds
>
>1-1/3 Tbsp. sea salt

Wash seeds, place in a dry skillet and roast over a low flame. Stainless steel skillets work best, since cast iron skillets take longer to heat up; but once they do, they become very hot and heat longer. Stir constantly with a rice paddle or wooden spoon, shaking the pan occasionally so that seeds will roast evenly. Roast until they give off a nutty fragrance, turn golden brown and begin to pop. They should be easily crushable if you squeeze them between your thumb and index finger.

Remove the seeds immediately from the skillet to prevent burning, and place in a suribachi. Add sea salt and grind slowly with even, gentle pressure in a circular motion until each seed is about half-crushed. Store in a glass jar. Sprinkle on grains, etc.

Use much less sea salt in children's gomashio. Adults should generally use a proportion of one part salt to 8–14 parts seeds. Children love gomashio, and often eat too much of it. Our children are two and five years old, and I use about a cup of seeds to a teaspoon of sea salt for their gomashio.

This is the most commonly used condiment, but others should be used as well, especially seaweed powders.

Gomashio is an excellent way to take in salt, as the oil from the seeds coats and balances the more yang salt. It is very high in calcium, iron and Vitamins A and B, and also aids in digestion.

Make gomashio in small amounts every week or week and a half. If it is not prepared slowly and patiently and in the proper way, it will not keep for long periods.

Tekka
Refer to *Introducing Macrobiotic Cooking* or other macrobiotic cookbooks for this recipe.

Green Nori Flakes
These are available prepackaged in some natural food stores. This particular type of nori is very high in iron and calcium. It comes in small flakes which are bright green in color. It is very good for pregnant women or anemic persons.

Miso Condiments
A variety of condiments can be made from combinations of miso and vegetables. Please refer to *How to Cook with Miso* by Aveline Kushi, published by Japan Publications, Inc., for recipe suggestions.

Umeboshi
Umeboshi are made from small plums that grow in Japan. They are pickled with shiso leaves (beefsteak plant) and sea salt brine, and have a salty and slightly

bitter flavor. (They have a reddish or pinkish color after being processed.) Umeboshi aids in digestion and has many medicinal properties. It can be eaten as a condiment with rice, other grains, rubbed on sweet corn or used in a number of other ways.

Tamari

Tamari is used more as a seasoning than as a condiment. Occasionally, however, you may add a drop or two to your soup or noodles, or to foods like natto or tofu. It should not be poured over rice, other grains, or vegetables, as it will produce an overly salty condition when eaten regularly in this manner.

Moromi

Moromi, a by-product of the miso-making process, can be used in small quantities both as a condiment or in making other condiments. It is available prepackaged in small, glass jars in some natural food stores. It can also be used in vegetable cooking and in sauces, dressings, etc.

Shiso Leaves

These are the leaves which are used to process umeboshi. They are available prepackaged or in kegs of umeboshi. They can be sliced and used as a condiment or in making other condiments, in sushi, salad dressings, etc.

Please refer to Introducing Macrobiotic Cooking for miso-scallion condiment, gomashio, and tekka recipes.

11. Pickle-Making

Pickles are said to have originated thousands of years ago in the Far East. Many ancient cultures developed various pickling methods as a way of naturally storing vegetables. Our ancestors were also aware that pickles are an aid to digestion. The fermentation process requires bacteria which change the natural sweetness or sugar of the vegetables into lactic acid. Lactic acid is a helpful enzyme, which aids in digestion and strengthens the intestines and stomach. Pickles are a good source of Vitamins B and C as well.

Pickles may be eaten year-round, but you may want to vary your selection according to seasonal change and your own needs. For example, quickly made, lighter pickles should be eaten more often in hot weather or by persons who need to restrict their salt intake, while saltier or long-time pickles should generally be eaten more during the colder months.

When you choose vegetables for pickling, make sure that they are freshy harvested. For instance, cucumbers which are one or two weeks old may become soft and hollow in the center when pickled. Your vegetables should be firm, crisp and brightly colored when bought. Dull or limp vegetables do not pickle as well.

Cooler weather is better for preparing *nuka*, salt, *takuan*, some miso pickles, and others which require a longer time to ferment. If pickles such as these are exposed to warmer temperatures, they may start to mold. A cool room or basement is best for storing your pickles. However, some varieties of pickles, such as those which can be prepared in a shorter time, ferment better in slightly warmer temperatures. Dill pickles are a good example of this.

While in Japan, I had the opportunity to become friends and study with a woman who was an expert on the traditional methods of pickle-making. She made some of the most delicious pickles I have tasted so far. While in college, she wrote her thesis on pickling, and researched and experimented with a variety of ingredients and pickling methods. As a part of her research, she visited various places throughout Japan that were famous for their pickles and studied their methods. Following her study, she came to the conclusion that the best tasting and most healthful pickles are those which are made with natural sea salt, organic vegetables and other natural ingredients, in ceramic or wooden kegs. She also discovered that pickles made with commercial salt and non-organic ingredients cause unhealthy and often poisonous chemicals to be released from the plastic kegs that they are made in. This has become a serious problem in modern Japan, as plastic kegs are used more often than wooden or ceramic ones, while natural sea salt is seldom used by the average person.

Several of the methods that I will explain in this chapter were taught to me by this woman, Sachiko-san. She regularly brought pickles for us to taste, and encouraged me to begin experimenting on my own. Since returning to America, I have begun to do this and am still learning. Many of the methods that she explained produce lighter, sweeter and less salty pickles. I hope that you will enjoy experimenting with pickling as I am now doing.

Do not be discouraged if your pickles do not turn out well the first time. As with all things, the longer you continue to experiment and accustom yourself to working with the ingredients involved in pickling, the better your end result will be.

Many vegetables, flowers, fish and some sea vegeatbles and fruits can be pickled, using one or a combination of ingredients to produce fermentation. Some of the ingredients used in pickling are sea salt, rice bran (*nuka*), rice flour, miso, tamari, umeboshi, shiso leaves and seeds, juices from other pickles, sake lees, white miso, rice *koji*, wheat bran, and others.

We usually do not use spices in making pickles. Instead, I use various foods such as fresh ginger, shiso, parsley, celery leaves, fresh or dried dill, lemon or orange rinds, etc. Sweeteners such as yinnnie syrup or rice honey can also be used occasionally in making sweet pickles.

When experimenting with pickles it is often difficult to discover the correct amount of salt to use to produce the best results. Large amounts of salt may cause spoilage or overly salty pickles. If your pickles are too salty, soak them for about half an hour before slicing and serving. In some cases, too little salt will also cause spoilage, as the water will not be drawn out of the vegetables and they will not ferment properly and will start to decay.

Make sure that your kegs, crocks or glass jars are very clean before placing the vegetables in them. Unclean containers may cause inferior or moldy pickles.

Always make sure that you have thoroughly washed your vegetables before pickling them. Some pickling methods require that you dry the vegetables for one or two days before pickling to remove excess liquid.

We do not boil or pasteurize natural pickles, as the heat will kill all the healthful enzymes and bacteria. In some cases, we boil the water and salt and allow it to cool before pouring it over the vegetables, but never cook the vegetables or pickles once they are done.

Not all pickles require that you place a weight on them during fermentation. If water is supposed to rise in a particular recipe but does not, you may need to increase the weight used or you may not have added enough sea salt to draw out the water. It is also possible that the vegetables are old and do not contain enough water, but in most cases this is not the major problem. If water is supposed to rise, it should do so usually within 10 hours after the weight has been placed on the pickles. If water rises too quickly and covers the wooden disc or plate, you may have added too much weight. At this time, reduce the weight until the water level just covers the pickles and is below the disc.

If mold surfaces, as it does in some types of pickles, it should be removed regularly. If left on for one or two days, the flavor of the mold will spread through your pickles and cause unappetizing flavors or spoilage. So be sure to remove mold as soon as it appears. Also, if the ceramic plates that you place on top of your pickles come in contact with the pickle brine, they may promote the development of mold. Wooden discs are the best to place on top of your pickles. If you do not have a wooden disc, you can place several layers of cheesecloth under the ceramic plate to keep if from coming in contact with the brine. In any case, if you watch your pickles daily and check them regularly for mold, you should not have a problem with this.

After you have placed your pickles in the crock or keg, it is often a good idea to cover the top of it with a thin layer of cheesecloth to keep dust, etc. out of the pickles.

If mold surfaces on nuka or rice flour pickles, you may not have used enough sea salt in the nuka mixture. If mold appears in miso pickles, your vegetables may have contained too much liquid or been improperly dried. This may also happen if the temperature of the room is too warm.

Pickles can be served on a daily basis to aid in digestion. Make sure that you always have a plentiful supply on hand. Children do not need to eat them as often, and should eat the less salty varieties. Be careful not to give your children too many pickles, as their condition may become overly yang.

Ginger Pickles
2 pieces of fresh ginger, about 2-1/2″–3″ long
several shiso leaves

Remove skin from ginger and slice into thin diagonals. Then cut each diagonal into thin, short matchsticks.

Wrap ginger in shiso leaves, place in a shallow bowl or container with a very light weight placed on top. Make sure that you have enough shiso to completely surround the ginger.

Leave for about 3 days or until the ginger turns dark pink. They are now ready to eat.

These pickles are somewhat hot but are quite delicious once you adjust to their flavor. Eat small quantities with rice, on noodles, or placed inside of norimaki.

Shiso leaves are packed with umeboshi plums or are sometimes packaged separately and sold in natural food stores. In English, the plant is known as "beefsteak."

If you do not have shiso leaves, umeboshi will suffice. Pack the ginger well with umeboshi. The ginger may have a lighter color and a spicier and less salty flavor if you use umeboshi. Refrigerate after pickling to store.

Turnip-Kombu Pickles
> **3 medium turnips**
> **2–3 12″ strips of kombu, soaked until soft enough to slice**
> **1/8 cup of sea salt**

Wash the tunips and slice in half. Cut each half into thin slices. Place a thin layer of sea salt on the bottom of a small crock. Then place a layer of turnip slices on top of the sea salt. Continue to alternate layers of sea salt and turnips until all ingredients are used up. The top layer should be sea salt.

Place a wooden disc or a plate on top. Then place a stone or brick on top of the disc or plate to add weight. The disc should fit down inside the crock, resting on top of the salt and turnips. In 8–10 hours or less, water will rise to the surface. When it rises to the level of the disc, drain off all water and discard.

Remove the turnips from the crock. Slice the kombu into rectangular shapes about 1/4-inch wide and 1-1/2 inches long. Mix the kombu and turnips together and place back in the crock. Replace the disc and stone on top. Keep in a cool place for one or two days. When pickles are ready to eat, the liquid surrounding the turnips will thicken and become very slippery. This is how they should turn out if correctly made.

They are now ready to eat. Refrigerate to store.

Daikon-Lemon Pickles
> **one 12″ piece of daikon**
> **3–4 pieces of lemon rind, about 1-1/2″–2″ long**
> **1–1-1/2 tsp. sea salt**

Wash daikon and slice diagonally into rounds. Cut each round into 1/8–1/2 inch wide rectangles.

Evenly mix sea salt with daikon. Place lemon or orange rind in with daikon. Remove lemon after 3–4 hours or if lemon taste becomes too strong.

Place a disc and small weight on top of the daikon as above. Leave for 1–2 days. They are now ready to eat. Keep in a cool place or refrigerate to store.

You may add a few shiso leaves instead of lemon or orange rind. You may also use turnips for this recipe instead of daikon.

Daikon-Umeboshi Pickles
> **1 piece of daikon (about 12″–14″ long)**

1-1/2 cups water
5–6 umeboshi plums

Wash daikon and grate on a Western-style (not a flat Japanese) grater. Place the daikon in a bowl.

Place water in a saucepan. Separate plums into pieces and place along with pits in water. Bring to a boil, reduce flame to low and simmer several minutes. Remove from flame and cool slightly.

Pour warm liquid over the daikon to almost cover it. Leave for at least 1-1/2 hours before serving. Your pickles are now done and will keep for a few days if kept in a cool place. These are very light pickles and are not salty.

Do not throw away the umeboshi water once pickles have been used. Save it and use again or for salad dressings or in making pressed salad.

Pressed Pickles

1 cup umeboshi juice
1 cup daikon, sliced into thin rectangles
2 cups Chinese cabbage, sliced thin diagonally
1 cup cucumber, sliced into thin rounds
1 small onion, sliced into thin rounds

Wash vegetables and slice as directed. Place in a pickle press. Add umeboshi juice. Screw down the press top until juice covers the vegetables. Leave for 1–2 days. They are now ready to eat. Keep in a cool place to store.

Save the juice and reuse or use for salad dressings.

Pressed Salt Pickles

Use any green such as diced or finely chopped daikon, turnip, or radish greens; thinly sliced cabbage, Chinese cabbage, celery, mustard greens, radish, daikon, turnip, carrots, cucumber, lettuce, etc.

Place sliced vegetables in a pickle press or crock and sprinkle with a little sea salt. Apply pressure or weight down and leave for about 3 days. If too salty, rinse before eating. Keep in a cool place to store.

Cucumber-Umeboshi Pickles

2 cucumbers, sliced into lengthwise quarters or thick rounds
1 quart umeboshi juice
1 small onion, sliced into thin rounds or half-moons

Place cucumbers and onion in a quart glass jar. Completely cover with umeboshi juice. Let sit for 2–3 days. They are now ready to eat.

Shiso-Cucumber Pickles

4–5 cucumbers, quartered lengthwise
shiso leaves
1 Tbsp. ginger, peeled and cut into thin, short matchsticks
sea salt

Place layers of cucumber, shiso and ginger in a bowl. Sprinkle with a small amount of sea salt. Place a plate and stone on top of the vegetables to weight down. Let sit for one day. They are now ready to eat. Refrigerate to store.

Rutabaga-Tamari Pickles

1/2 rutabaga, halved or quartered and thinly sliced
1 cup water
1 cup tamari

Wash, peel (if waxed) and slice rutabaga. Place in a pickle press with tamari and water and screw down top. If you do not have a press, use a bowl and a plate to weight down. Pickles are ready to eat in about 4 hours. These pickles will keep for about 1-1/2–2 weeks in a cool place, and may become saltier the longer they sit. Before serving, rinse off if too salty.

You may use other root vegetables such as daikon, turnip, carrots, or onions.

Mustard, Daikon, or Turnip Green Pickles

1 bunch mustard, daikon, or turnip greens, cut into 1″ slices
1/2 cup tamari (or half water—half tamari)
2 tsp. yinnie syrup or barley malt
2 tsp. roasted sesame seeds
1/2–1 Tbsp. fresh grated ginger (remove skin before grating)

Wash and cut greens. Drain and pack tightly into a quart glass jar. Place tamari and yinnie syrup in a saucepan. Bring to a boil, reduce flame to low and simmer about 1–2 minutes to dissolve yinnie syrup. Place roasted sesame seeds in the jar and add the grated ginger. Pour warm, not hot, tamari mixture over the greens, seeds, and ginger. Cover the jar and refrigerate for a day. They are now ready to eat. These will keep in the refrigerator for about a week.

Pickled Mustard or Broccoli Flowers

2–3 cups of small mustard or broccoli flowers
sea salt
nuka or rice flour

In this recipe, use only the broccoli or mustard flowerettes with a little of the stem attached. Place flowers in a small crock or bowl. Sprinkle with a little sea salt. Place a disc and weight on top. When water rises to the disc, drain off and remove flowers to drain. Place flowers back in crock or bowl. Wrap a small amount of nuka or brown rice flour in cheesecloth and set on top of flowers. Put disc and weight back in place. Leave for a day or two. They are now ready to eat. Refrigerate to store.

Pickled Cherry Blossoms (for making light spring tea)

cherry blossoms, washed quickly and drained
shiso leaves (or small amount of cool umeboshi juice)

Place blossoms in a small bowl. Cover with shiso leaves or a small amount of umeboshi juice. Apply a light lid with just enough weight to hold the blossoms down. Leave for several hours. Store in refrigerator.

To make tea, boil water and pour over blossoms. Place one or two blossoms in each cup of tea. Let steep.

This tea is very light and delicious. I am sure that apple or peach blossoms could be used as well.

Pickled Mackerel
3–4 mackerel fillets (or other oily fish)
white miso
small amount of rice koji

Wash fish. Leave skin on. Purée white miso with a little water to make a thick paste. Mix in a small amount of rice koji. Surround the fish with the miso-koji mixture. Leave for one day. Miso will draw the oil out of the fish.

To prepare, wipe off some of the miso and koji mixture with your fingers, but do not wash the fish. Some miso should remain on it. Broil or bake the fish until done and serve. Refrigerate to store.

Other Pickled Fish
Other types of fish can be pickled in mugi miso. Simply wash the fish fillet (leave skin on) and drain off water. If you wish, rub a little grated ginger into the fish and place in the miso, making sure it is well covered. (You may omit the ginger if desired.) Leave about one week, remove, and store in the refrigerator.

Quick Miso Pickles
Wash, drain and slice root vegetables into thin pieces. Insert in a jar of miso and cover. (You may also tie the vegetable slices in cheesecloth sack before inserting.) Leave for 2–3 days. Wash and serve.

If you use leafy greens, wash and allow them to dry for about one day before placing them in the miso. If you do not allow them to dry properly, the water from the vegetables will cause the miso to spoil. Leave 1–3 days, depending on the type of green used. More hard greens take longer, while softer ones require a shorter time.

Larger slices of vegetables may require as much as one week to pickle. To pickle whole vegetables such as carrots and daikon, make a few lengthwise slits in the skin before inserting them in the miso. Leave for 1–2 weeks. Wash, slice and serve.

Other miso pickles can be made by combining several cups of nuka or rice flour with equal amounts of miso and sea salt. Use about 1/5 as much miso and salt as you do flour or nuka.

You may use mugi, Hatcho, *genmai*, *kome*, or combinations of these various misos to prepare your pickles.

Dill Pickles
2–3 lbs. pickling cucumbers
12 cups water

1/3 cup sea salt
1 large onion
3 sprigs of fresh or dry dill

Wash cucumbers. Peel onion, halve, and then quarter each half. Place cucumbers and onions in a crock or gallon glass jar. Place dill in jar.

Bring salt and water to a boil, reduce flame to low and simmer until salt is dissolved. Remove from flame and allow to cool. When water is cool, pour it over the cucumbers. If necessary, place a lid on top to keep the vegetables submerged in brine. Cover with a thin layer of cheesecloth to keep dust out. Place in a cool, shaded place for 3–4 days. If a film rises to the surface, skim it off. Cover and refrigerate to store. These will keep about one month in the refrigerator.

Other vegetables such as carrot slices, broccoli stems and flowerettes, cauliflower, watermelon rind, etc. may be pickled in the same manner.

The juice from these pickles makes a good base for salad dressings, so do not throw it away.

Kyoto Style Chinese Cabbage Pickles
2 heads Chinese cabbage
1/4–1/3 cup sea salt
nuka or brown rice flour

Cut away just enough base from the cabbages to remove leaves. Peel leaves and wash under cold water. Discard any yellow or dry leaves. The heart or core of the cabbage should be quartered and washed. Dry in the sun for two days. This will make the cabbage very sweet.

Sprinkle a thin layer of sea salt on the bottom of a crock or keg. Next, place a layer of cabbage leaves on top of the salt. Then add a thin layer of sea salt on top of cabbage leaves. Repeat, alternating between cabbage and sea salt until all ingredients are used up. The top layer should be sea salt, as should the bottom layer. Place a lid or disc inside the crock so that it rests on top of the cabbage. Weight down by placing a heavy stone or brick on top of the lid.

Water should rise to the level of the lid within 10 hours. If water does not rise after this amount of time, apply additional weight. (It may also be that you have used too little salt.) Drain cabbage thoroughly when water rises to the level of the lid. Remove cabbage from the crock.

Layer the cabbage in the crock once again, this time placing nuka or rice flour between layers of cabbage. (Top layer should be nuka or flour.) Replace the lid and stone. Keep in a cool place for about a week. Your pickles are now ready to eat. Wash under cold water to remove bran, slice, and serve.

Keep pickles in the crock and store in a cool place until you are ready to serve them. They should keep for about one month.

For additional pickle recipes, including those for salt, miso, mustard green, rice bran, cucumber, and umeboshi pickles, as well as sauerkraut and daikon-sauerkraut, please refer to *Introducing Macrobiotic Cooking*.

12. Dressings, Spreads, Sauces and Dips

The following are just a few of the wide variety of dressings, spreads, sauces and dips that can be made with natural ingredients. Many delicious dishes can be invented by slightly changing your ingredients or proportions.

These dishes are better when made without spices, which are very yin. It is better to use ingredients like fresh ginger, lemon or orange rinds, kelp powders, onions, parsley, chives, celery leaves, dill leaves, shiso, etc. for more zesty flavors. When dining out, it is best to avoid salad dressings and sauces made with sugar, large amounts of spices, dairy food, butter, vinegar, etc.

I usually grind and mix dressings in a suribachi and use a food mill for making spreads and dips. However, if you are making larger quantities for a party, it may be more practical to use a blender. Blenders should not be used daily, however, as electric currents upset the vibrational quality of your food. Slower and more peaceful ways of mixing, grinding, and puréeing are recommended for daily use. Please experiment with your own variations of any of the following recipes.

DRESSINGS

Sesame-Umeboshi Dressing
> 1/8 onion, grated or minced
> 1/2 cup water
> 2 tsp. sesame butter
> 1 Tbsp. lemon juice
> 2 umeboshi plums

Place umeboshi, onions, and sesame butter in a suribachi and purée. Add lemon juice and water. Purée once again to mix well.

Tofu-Tamari Dressing
> 1-1/2 cakes tofu
> 1/2 grated onion
> 1/2 cup water
> a little tamari

Place onion, tofu and tamari in a suribachi and blend until very smooth. Add water and blend again until very creamy.

You may mix in a few sliced scallions, chopped chives, or minced parsley if desired.

Tahini Dressing
> 2 Tbsp. tahini
> 1 Tbsp. grated onion
> 2-1/2 umeboshi plums

1/2 cup water
a little lemon juice

Purée umeboshi and onions in suribachi until smooth. Add tahini and lemon juice, and purée again until smooth. Add water and mix well.

Tofu-Sesame Dressing
1/2 cake tofu
1 Tbsp. grated onion
2 umeboshi plums
1/2 cup water (you may use 1 cup for thinner dressing)
1/2 tsp sesame butter
a little lemon juice (1/2 tsp.)

Blend onion, umeboshi and sesame butter in a suribachi. Add tofu and lemon juice. Blend until smooth. Add water and blend again.

This dressing is very good on Waldorf salads.

Shiro-Miso-Tofu Dressing
1 cake tofu, drained
1-1/2 Tbsp. *Shiro* (white) miso
1 Tbsp. toasted sesame seeds
1 thinly sliced scallion
pinch of sea salt or a little tamari

Toast sesame seeds in a dry skillet. Place in a suribachi and grind thoroughly. Add miso and blend in. Add tofu and sea salt. Blend until very smooth. Place in an attractive serving bowl and garnish with sliced scallions.

This dressing is good when served with salads, sprouts, in sandwiches, or as a dip for party snacks.

Miso Dressing
3 Tbsp. red, white, yellow, or brown rice miso
2 Tbsp. brown rice vinegar
2–3 Tbsp. water
1/2 diced or grated onion
1 tsp. minced parsley or chopped scallion

Place onion in suribachi and grind until smooth. Add miso and blend again. Add water and brown rice vinegar and purée until creamy. Mix in parsley or scallions.

Green Goddess Dressing
3 umeboshi plums
2 Tbsp. minced or grated onion
1 cup water
1/2 cup finely chopped parsley
3/4 cup cooked brown rice (grind first in Foley food mill)
2 Tbsp. tahini (or small amount of heated sesame oil)
1 Tbsp. tamari

Boil umeboshi plums for one minute. Add onions and boil 1–2 minutes. Add persley and simmer one minute. Remove from flame. Mix with rice and blend through a Foley food mill. Place in a suribachi and purée until creamy. Heat oil for about one minute on a low flame. Add oil, tahini, and tamari to rice mixture. Blend again and serve.

Umeboshi-Parsley Dressing
    1-1/2 umeboshi plums
    1/4 cup umeboshi juice
    1/2 cup water
    1 tsp. chopped parsley
    1 scallion, sliced thin
    1/4 cup minced cucumber
    1/2 tsp. sesame oil, heated 1 minute on low flame

Boil umeboshi and juice for 1–2 minutes. Place in a suribachi and add the scallion and cucmber. Blend well. Add parsley and oil and blend again. Add water and mix well.

Tamari-Lemon Dressing
    1/2 cup water
    1 Tbsp. grated onion
    2 Tbsp. tamari
    a little lemon or orange juice
    1/4–1/2 tsp. sesame oil, heated for 1 minute on low flame

Blend all ingredients together in a suribachi and serve.

Tamari-Rice Vinegar Dressing
    1 Tbsp. tamari
    4 Tbsp. brown rice vinegar
    1 Tbsp. grated onion
    1/4–1/2 tsp. sesame oil, heated for 1 minute on low flame
    1/2 cup water

Prepare same as previous recipe.

Umeboshi-Lemon Dressing
    2 umeboshi plums
    1/2 cup water
    1 Tbsp. lemon juice
    1/2 tsp. oil, heated for 1 minute on low flame
    1 Tbsp. grated onion

Place umeboshi, onion, and oil in a suribachi and purée well. Add water and lemon juice and purée again.

Miso-Tahini Dressing
    3 tsp. tahini
    1 tsp. miso

1 tsp. grated onion
1/2 cup water

Blend all ingredients together in a suribachi and serve.

Miso-Rice Vinegar Dressing

2 Tbsp. miso
2 Tbsp. brown rice vinegar
1/2 cup water

Blend all ingredients together in a suribachi and serve.

Miso-Walnut Dressing

1/2 cup roasted, finely chopped walnuts
1 Tbsp. miso
1/4–1/2 cup water

Roast nuts and chop very finely. Place in a suribachi and grind until similar to nut butter. Add miso and purée. Add water and purée again until all ingredients are thoroughly mixed.

SPREADS

Miso-Tahini Spread

6 Tbsp. tahini
1 Tbsp. miso
2 Tbsp. chopped scallions or chives

Roast tahini in a dry cast iron skillet until golden brown. Stir constantly to prevent burning. Remove from flame and stir in miso. Add scallions or chives and mix.

Sesame-Miso Spread

6 Tbsp. sesame butter
1 Tbsp. miso
2 Tbsp. sautéed minced onion

Using a low flame, sauté onions in a small amount of sesame oil until translucent. Add sesame butter and stir 2–3 minutes. Remove from flame and add miso. Mix well.

Miso-Nut Spread

1 cup roasted walnuts or pecans (very finely chopped)
2 Tbsp. miso
1/4 cup water

Roast nuts in a dry skillet, stirring constantly to prevent burning. Chop nuts very finely. Place in a suribachi and grind until like nut butter. Add miso and purée. Add water and purée again until smooth.

Lentil-Miso Spread
    1 cup cooked lentils
    1–2 Tbsp. miso
    2 Tbsp. minced scallions or chives
    a little water

Place lentils in a food mill and purée. Remove and place in a suribachi. Add miso and blend together. Add scallions or chives and mix in. Place in a bowl and garnish with chopped parsley.

Lima Bean-Miso Spread
    1 cup cooked lima beans
    1–2 Tbsp. miso
    a little water if necessary
    2 Tbsp. minced sautéed onions

Purée beans in a food mill until creamy. Sauté onions in a little sesame oil until translucent. Place onions and beans in a suribachi. Add miso and water and purée until smooth and creamy.

You may add scallions or chives instead of onions or use other beans, such as kidney, pinto, chickpeas, etc. Garnish with chopped parsley.

FRUIT BUTTERS, JELLIES AND JAMS

Various fruit butters can be made very simply at home. In most cases, you need only slice the fruit, add a little water and a pinch of sea salt, and cook until very sweet and soft. You can also purée the cooked fruit in a food mill if necessary. Refrigerate to store. If additional sweetness is desired, you may add yinnie syrup, ame, or barley malt while cooking.

Jellies can be made by either boiling down cider or fruit juice or by combining fruit with juice, adding a pinch of salt, and cooking it down until it becomes thick, skimming off foam when it rises. Natural sweeteners may be added if necessary.

Jams can be made simply by cooking a variety of local berries and fruits. (If they contain seeds which you may wish to remove, place the cooked berries in a strainer and squeeze out the pulp and juice. The seeds will remain in the strainer.) To cook down, place berries on a low flame, adding sweetener when necessary, and simmer until very thick. You may add a little arrowroot flour or diluted kuzu to thicken if necessary.

Squash-Apple Butter
    1 small buttercup squash
    2–3 apples, diced (peeled)
    pinch of sea salt
    1/2 cup water

Peel squash, remove seeds and cut into cubes. Peel apples, remove skin and core. Cut into chunks or thin slices. Place squash and apples in a pot with a pinch of sea salt and very little water. Bring to a boil. Reduce flame to low, cover and simmer until squash is soft. Purée in a food mill until creamy. Place back in pot and simmer on a low flame, stirring occasionally, for 30–45 minutes or until thick. Refrigerate to store.

Apple Butter

2 lbs. cooking or baking apples
a little water
pinch of sea salt

Peel, core and slice apples. Place in a pot with a pinch of sea salt and a very small amount of water. Bring to a boil, cover and reduce flame to very low. Place a flame-deflector under the pot. Stir occasionally to prevent burning. Cook on a low flame until thick and brown. Refrigerate to store.

SAUCES

Bechamel Sauce

1/2 cup whole wheat pastry flour
3 cups vegetable or kombu stock
1 medium onion
sesame oil
2 Tbsp. tamari

Lightly brush a skillet with sesame oil and sauté onions until translucent. Stir in pastry flour and sauté 2–3 minutes, stirring constantly to mix in well and prevent burning. Gradually add stock or water and mix well. Bring to a boil, reduce flame to low, cover and simmer on a low flame 2–3 minutes. Add tamari to taste and simmer another 10–12 minutes. Stir occasionally to prevent sticking.

Other flours such as rice, sweet rice, corn, or winter wheat flour may be used instead of pastry flour, while seitan starch water may be substituted for flour and water. You can also add vegetables such as parsley, scallions, chives, mushrooms, celery, etc.

Mushroom Sauce

1/2 cup pastry or rice flour
3 cups kombu-shiitake stock
1–1-1/2 cups chopped fresh mushrooms
1/2 grated onion
sesame oil
2 Tbsp. tamari

Lightly brush skillet with sesame oil and sauté mushrooms and onions until onions are translucent. Cook as above.

White Sauce

1/2 cup brown rice flour
3 cups water
corn oil

1 onion, diced
1 Tbsp. chopped parsley
sea salt to taste

Sauté onion in corn oil until translucent. Add rice flour and cook as above. Season with sea salt to taste. Add chopped parsley during the final 1–2 minutes.

This sauce is very delicious when served with onions, carrots, cauliflower, mushrooms, green peas, etc.

Seitan-Kuzu Sauce

3 cups seitan-tamari cooking water
2–2-1/2 Tbsp. kuzu, diluted in a little water
1 onion, diced
1 tsp. fresh grated ginger

Place seitan-tamari water and onions in a pot. Bring to a boil, reduce flame to low and simmer 10 minutes. Slowly add diluted kuzu, stirring constantly to mix well. Simmer 10–15 minutes on a low flame. Add ginger and cook 1–2 minutes longer.

Seitan Gravy

(see Thankgiving Holiday Menu for recipe)

Kuzu Sauce

3 cups kombu-shiitake or kombu-shiitake-bonito stock
2–2-1/2 Tbsp. kuzu, diluted in a little water
tamari or sea salt to taste (miso can also be used)

Bring stock to a boil. Reduce flame to low, add diluted kuzu, and stir in well. Simmer about 10 minutes. Season with sea salt, tamari, or miso and serve over vegetables or noodles.

Fish Sauce

1/2 cup brown rice flour
3 cups water or kombu stock
1/4 lb. white meat fish, boned and cut into small pieces (or tie leftover fish, bones, etc. in a cheesecloth sack)
1/2 cup diced onion
1 Tbsp. minced parsley
sea salt to taste
sesame or corn oil

Sauté onions and fish (if using fish fillet) in corn or sesame oil for several minutes. If you are using leftover fish and fish bones, put them in a cheesecloth sack and boil to remove fish flavor. Remove sack and discard.

If using fish fillet, cook as for other sauce recipes. If using leftover fish, cook as for other sauce recipes after boiling. Garnish with chopped or minced parsley.

Dip Sauces

(see tempura recipe in vegetable chapter)

DIPS

Tofu Dip
>   1 cake tofu
>   1/2 tsp. puréed umeboshi paste
>   1/4 small onion, grated
>   1/4 cup water
>   2 Tbsp. chopped chives
>   1 Tbsp. minced parsley

Purée onion and umeboshi in a suribachi or use a blender to make smoother. Add tofu and water. Blend and remove. Mix in parsley and chives. Chill, garnish, and serve with chips, crackers, or bread.

Bean Dips
>   2 cups cooked kidney, pinto or lima beans
>   1/4 cup minced onion
>   1/2 cup chopped scallions
>   a little water for desired consistency

Mix ingredients in a blender until smooth, adding a little water if necessary for desired thickness.

When cooking the beans, you may season with sea salt or puréed miso to create different flavors.

Serve with bread, crackers, or chips.

Chickpea Dip
>   2 cups cooked chickpeas
>   2 umeboshi plums
>   1 small onion, diced
>   1 Tbsp. chopped chives
>   2 Tbsp. tahini
>   a little chickpea water or plain water if necessary for desired thickness

Mix chickpeas, umeboshi, tahini and onions in blender, adding water if necessary. Remove and mix in chives. Garnish and serve with bread, crackers, or chips.

Please refer to *Introducing Maerobiotic Cooking* for additional recipes, including those for tofu, umeboshi, scallion-parsley, and tahini dressings; miso-tahini spread; bechamel, kuzu, and lemon-miso sauces; and chickpea and tofu dips.

13. Beverages

The beverages that we use most often in our home are those which are non-aromatic, non-stimulating and which contain no sugar, caffeine, artificial coloring agents, preservatives or other additives. The main drink which we prepare is bancha, a very mild, balanced tea. Other teas come prepared, or you may prepare your own by using grains, beans and other ingredients. Grain coffee can also be used, and should be of high quality, without ingredients such as dates, figs, and spices. It should be made from roasted, ground grains, beans, chicory, vegetables and other, more yang, ingredients. There are a few good brands available in natural food stores across the United States. Occasionally, fruit juices may be used, but they should not usually be taken in large quantities or too frequently. Among these, apple cider is probably the best. Amazake is another suitable drink, made from sweet rice and rice koji.

All of the drinks listed above should generally be served hot, warm, or at room temperature. Cool drinks can be used occasionally in the summer, but your beverages should not be served ice-cold. Iced drinks tend to stop digestion, paralyze the stomach, and can produce head and eye aches and other problems.

Mineral water may also be used occasionally with a little lemon or lime juice squeezed in it. The mineral water should be of the high quality, naturally carbonated variety, without sodium bicarbonate or other ingredients added to it.

Occasionally at parties, social gatherings of simply for your enjoyment, good quality beer or *sake* (Japanese rice wine) may be used in moderate quantities. However, it is not advisable to drink these daily or in excessive quantities.

BANCHA

Bancha is made from the older leaves and twigs of a tea bush grown in Japan. This bush is said to have originated in China. Sometimes the tea is packaged under the name *kukicha* instead of bancha. (*Cha* is the Japanese word for "tea"

	Protein	Calcium	Iron	Vit. A	Niacin	Vit. C
Bancha	20.3 g.	720 mg.	37 mg.	9000 I.U.	9.0 mg.	130 mg.
Whole Milk	3.5 g.	118 mg.	trace	140 I.U.	0.1 mg.	1 mg.
Condensed Milk	8.1 g.	262 mg.	0.1 mg.	140 I.U.	0.2 mg.	1 mg.
Skim Milk	3.6 g.	121 mg.	trace	trace	0.1 mg.	1 mg. *

---

* Information taken from *The Book of Macrobiotics* by Michio Kushi, published by Japan Publications, Inc. Based on information obtained from U.S. Department of Agriculture and Japan Nutritionist Association food composition tables.

and *ban* refers to the particular variety of plant.) Bancha contains no caffeine, is not aromatic and contains no artificial colorings or dyes.

To prepare bancha, roast in a dry skillet for 3–4 minutes. Place 1-1/2 quarts of water in a teapot and add 1–2 tablespoons of bancha. Bring to a boil, reduce flame to very low and simmer 2–3 minutes. Pour through a bamboo tea strainer into individual cups.

While in Japan, I had the opportunity to see tea bushes growing in the fields and to learn how they are harvested and prepared. There are many different types or grades of tea which can be obtained from one type of bush such as bancha, and all are harvested at different times of the year to produce the different qualities of tea. For example, the tea that is prepared especially for the Japanese tea ceremony is prepared from the very top, or most yin part, of the tea bush. Only tiny, young leaves are chosen, and these are then ground into a powder. It is very high in caffeine, which is yin. Other grades of green tea are also selected at various times from the bush. Depending on the age and color of the leaves, the tea is then graded and sold dried. All other green teas contain various degrees of caffeine. Older and drier leaves generally contain less caffeine than younger and fresher leaves. Bancha is the last tea to be harvested, and it consists of older dried leaves and twigs. By the time bancha is harvested, no caffeine remains in the leaves and twigs.

All the tea in Japan is harvested by hand. The tea grows mainly in mountainous areas, as it needs the dew and moisture of the mountains and valleys to grow well. It is usually grown on terraces up the sides of the mountains. The bushes are kept fairly short. They average about 2–3 feet high and are kept well trimmed.

Mugicha

This tea is made from unhulled, roasted barley, and is usually sold pre-roasted and prepackaged in natural food stores. *Mugi* is the Japanese word for barley. To prepare mugicha, simply place a couple of tablespoons in 1-1/2–2 quarts of water. Bring to a boil, reduce flame to low and simmer several minutes. This tea is very delicious and can also be mixed with bancha to produce a different flavor.

If you cannot obtain the prepackaged tea, try to purchase some unhulled barley. To prepare, simply roast the unhulled barley in a dry skillet until it becomes very dark brown and releases a nutty fragrance. Store in an airtight container and cook as above when desired.

Brown Rice Tea

This tea is very delicious and light, and is especially good in the summer. To prepare, simply roast some washed brown rice in a dry skillet until it becomes a golden brown and releases a nutty fragrance. Stir constantly to prevent burning. To make tea, simply add a couple of tablespoons of roasted rice to 1-1/2–2 quarts of water. Bring to a boil, reduce flame to low and simmer about 10 minutes or so. You can also mix in a little bancha or mix mugicha and rice together for a different tea.

Other Grain Teas

Other grains such as millet, oats, wheat, etc. can also be dry-roasted and prepared as above. You can also separately roast several grains and prepare a tea made by mixing two or more varieties.

Umeboshi Tea

This tea is used more during the summer months. It produces a cooling effect on the body and helps to replace minerals lost through perspiration. However, it should not be overly salty. It should have a slightly salty and refreshing taste, and should not be made so strong that it makes you desire to drink cold water or eat fruit.

To prepare, use leftover umeboshi pits. Place 3–4 umeboshi pits in a tea pot with 1-1/2–2 quarts of water. You can add a couple of shiso leaves as well. Bring to a boil, reduce flame to low and simmer for 20 minutes or so. Drink at room temperature or slightly cool. It can also be served warm if desired.

Mu Tea

Mu Tea is sold prepackaged in most natural food stores. It comes in teabag form. Mu tea is prepared from a combination of about 16 different herbs. It is mainly used for its medicinal properties instead of as a daily beverage. It is especially good for the stomach. However, mu tea is a yang tea and should not be used regularly or in large quantities. Follow directions on package to prepare.

Mugwort Tea

This tea is made from a plant by the same name which has been dried. It is not recommended for daily use as it is quite yin, and may cause constipation if used regularly or in large quantities. It is mainly used as a medicinal tea, as it is beneficial in treating overly yang conditions, such as jaundice, and in ridding the body of worms. To prepare, place about one tablespoon of tea into a quart of water. Bring to a boil, reduce flame and simmer 5–10 minutes.

Other Teas

There are a number of other teas which we use mainly for medicinal purposes. They include lotus root tea, which is good for upper respiratory problems; daikon tea, which is used to treat overly yang conditions or to help rid the body of excess fat, mucus, or salt deposits; shiitake mushroom tea, which is used to help eliminate or rid the body of excess salts and mineral-fat deposits, or to treat overly yang conditions; raspberry leaf tea, which is sometimes used by women during labor as it is yin and helps them to relax; ume-shoyu-bancha tea, which is prepared from umeboshi, tamari, and bancha and which is good for digestive problems, some types of headaches, etc.

Yannoh

Yannoh is a type of coffee prepared from roasted grain, beans, and chicory. This tea is not sold in many natural food stores in this country, but is widely sold in Japan and in Europe.

To prepare yannoh, simply wash three cups of brown rice, 2-1/2 cups of winter wheat, 1-1/2 cups Japanese azuki beans, 2 cups chickpeas, and a cup of chicory root. Dry-roast all ingredients separately in a skillet until they are dark brown in color, stirring to prevent burning. Then mix them together and grind into a fine powder in a grain mill. Use one tablespoon of yannoh per cup of water. Bring the water to a boil and very quickly reduce the flame. If allowed to boil, the coffee will bubble and foam out of the tea pot. Simmer on a low flame for 5–10 minutes or until dark brown in color. Store remaining yannoh in an airtight container.

You can prepare other grain coffees simply by using different grains, beans, or vegetables such as burdock, or by varying the amounts and proportions of the ingredients. Please experiment and discover many wonderful and delicous grain coffees to prepare.

Fruit Juice and Cider

Among fruit juices, I recommend that you primarily use apple juice or cider, as these are generally more yang than other varieites. Apple juice or cider should be of very high quality, with no preservatives, sugar or other ingredients added. Unpasteurized varieties are preferable. You may serve juice cool, but never iced.

For overly yang conditions resulting from too much salt, hot apple juice can be used very effectively as medicine. However, persons with more yin illnesses should try to avoid all fruit juices until their condition improves.

Mineral Water and Fruit Juice

Occasionally, for parties or during the hot summer months, a punch can be prepared by combining apple or other juices with mineral water. For every gallon of juice, add about half a gallon of mineral water. You can add several thin slices of lemon, lime or orange to the punch bowl for more festive occasions.

Plain mineral water served with a twist of lemon or lime can be very refreshing on a hot summer day or even occasionally during the winter if your condition becomes overly yang.

Amazake

Amazake is a drink prepared from fermented sweet rice. Fermentation is produced by adding rice koji to the cooked sweet rice. (Amazake is also used as a natural sweetener for cookies, breads, cakes, doughnuts, puddings, etc.) We find it especially good when served hot during the autumn and winter months. It is also delicious when served slightly chilled in the summer. To prepare amazake beverage, first wash 4 cups of sweet brown rice, drain it and let it sit overnight in 8 cups of cold water. Then place the rice in a pressure-cooker and bring to pressure. Reduce the flame to low and simmer for about 20 minutes. Remove from flame and allow to sit for about 45 minutes. Remove rice and place in a bowl. When rice becomes cool enough to handle, mix in 1/2 cup koji (a special bacteria used to produce fermentation). Allow the rice to sit in a warm place, covered with a towel, for at least 4 hours. (Don't let it sit for more than 8 hours, as it will begin to turn sour.) Make sure to place the rice and koji in a glass bowl to ferment. (Do not use a metal pot or mixing bowl.) Several times during the fermentation process, mix the rice and koji with a bamboo rice paddle or wooden spoon so that the koji will melt. Then place the rice in a pot, add a little water and bring to a boil. Turn the flame off as soon as it starts to bubble.

To use as a drink, grind through a Foley food mill, mix with enough water for desired consistency and add a pinch of sea salt. Bring to a boil, reduce flame to very low and simmer for several minutes. Store in a glass jar in the refrigerator.

A very delicious beverage can be made by heating amazake and adding a little freshly grated ginger to it. (A pinch of cinnamon can also be added.)

For use as a sweetener, it can be used as is or blended to make it smoother.

Amazake will keep for several days in the refrigerator. If you wish to keep it for longer periods, it should be cooked over a low flame until it becomes a dark, brown color.

14. Holiday Cooking

Holidays are wonderful times to get together with family and friends to share in celebration, conversation and giving thanks. They are times of much happiness and joy, as well as for self-reflection. Whether you are cooking for a holiday or just any day of the week, your food should always be orderly, beautifully prepared and attractively arranged. When you are cooking, always be thankful for the food that has come from nature and the universe for you to prepare for your family and friends. Maintain a happy and peaceful attitude while cooking and you will bring much joy, happiness, and health to all who eat from your table.*

THANKS GIVING MENU

Squash Turkey
Brown Rice
Seitan-Mushroom Gravy
Cranberry Sauce
Baked Wild Rice

---

* For the specific recipes presented in the Christmas, New Year's Eve, New Year and picnic menus, please refer to the main text of this book.

Clear Broth Soup w/Watercress
Boiled Carrots
Raw Salad w/Umeboshi Dressing
Yeasted Rolls
Dill Pickles
Apple Pie
Pumpkin Pie

Squash Turkey

    1 medium blue Hubbard Squash
    9 cups whole wheat bread cubes (toasted in a dry skillet)
    1 cup diced onion
    1 cup diced celery
    1-1/2 cups sliced mushrooms
    1 cup cooked seitan, chopped or cubed
    1 Tbsp. corn oil
    pinch of sea salt
    1 cup seitan-mushroom gravy

Remove top from squash and clean out seeds. Save seeds and roast later for a snack. Pre-bake the unstuffed squash at 350° F. for approximately 45 minutes to remove any excess liquid, as Hubbard squash tend to be more watery. Dry-roast the bread cubes until golden brown and place in a bowl. Sauté vegetables in corn oil until onions are translucent. Mix vegetables, sea salt and bread cubes together. Add in cooked seitan and mix again. Stuff the squash until full. Bake at 325° F. for 2 hours. Remove top and pour a cup of seitan-mushroom gravy over the stuffing. Continue to bake 30–45 minutes more, without top. Remove from oven and arrange attractively on a large serving platter. Serve with seitan-mushroom gravy.

Seitan-Mushroom Gravy

    5 cups tamari-seitan cooking water
    1 cup cooked, chopped seitan
    1 cup diced onion
    1 cup halved and sliced mushrooms
    4 cups seitan-starch water

Combine ingredients, except for the starch water, in a pot. Bring to a boil, reduce flame to low and cover. Simmer 30 minutes. Add in starch water and bring to a boil again. Reduce flame to low and simmer 15–20 minutes or until thickened. Serve over stuffing in squash.

Cranberry Sauce

    4 cups cranberries, washed and cleaned
    1 cup raisins
    1/2 cup barley malt
    4-1/2 Tbsp. kuzu
    3 cups water

Cook raisins in 1 cup water for about 10 minutes. Add cranberries, remaining water, pinch of sea salt and barley malt. Simmer about 10 minutes. Dilute kuzu in a little water and add to the cranberries. Stir to prevent lumping. Simmer about 5–7 minutes. Pour into a bowl or mold and allow to harden.

Baked Wild Rice

 3 cups kombu soup stock
 1 onion, diced (about 1/4–1/3 cup)
 1 stalk celery, diced (about 1/2 cup)
 1-1/2 cups fresh mushrooms, thinly sliced
 1/2 cup slivered almonds
 1-1/2 tsp. sesame oil
 1 cup wild rice
 pinch of sea salt
 1-1/2 tsp. tamari

Sauté onions, celery and mushrooms in a little oil until onions are translucent. Bring kombu stock to a boil. Mix all ingredients together and place in a casserole or baking dish. Cover and bake at 350 °F. for 1-1/2 hours. Remove cover and bake another 15–20 minutes to remove any excess liquid. Serve.

Clear Broth Soup

 8 cups water
 6″ strip of kombu
 1/4–1/3 cup chuba (dried fish)
 1 cup cubed tofu
 1 bunch watercress, separately boiled less than 1 minute and rinsed
 tamari to taste

Place kombu, chuba and water in a pot. Bring to a boil, cover and reduce flame to low. Remove kombu after one minute. Remove chuba after 3–4 minutes. Season broth with tamari to taste. Add tofu during the final two minutes. Place in serving bowls and garnish with watercress.

Boiled Carrots

 10–12 carrots
 one 6″ strip of kombu
 water
 sea salt

Place kombu in the bottom of a pot. Place carrots on top and add water to about half-cover. Season with a pinch of sea salt. Bring to a boil, reduce flame to low, cover and simmer until carrots are done. Carrots should be tender and sweet but not too soft. Place in a serving bowl.

Raw Salad

 1 head iceberg or Romaine lettuce
 4 red radishes

1/2 cup alfalfa sprouts
2 sprigs of parsley
1 cucumber, halved and thinly sliced

Mix ingredients together and place in a bowl or attractively arrange on a platter or in a bowl, keeping each ingredient separate. Serve with umeboshi dressing.

Umeboshi Dressing

1 sprig parsley, chopped
2 scallions, sliced
2 umeboshi plums
1/8-1/4 cup umeboshi juice
1/2–1 cup water

Place umeboshi in a suribachi and purée. Add umeboshi juice and purée again. Add parsley, scallion, and water and purée again. Serve over salad.

Yeasted Rolls

3 cups whole wheat flour
3 cups unbleached white flour
1-1/2 tsp. dry yeast
1/2 tsp. sea salt
1/4 cup water, warm
2 cups water
1/4 cup barley malt

Mix yeast with 1/4 cup warm water and let sit for 10 minutes. Mix remaining water with barley malt and salt. Add yeast. Gradually add in flours and form a ball of dough. Knead the dough, adding flour when necessary to keep the dough from sticking to the kneading surface. Knead until stiff and elastic. Oil a bowl with sesame oil and roll dough in it to coat it with oil. Cover the bowl with a damp cloth and set in a warm place until double in size. (About 1-1-1/2 hours.) Punch down and form into a ball again and knead. Pull apart and form into small balls. Place three balls in each section of an oiled muffin tin. This will produce a clover-leaf effect as the dough rises again. Allow to rise in muffin tins for 45 minutes to an hour. Bake at 350° F. for 25–30 minutes or until golden brown. Cool slightly before serving.

Dill Pickles

(refer to pickle chapter for recipe)

Apple Pie

(refer to dessert chapter for recipe)

Pumpkin Pie

1 medium Hokkaido pumpkin
1 cup water
pinch of sea salt

1/2 tsp. cinnamon (optional)
1/2 cup barley malt
1 cup chopped walnuts

Wash pumpkin and remove skin. Cut into 1–1-1/2 inch cubes. Place cubes, a pinch of sea salt and water in a pot. Bring to a boil. Cover, reduce flame to low and simmer until pumpkin is soft. Remove and purée in a Foley food mill. Place back in the pot, add barley malt and cinnamon. Bring to a boil again and simmer, covered, on a low flame for 10 minutes or so. Remove from flame when pumpkin becomes very thick. Place filling in a pre-baked pie shell. Sprinkle chopped walnuts on top of pie filling. Bake at 350° F. about 30 minutes or until crust is golden brown. Slice and serve.

CHRISTMAS MENU
Chestnut Rice
Clear Broth Soup w/Tofu and Scallions
Broiled Fillet of Sole
Pressed Salad
Nori-Maki
Boiled Watercress and Carrot Slices
Sauerkraut
Squash Pie
Apple Strudel
Tea

Clear Broth Soup with Tofu and Scallions
    5–6 cups water
    6 shiitake mushrooms, soaked, destemmed and sliced
    one 6″ strip kombu
    1–2 Tbsp. bonito flakes
    1 cake tofu, cubed (1-1/2″ × 1″ × 1/2″)
    2 scallions, thinly sliced
    tamari to taste

Place water, kombu and bonito in a pot. Bring to a boil, reduce flame and simmer 2–3 minutes. Remove kombu. Simmer about 5 more minutes. Remove bonito with a wire skimmer or strain. Add shiitake, cover and simmer about 10–15 minutes. Add tofu and simmer 1–2 minutes. Season with tamari to taste. Add sliced scallions just before serving.

NEW YEAR'S EVE
Served at 12:000 Midnight

Last year, we had the opportunity to oberve the New Year in Japan. Of the many holidays celebrated in that country, New Year's is perhaps the most important.

Two aspects of our New Year experience in Japan stand out most vividly in my mind. First, food plays a central role in the celebration of the holiday; and, secondly, the New Year's celebration has a deep, spiritual meaning.

About a week before the holiday, the macrobiotic center in Kyoto held a brown rice mochi-pounding party, to which all friends were invited. Of all the traditional dishes prepared during the holiday, mochi is perhaps the most important. It is served in soups, with tamari, dipped in ame and rolled in *kinako* (roasted soybean flour) and in a number of other ways.

Most of the mochi eaten nowadays in Japan is made from pounded, refined sweet rice rather than the more traditional brown rice. Our *genmai* (brown rice) mochi came from the macrobiotic center, which was one of the few places where it could be found.

Another New Year's food that we enjoyed is known as *Toshikoshi Soba*. The dish itself is simply a bowl of soba served in tamari broth and garnished with scallions and perhaps a little ginger, and is similar to what you find in the countless noodle shops which are all over Japan. The name *Toshikoshi Soba* means something like "long life soba," and its significance comes from the fact that the noodles are eaten right before and during midnight on New Year's Eve. According to tradition, if you eat these noodles as you enter the New Year, you will pass through the coming year without sickness or harm.

Perhaps the deeper meaning is that by eating whole grains (represented by buckwheat noodles) you will enjoy a long and healthy life. While in Japan, I began to wonder whether this idea was perhaps similar to the Jewish custom of eating unleavened bread during the celebration of Passover.

Several of the other foods which play an important part in the New Year's celebration are the small Japanese tangerines known as *mikan*, a variety of special miso soups and, of course, sake. Interestingly, *mikan* grow throughout most of Japan, and are harvested during the autumn and winter.

As you can probably imagine, children are involved in all of these activities, especially the pounding of sweet rice into mochi. In this way, many of these wonderful customs are passed from generation to generation into the future.

At the same time, the Japanese celebration of New Year's involves a deep sense of connection with the past. Millions of people visit various Buddhist and Shinto shrines during the holiday, and mochi and other types of food are offered to ancestors and various spirits of nature in millions of household shrines throughout the country.

MENU
Soba and Broth (called Toshikoshi Soba)
Mochi
Sake

NEW YEAR'S DAY
Ozoni
Azuki Bean Ohagi
Walnut Ohagi
Sesame Ohagi
Chestnut Ohagi

Black Bean Mochi
Plain Brown Rice Mochi
Black Beans (Japanese Soybeans)
Soba Nori-Maki
Somen Nori-Maki
Sashimi
Sautéed Mustard Greens
Steamed Chinese Cabbage
Pickles
Sake
Tangerines
Bancha Tea

PICNIC (Summer Menu)
Sushi
Nori-Maki
Noodle Salad
Baked Beans
Fruit Salad
Dill Pickles
Crab Stuffed Cucumbers
Grilled Tofu
Pressed Salad
Blueberry Pie
Cool Bancha with Lemon

Noodle Watercress Salad
  8 oz. whole wheat or Jerusalem artichoke shells
  1/2 cucumber, quartered and sliced thin
  1/2 stalk celery, halved and sliced thin
  2 Tbsp. sliced scallions
  1/2 carrot, quartered and thinly sliced
  cup watercress, cut into 1/2″ pieces
Cook, rinse and drain shells. Mix shells together with all other ingredients. Serve with tahini dressing.

  You may also add a few cooked chickpeas to this recipe if desired.

Tahini-Umeboshi Dressing
  3 Tbsp. tahini
  3/4 cup water
  1/3 onion, diced
  2 umeboshi plums
  2 tsp. lemon juice
  1/4 tsp. tamari
Place onion and umeboshi in a suribachi and grind until smooth. Add tahini and mix. Add lemon juice and tamari and blend again. Add water and blend well. Mix in with noodle or raw salad.

15. Menu Suggestions

The following menus are based on dinners served in out home over a period of two weeks. Generally, breakfast should be a light meal with miso soup, using the various types of miso available and a variety of vegetables, seaweeds, tofu, etc. A grain cereal such as soft whole oats, soft rice, soft barley, soft millet, oatmeal and rice, miso rice, fried rice, etc. can also be served for breakfast. Breakfast in our home also usually includes one vegetable, either freshly prepared or leftover from dinner the night before. Lunches are also generally light. They usually consist of fried rice, riceballs, any type of noodles with or without broth, a sandwich, fried noodles, bread, maybe a leftover soup, some type of lightly cooked vegetable and either bancha tea, grain tea or coffee. Make sure you regularly vary your breakfast, lunch and dinner menus so that your meals do not become repetitive or boring.

Keep in mind that these menus are only general suggestions and should not be followed exactly or rigidly adhered to. Vary your menus to fit changes in your own personal condition, your environment, etc.

Monday Dinner
> Brown Rice
> *Aka* (red) Miso Soup
> Unsweetened Squash Pie with Oatmeal Crust
> Pressed Salad
> Sautéed Savoy Cabbage
> Bancha Tea

Tuesday Dinner
> Brown Rice
> Soba Sushi
> Lima Bean Soup
> Chinese Cabbage Rolls
> Sautéed Kale

Apple/Pear Kanten
Mugicha or Bancha

Wednesday Dinner
Mixed Brown and Sweet Rice
Barley-Lentil Soup
Burdock Eel
Boiled Broccoli
Grated Daikon/Umeboshi Pickles
Applesauce
Bancha Tea

Thursday Dinner
Brown Rice
Tofu-Scallion Soup
Boiled Watercress
Baked Squash
Baked Mochi
Bancha

Friday Dinner
Brown Rice w/Wild Rice
Cream of Mushroom Soup
Sautéed Cabbage and Carrots
Boiled Mustard Greens
Azuki Beans
Stewed Apples w/Kuzu Sauce

Saturday Dinner
Brown Rice
Millet Soup
Seitan and Vegetables
Puréed Buttercup Squash
Wakame and Onions
Apple Pie
Tea

Sunday Dinner
Brown Rice
Kenchin Soup w/Deep Fried Tofu
Sautéed Kale
Steamed Broccoli and Cauliflower
Popcorn Balls
Tea

Monday Dinner
    Brown Rice
    Ramen Soup w/Watercress
    Red Lentils
    Sautéed Collard Greens and Onions
    Steamed Broccoli Rappia and Carrots
    Tea

Tuesday Dinner
    Brown Rice
    Tofu Clear Broth Soup
    Boiled Watercress
    Steamed Squash
    Carrot Burdock Kinpira
    Apple-Cou Cous Kanten
    Tea

Wednesday Dinner
    Brown Rice
    Baked Kasha w/Sauce
    Boiled Turnips, Carrots and Onions
    Navy Bean Soup
    Steamed Chinese Cabbage
    Tea

Thursday Dinner
    Brown Rice
    Yellow Miso Soup
    Boiled Brussels Sprouts and Turnips
    Baked Black Bean Mochi
    Carrot/Sesame Seed Kinpira
    Tea

Friday Dinner
    Chickpea Soup
    Brown Rice
    Sautéed Kale
    Noodle Salad
    Boiled Buttercup Squash and Onions
    Tea

Saturday Dinner
    Brown Rice
    Clear Broth Fish and Watercress Soup

Baked Hubbard Squash
Steamed Mustard Greens
Kanten
Tea

Sunday Dinner
Brown Rice
Barley Soup
Kidney Beans
Sautéed Carrots and Kale
Steamed Cauliflower and Greens
Homemade Rice Bread
Tea

Special Note: These menus were prepared in New England during the months of December and January. Please adjust them to reflect seasonal change and the environment in which you live.

Principles of the Order of Universe

Seven Universal Principles of the Infinite Universe

1. Everything is a differentiation of one Infinity.
2. Everything changes.
3. All antagonisms are complementary.
4. There is nothing identical.
5. What has a front has a back.
6. The bigger the front, the bigger the back.
7. What has a beginning has an end.

Twelve Laws of Change of the Infinite Universe

1. One Infinity manifests itself into complementary and antagonistic tendencies, yin and yang, in its endless change.
2. Yin and yang are manifested continuously from the eternal movement of one infinite universe.
3. Yin represents centrifugality. Yang represents centripetality. Yin and yang together produce energy and all phenomena.
4. Yin attracts yang. Yang attracts yin.
5. Yin repels yin. Yang repels yang.
6. Yin and yang combined in varying proportions produce different phenomena. The attraction and repulsion among phenomena is proportional to the difference of the yin and yang forces.
7. All phenomena are ephemeral, constantly changing their constitution of yin and yang forces; yin changes into yang, yang changes into yin.
8. Nothing is solely yin or solely yang. Everything is composed of both tendencies in varying degrees.
9. There is nothing neuter. Either yin or yang is in excess in every occurrence.
10. Large yin attracts small yin. Large yang attracts small yang.
11. Extreme yin produces yang, and extreme yang produces yin.
12. All physical manifestations are yang at the center, and yin at the surface.

* Adapted from the *Book of Macrobiotics: The Universal Way of Health and Happiness* by Michio Kushi.

Classification of Yin and Yang

Characteristic	YIN (▽) Centrifugal Force	YANG (△) Centripetal Force
Tendency	Expansion	Contraction
Function	Diffusion	Fusion
	Dispersion	Assimilation
	Separation	Gathering
	Decomposition	Organization
Movement	More inactive and slower	More active and faster
Vibration	Shorter wave and higher frequency	Longer wave and lower frequency
Direction	Ascent and vertical	Descent and horizontal
Position	More outward and periphery	More inward and central
Weight	Lighter	Heavier
Temperature	Colder	Hotter
Light	Darker	Brighter
Humidity	More wet	More dry
Density	Thinner	Thicker
Size	Longer	Smaller
Shape	More expansive and fragile	More contractive and harder
Form	Longer	Shorter
Texture	Softer	Harder
Atomic particle	Electron	Proton
Elements	N, O, K, P, Ca, etc.	H, C, Na, As, Mg, etc.
Environment	Vibration . . . Air . . . Water . . . Earth	
Climatic effects	Tropical climate	Colder climate
Biological	More vegetable quality	More animal quality
Sex	Female	Male
Organ structure	More hollow and expansive	More compacted and condensed
Nerves	More peripheral, orthosympathetic	More central, parasympathetic
Attitude	More gentle, negative	More active, positive
Work	More psychological and mental	More physical and social
Dimension	Space	Time

Yin and Yang Guidelines:
The Vegetable and Animal Kingdoms

Yin and Yang in the Animal Kingdom*

Characteristic	YIN ($\triangledown$) Centrifugal (Earth's Force)	YANG ($\triangle$) Centripetal (Heaven's Force)
Environment:	Warmer and more tropical; also, in warm current.	Colder and more polar; also, in cold current.
Air humidity:	More humid	More dry
Species:	Generally more ancient	Generally more modern
Size:	Larger, more expanded	Smaller, more compacted
Activity:	Slower moving and more inactive	Faster moving and more active
Body temperature:	Colder	Warmer
Texture:	Softer, more watery and oily	Harder and drier
Color of flesh:	Transparent . . . white . . . brown . . . pink . . . red . . . black	
Odor:	More odor	Less odor
Taste:	Putrid . . . sour . . . sweet . . . salty . . . bitter	
Chemical components:	Less sodium (Na) and other yang elements.	More sodium (Na) and other yang elements.
Nutritional components:	Fat . . . Protein . . . Minerals . . .	
Cooking time:	Shorter	Longer

* Adapted from the *Book of Macrobiotics: The Universal Way of Health and Happiness* by Michio Kushi.

Yin and Yang in the Vegetable Kingdom*

Characteristic	YIN (▽) Centrifugal (Earth's Force)	YANG (△) Centripetal (Heaven's Force)
Environment:	Warmer, more tropical	Colder, more polar
Season:	Grows more in spring and summer	Grows more in autumn and winter
Soil:	More watery and sedimentary	More dry and volcanic
Growing direction:	Vertically growing upwards; expanding horizontally underground.	Vertically growing downwards; expanding horizontally above the ground.
Growing speed:	Growing faster	Growing slower
Size:	Larger, more expanded	Smaller, more compacted
Height:	Taller	Shorter
Texture:	Softer	Harder
Water content:	More juicy and watery	More dry
Color:	Purple . . . blue . . . green . . . yellow . . . brown . . . orange . . . red	
Odor:	Stronger smell	Less smell
Taste:	Spicy . . . sour . . . sweet . . . salty . . . bitter	
Chemical components:	More K and other yin elements	Less K and other yin elements
Nutritional components:	Fat . . . Protein . . . Carbohydrate . . . Mineral	
Cooking time:	Faster cooking	Slower cooking

North American Macrobiotic Congress, Case History Project

During the 1979 North American Macrobiotic Congress held in Boston, the Committee for Medical, Scientific, and Governmental Affairs established as a priority the regular collection and publication of macribiotic case histories. In cooperation with this project, we would like to encourage all readers of this book who have experienced the benefits of improved health and well-being through macrobiotics to contribute a brief written report describing your experiences.

Kindly include the following or any other information in your case history:

1.   General information: name, permanent address, date and place of birth, marital status, occupation, etc.

2.   Personal history: family background, previous dietary habits, living environments, education, type of work and activities, etc.

3.   Medical history: general description of any sickness or problems of a physical or psychological nature, previous medical treatment such as medication, surgery, natural therapies, etc., and the effects of these treatments.

4.   The nature of your macrobiotic practice, including selection of foods, manner of cooking, supplemental treatments such as ginger compresses, Shiatsu massage, etc. When, where, and how you discovered macrobiotics, and the type of studies you have pursued.

5.   Changes in your condition, including relief from negative symptoms and changes in your life as a whole. This can include physical, mental, and spiritual changes. Examples are changes in sleeping habits, bowel movements, menstruation, patience, energy level, mental clarity, general life direction, etc.

6.   If available, copies of medical records verifying the diagnosis of your medical problems and their subsequent improvement. Please include name of hospital or medical center, types of tests, etc.

7.   Any photographs which document changes as a result of practicing macrobiotics.

8.   Any advice or suggestions you have for others wishing to deal with their problems and pursue their dream through the way of macrobiotics.

Please send your case history to:
 Case History Project
 Secretariat, Macrobiotic Congress
 c/o East West Foundation
 240 Washington Street
 Brookline, MA 02146
 (617) 566–0081

Your kindness and cooperation in this project will be gratefully appreciated.

Glossary

aburage Deep fried tofu.

agar-agar A white gelatin derived from a species of seaweed. Used in making *kanten* and aspics.

age Abbreviation for *aburage*,

ai knife A Japanese vegetable knife with a pointed tip.

ame A natural grain sweetener made from either rice, barley or wheat, or a combination of grains. Frequently called rice honey or yinnie syrup.

amazake A sweetener or refreshing drink made from fermented sweet rice.

arrowroot A starch flour processed from the root of a native American plant. It is used as a thickening agent, similar to cornstarch or *kuzu*, for making sauces, stews, gravies or desserts.

azuki beans A small, dark red bean imported from Japan, but also grown in this country. Especially good for the kidneys.

bancha tea Correctly named *Kukicha*, *bancha* consists of the stems and leaves from tea bushes that are at least three years old. It is grown in Japan. *Bancha* tea aids in digestion and is high in calcium. It contains no chemical dyes or caffeine. *Bancha* makes an excellent after-dinner beverage.

bok choy A leafy green vegetable.

bonito flakes Fish flakes shaved from dried bonito fish. Used in soup stocks or as a garnish for soups and noodle dishes.

brown rice miso A fermented soybean paste made from brown rice, soybeans and sea salt.

burdock A wild, hardy plant that grows throughout most of the United States. The long, dark root is highly valued in macrobiotic cooking for its strengthening qualities. The Japanese name is *Gobo*.

chirimen iriko Very small dried fish. High in iron and calcium.

chow mein Chinese style deep fried noodle dish served with a vegetable sauce over it.

chuba Small dried sardines, used for seasoning soups, making condiments, in salads, etc.

cous-cous Partially refined, cracked wheat.

daikon A long, white radish. Besides making a delicious side dish, *daikon* is a specific for cutting fat and mucus deposits that have accumulated in our bodies as a result of past animal food intake. Grated *daikon* aids in the digestion of oily foods.

dentie A black tooth powder made from sea salt and charred eggplant.

dulse A reddish-purple seaweed. Used in soups, salads, and vegetable dishes. Very high in iron.

Foley food mill A special steel food mill, which is operated by a hand crank to make purées, sauces, dips, etc.

fu Dried wheat gluten cakes or sheets. Very high in protein.

furikake Dried *shiro* leave condiment. The leaves are dried and ground to a powder. Sometimes contains other ingredients such as bonito flakes or sesame seeds, etc.

ganmodoki A deep-fried cake made from *tofu* and a variety of different vegetables.

gazpacho Cold chickpea soup. Usually served in the summer with raw vegetables cut into very small pieces and served on top of the soup.

genmai miso — *Miso* made from brown rice, soybeans, and sea salt.

ginger — A spicy, pungent, golden-colored root, used in cooking and for medicinal purposes.

ginger compress — Sometimes called a ginger fomentation. A compress made from grated ginger root and water. Applied hot to an affected area of the body, it will stimulate circulation and dissolve stagnation.

gluten — The sticky substance that remains after the bran has been kneaded and rinsed from flour. Used to make *seitan* and *fu*.

gomashio — A condiment made from roasted, ground sesame seeds and sea salt.

Hatcho miso — A soybean paste made from soybeans and sea salt and aged for at least 3 years. Used in making condiments, soup stocks, seasoning for vegetable dishes, etc.

hijiki — A dark brown seaweed which, when dried, turns black. It is strong and wiry. *Hijiki* is native to Japan but also grows off the coast of Maine.

Hokkaido pumpkin — A round, dark green or orange squash, which is very sweet. It is harvested in early fall. Originated in New England and was introduced to Japan and named after the island of Hokkaido.

Irish moss — Type of seaweed found in the Atlantic Ocean and used for centuries in Europe. Known for its natural gelatinous properties.

ito soba — A very thin, short *soba* noodle.

jinenjo — A light brown Japanese mountain potato which grows to be several feet long and two to three inches wide.

jinenjo soba — Noodles made in Japan from *jinenjo* (mountain potato) flour and buckwheat flour.

kanpyo — Dried gourd strips. Used to tie cabbage rolls, etc.

kanten — A jelled dessert made from fruit and agar-agar.

kasha knishes — Cakes made from buckwheat and vegetables, wrapped in a pastry dough and baked.

kasha varnitchkes — Fried buckwheat, noodles, and vegetables.

kayu — Long-cooked grain prepared with approximately five times as much water as grain. *Kayu* is ready when it is very soft and creamy.

kenchin soup — Soup made from left-over vegetable ends and pieces which often contains *tofu* or deep fried tofu.

kinako — Roasted soybean flour.

kinpira — A sautéed burdock or burdock and carrot dish, which is seasoned with *tamari*.

koi-koku — *Miso* soup made from carp, burdock, *bancha* leaves and *miso*. Known for its medicinal properties.

koji — Grain that has been innoculated with the same type of bacteria that is used in making such fermented foods and drinks as *miso, tamari, amazake* and *sake*.

kombu — A wide, thick, dark green seaweed which grows in deep ocean water. Used in making soup stocks, cooked with vegetables, in soups, condiments, candy, etc.

kombu dashi — A soup broth made from *kombu* and water.

kome miso — Rice *miso*. Usually white rice *miso*, made from white rice, soybeans and sea salt.

kukicha — Usually called *bancha*. Older stems and leaves of a tea bush grown in Japan.

kuzu — A white starch made from the root of the wild *kuzu* plant. In this country the plant is called "kudzu." Used in making soups, sauces, gravies, desserts, and for medicinal purposes.

layering method — A method of cooking soups, vegetables, beans, grains, etc., in which ingredients are layered in ascending order in the cooking pot from yin to yang.

lotus root — The root of a variety of water lily which is brown-skinned with a hollow, chambered, off-white inside. Especially good for respiratory organs.

mekabu	Roots of the *wakame* seaweed plant. Used in making soups and soup stocks. Has a very strong flavor.
mirin	A sweet Japanese cooking wine or sherry made from rice.
mochi	A rice cake or dumpling made from cooked, pounded sweet rice.
moromi	By-product of making miso. Usually used as a condiment or in preparing condiments.
mugicha	A tea made out of roasted, unhulled barley and water.
mugi miso	Soybean paste made from barley, soybeans, sea salt and water.
mugwort	A wild plant which can be dried and made into tea, or pounded with sweet rice to make mugwort *mochi*. Has medicinal properties.
mu tea	A tea made from 16 different herbs. It is very yang and has certain medicinal values.
nabe	A one dish meal, prepared and served in a colorfully decorated earthenware cassarole and served with a dipping sauce or broth made of either *tamari* or *miso*.
natto	Soybeans which have been cooked and mixed with beneficial enzymes and allowed to ferment for 24 hours under a controlled temperature.
natto miso	A condiment *miso*, which is not actually *natto*. It is made from soybeans, grain, ginger and *kombu*, and fermented for a very short time.
nigari	Hard, crystallized salt made from the liquid drippings of dampened sea salt. Used in making *tofu*.
nori	Thin sheets of dried seaweed. Black or dark purple when dried. Roasted over a flame until green. Used as a garnish, wrapped around rice balls, in making *sushi*, or cooked with *tamari* and used as a condiment.
nori maki	Often called *sushi*. Rice rolled up in nori with a combination of ingredients such as vegetables, pickles, fish, *shiso* leaves fried *tofu*, etc. rolled inside the rice. Sliced into small bite-sized rounds.
ohagi	A rice cake made from cooked, pounded sweet rice and coated with items such as *azuki* beans, chestnuts, roasted, chopped, ground nuts, sesame seeds, soybean flour, etc.
ojiya	Soft rice and vegetables which have been cooked for a long time. Usually seasoned with sea salt, *tamari*, or *miso*. Fish, shellfish, beans, and fried *tofu* are often used in preparing different kinds of *ojiya*. Known for its medicinal properties.
okara	The coarse soybean pulp left over when making *tofu*. Cooked with vegetables.
ozoni	A miso soup made from white *miso*, vegetables, and *mochi*. Traditionally served in Japan on New Year's.
ramen	A Chinese style noodle which has been previously deep fried and then dried. It cooks very quickly. Made from buckwheat flour or white flour.
red (aka)miso	A short-time fermented *miso*, made from rice *koji*. soybeans, and sea salt.
saifun	A clear noodle made from mung beans. Used in salads, soups, and vegetable dishes. Sometimes called *Beifun*.
sake	A Japanese wine made from rice. Usually served warm in small cups but can sometimes be served room temperature or cold.
sake lees	Fermented residue left after making *sake*. Used in soups and in vegetable and pickle dishes.
sake-no-kasu	Soup made from vegetables and *sake* lees. Sometimes contains fish or shellfish. Usually prepared in winter. Known for its warming effect on the body.
sashimi	Raw, sliced fish.
sea salt	Salt obtained from the ocean as opposed to land salt. It is either sun baked or kiln baked. High in trace minerals, it contains no chemicals, sugar, or iodine.
seitan	Wheat gluten cooked in *tamari*, *kombu* and water.
shiitake	A medicinal, dried mushroom imported from Japan.

shio kombu   Pieces of *kombu* cooked for a long time in *tamari* and used in small amounts as a condiment.

shio nori   Pieces of *nori* cooked in *tamari* or *tamari* and water. Used as a condiment.

shiso   Pickled beefsteak plant leaves.

soba   Noodles made from buckwheat flour or a combination of buckwheat flour with whole wheat flour or *jinenjo* flour.

somen   Very thin, white, or wholewheat Japanese noodles. Often served during the summer.

su   Japanese rice or brown rice vinegar.

surikogi   A wooden pestle that is used with a *suribachi*.

sukiyaki   A one-dish meal prepared in a large cast iron skillet, containing a variety of vegetables, noodles, seaweeds, *seitan*, *tofu*, fish etc.

suribachi   A special serrated, glazed clay bowl. Used with a pestle (called a *surikogi*) for grinding and puréeing foods.

sushi   Rice rolled with vegetables, fish, or pickles, wrapped in *nori* and sliced into rounds.

sushi mat   A mat made from strips of bamboo tied together with string. Used in making *sushi*, or as a cover for bowls.

takuan   *Daikon* which is pickled in rice bran and sea salt. Sometimes spelled "takuwan."

taro   A potato which has a thick, hairy skin. Often called *albi*. Used in making *taro* or *albi* plasters to draw toxins from the body, or can be eaten as a vegetable.

tamari   Name given to traditional, naturally made soy sauce to distinguish it from the commercial, chemically processed variety.

tekka   Condiment made from *Hatcho* miso, sesame oil, burdock, lotus root, carrot, and ginger root. Sautéed on a low flame for several hours.

tempeh   A dish made from split soybeans, vinegar, water and a special bacteria, which is allowed to ferment for several hours. Eaten in Indonesia and Ceylon as a staple food. Available prepacked, ready to make, in some natural food stores.

tempura   Sliced vegetables, fish, or patties made of grain, vegetables, fish *tofu*, etc., which are dipped into a batter and deep fried until golden brown.

tendon   A one-dish meal consisting of rice served with tempuraed vegetables with a light *tamari* broth served over it.

tentsuyu   A *tempura* dip sauce made with soup broth, *tamari*, *sake* and ginger.

tofu   A cake made from soybeans, *nigari*, and water.

toshi koshi soba   Plain *soba* and broth. Traditionally served at midnight on New Year's Eve in Japan. Literally means "long-life soba." Is also served often as part of the Japanese diet.

udon   Japanese noodles made from wheat, wholewheat, or wholewheat and unbleached white flour.

umeboshi   A salty pickled plum.

unohana   Another name for "okara," which is the soybean pulp left over from making *tofu*.

wakame   A long, thin, green seaweed used in making soups, salads, vegetable dishes, etc.

wasabi   A Japanese hot, green mustard.

white (shiro) miso   A sweet, short-time fermented *miso*, made from rice, soybeans, rice *koji*, and sea salt.

wok   A deep, round Chinese skillet.

yannoh   A grain coffee made from five different grains and beans which have been roasted and ground into a fine powder.

yellow miso   A short-time fermented *miso*, very mellow in flavor. Made from rice *koji*, soybeans, rice, and sea salt.

yuba   Dried soy milk.

Bibliography

Abehsera, Michel. *Cooking for Life*. Binghamton, N. Y.: Swan House.

Aihara, Cornellia. *Chico-San Cookbook*, Chico. Calif.: Chico-San, Inc.

Aihara, Cornellia, *The Dō of Cooking*, 4 vols. Oroville, Calif.: George Ohsawa Macrobiotic Foundation.

Carrel, Alexis. *Man the Unknown*. New York: Harper and Row.

Chishima, Kikuo. *Revolution of Biology and Medicine*. Gifu, Japan: Neo-Haematological Society Press.

Colbin, Annemarie. *The Book of Whole Meals*. Brookline, Mass.: Autumn Press.

Dufty, William. *Sugar Blues*. New York: Warner Publications.

East West Foundation. *A Dietary Approach to Cancer Accorldng to the Principles of Macrobiotics*. Brookline, Mass.: East West Publications.

East West Foundation. *A Nutritional Approach to Cancer*. Ibid.

East West Foundation. *Cancer and Diet*. Ibid.

East West Foundation. *Macrobiotic Case Histories*. Vols. I through VI. Ibid.

East West Foundation. *Report on the First North American Congress of Macrobiotics*. Ibid.

East West Foundation. *Standard Recommendations for Diet and Way of Life*. Ibid.

Esko, Wendy. *Introducing Macrobiotic Cooking*. Tokyo: Japan Publications, Inc.

Fukuoka, Masanobu. *The One-Straw Revolution*: *An Introduction to Natural Farming*. Emmaus, Pa: Rodale Press.

Gilbert, Margaret Shea. *Biography of the Unborn*. New York: Hafner.

Jacobsen and Brewster. *The Changing American Diet*. Washington, D. C.: Center for Science in the Public Interest.

Kohler, Jean and Mary Alice. *Healing Miracles from Macrobiotics*. West Nyack, N. Y.: Parker Publishing Co.

Kushi, Michio. *Acupuncture*: *Ancient and Future Worlds*. Brookline, Mass.: East West Foundation.

Kushi, Michio. *Oriental Diagnosis*. London: Sunwheel, Ltd.

Kushi, Michio. *How to See Your Health*: *The Book of Diagnosis*, Tokyo: Japan Publications, Inc.

Kushi, Michio. *Natural Healing Through Macrobiotics*. Ibid.

Kushi, Michio. *The Teachings of Michio Kushi*, Vols. I and II. Ibid.

Kushi, Michio. *The Book of Macrobiotics*: *The Universal Way of Health and Happiness*. Tokyo: Japan Publications, Inc.

Kushi, Michio. *The Book of Dō-In*: *Exercise for Physical and Spiritual Development*. Ibid.

Kushi, Aveline. *How to Cook with Miso*. Ibid.

Mendelsohn, Robert S., M. D. *Confessions of a Medical Heretic*. Chicago, Ill.: Contemporary Books.

Muramoto, Noboru. *Healing Ourselves.* New York: Avon; London: Michael Dempsey/Cassell.

Ohsawa, George. *Acupuncture and the Philosophy of the Far East.* Boston, Mass.: Tao Books.

Ohsawa, George. *The Book of Judgment.* Los Angeles: Ohsawa Foundation.

Ohsawa, George. *Cancer and the Philosophy of the Far East.* Binghamton, N. Y.: Swan House.

Ohsawa, George. *Guidebook for Living.* Los Angeles: Ohsawa Foundation.

Ohsawa, George. *Practical Guide to Far-Eastern Macrobiotic Medicine.* Oroville, Calif.: George Ohsawa Macrobiotic Foundation.

Ohsawa, George. *The Unique Principle.* Ibid.

Ohsawa, George. *Zen Macrobiotics.* Los Angeles: Ohsawa Foundation.

Ohsawa, Lima. *The Art of Just Cooking.* Tokyo: Autumn Press.

Sacks, Castelli, Donner, and Kass. "Plasma Lipids and Lipoproteins in Vegetarians and Controls." Boston: *New England Journal of Medicine.* May 29, 1975.

Sacks, Rosner, and Kass. "Blood Pressure in Vegetarians." *American Journal of Epidemiology*, Vol. 100, No. 5, Baltimore: Johns Hopkins University.

Sakurazawa, Nyoiti (George Ohsawa), edited by Dufty, William. *Macrobiotics.* London: Tandem Books. Published in the U.S.A. under the title *You Are All Sanpaku.* New York: University Books.

Select Committee on Nutrition and Human Needs, U.S. Senate. *Dietary Goals for the United States.* February 1977.

Stiskin, Nahum. *The Looking Glass God.* Tokyo: Autumn Press.

Surgeon General's Report on Health Promotion and Disease Prevention. *Healthy People.* Washington, D. C. September, 1979.

Veith, Ilza. *The Yellow Emperor's Classic of Internal Medicine.* Berkely, Calif.: University of California Press.

Wilhelm and Baynes. *I Ching.* Princeton: Princeton University Press.

Yamamoto, Shizuko. *Barefoot Shiatsu.* Tokyo: Japan Publications, Inc.

Periodicals

East West Journal. Brookline, Mass.

Kushi Institute Study Guide, Kushi Institute Newsletter, Brookline, Mass.

The Order of the Universe. Brookline, Mass. East West Foundation.

Nutrition Action, Washington D. C.: Center for Science in the Public Interest.

The Macrobiotic Review. Baltimore, Md.: East West Foundation.

Spiral. Community Health Foundation, London.

Le Compas. Paris.